~~TOP SECRET~~
Security Information

MEMORANDUM RE P.B. FORTUNE

8 March 1953

We now expect to be in a position to proceed with our phase of the project if desired. However, the chances of success would be greatly enhanced if there were a coordinated effort in the political field. The country in question is thoroughly dependent on its trade relations with us and has discounted the fact that we would do nothing. In effect they have flaunted us and consistently got away with it. It is time they were brought to realize that this could not continue.

While the exact steps which might be politically feasible are matters beyond our competence here, we have a legitimate interest, it seems to me, in seeing that the climate is right for the types of action in which we may be engaged.

Here are some of the measures which might be considered.

1. Recalling our ambassador for consultation and sending a two-fisted guy to the general area on a trip of inspection and to report to the President.

Our ambassador is timid and never recovered from his treatment at the hands of Anna Pauker. Further the whole Embassy should be given a look over. I just received the visit of two American citizens highly recommended who have large interests in the country. They indicated that they did not feel they could get anything whatever out of the Embassy in the way of protection of American interests and hinted at darker things. They came to me after talking with Herbert Hoover and Lewis Strauss, and the latter urged that I see them. Herman Pfleger knows about them through Herbert Hoover.

Bill Pawley or someone of his type might be considered. I recognize that Pawley is hard to control, but he is fearless and gets things done even though he may break a little crockery in doing it. I would suggest that he might also spend a little time in the countries bordering on the one of our chief concern.

2. In connection with the mission described in 1, the President in a press conference might express his concern at the Soviet Communist penetration and his desire to consult, in the spirit of the Rio Pact, with other Latin American countries affected thereby.

3. Appropriate speeches might be made by a couple of members of Congress. You may recall that this was done a year or

~~SECRET~~
Security Information

COLD WAR
PLANS
THAT NEVER
HAPPENED
1945–91

COLD WAR PLANS THAT NEVER HAPPENED
1945–91

MICHAEL KERRIGAN

amber
BOOKS

This edition first published in 2012

Published by
Amber Books Ltd
Bradley's Close
74–77 White Lion Street
London N1 9PF
United Kingdom
Website: www.amberbooks.co.uk
Appstore: itunes.com/apps/amberbooksltd
Facebook: www.facebook.com/amberbooks
Twitter: @amberbooks
Email: enquiries@amberbooks.co.uk

ISBN: 978-1-908273-78-9

Printed in China

Project Editor: Sarah Uttridge
Editorial Assistant: Kieron Connolly
Designer: Jerry Williams
Picture Research: Terry Forshaw

Contents

Introduction

'The Gulf War Did Not Take Place', the French thinker Jean Baudrillard notoriously claimed. So totally had TV and press pictures shaped our perceptions of that conflict, so real did the media imagery seem to us, he suggested, that what we read and saw supplanted what actually happened on the ground. But the West's war against Saddam Hussein's Iraq over the annexation of Kuwait had hardly been the first conflict that seemed somehow both to have taken place and to have not taken place. What are we to make of the Cold War, 1945–91?

Long before the advent of 24-hour TV news, its ins and outs were every bit as powerful in their impact – and as elusive. An enmity that, for a whole generation, more or less defined reality – not just military but political, economic and cultural – makes less sense to us with every decade that goes by. The conflict that never quite was, the entire Cold War can be seen as an 'operation that didn't happen'; indeed, it is starting to seem more and more that way.

A War With a Difference
This study was intended to be a sequel for *World War II Plans that Never Happened* – and it is. Yet in intriguing (sometimes perplexing) ways, it's a very different book. World War II very definitely did happen; it

Molotov's signature sealed the Nazi–Soviet Pact of 1939.

had a clear beginning, a middle and an end; we feel we understand it (however much we may simplify). Within that overall narrative, innumerable subplots are to be found: events and operations that had their place in the advancing drama as a whole. Those operations that were considered – perhaps planned in great detail and elaborately prepared-for, but then dismissed – offer a fascinating commentary on those that did ultimately go ahead. They're ironic asides to the main action; photographic negatives for the historical imagery; tantalizing glimpses of the war that might have been.

In the case of the Cold War, though, these non-operations come much closer to having

been the warp and woof of the unfolding conflict – its reality, in so far as there was such a thing. Granted, the argument can be carried too far: try telling a veteran of Vietnam or Korea that the Cold War didn't happen; or a Guatemalan villager or a soldier from the British Army of the Rhine. Nor, for that matter, did it seem so unreal to the ordinary civilian, whoever and wherever he or she might be – in America, Australia, Czechoslovakia or the Soviet Union. While the overarching opposition of the superpowers spanned the world, no country could long resist enlistment into one Cold War camp or other. The peoples of North America and Europe found themselves living beneath one or other of the rival's 'nuclear umbrella': if these provided shelter, they cast a considerable shadow too. And yet, horrific as it was in prospect, the feared inferno never came: this was the mass-destruction dog that didn't bark.

A Chilly Start

While what we call the 'Cold War' began in 1945, the *froideur* between the western capitalist countries and Communist Russia was as old as the Soviet Union itself. Few in the West had seen 1917's October Revolution as cause for celebration. Private ownership, property rights, market freedom, a non-interfering state . . . such things were the cornerstones of capitalism, and Lenin, Trotsky and co. were busily abolishing them all. Naturally, some in the labour movement looked on the Russian Reds as heroes, inspirational prophets of the socialist future, but these views weren't prevalent among the political elite. Winston Churchill spoke for them (as eloquently as ever) when, in June 1918, he called on Britain and her allies to 'strangle the Bolshevik baby in its cradle'.

By that time his country's soldiers and sailors were already in action attempting to overthrow the men who'd overthrown the Tsar. Britain, America and France led a coalition of no fewer than 14 nations that intervened in the Russian Civil War, attacking the

Reds in support of the Tsarist 'Whites'. While an Anglo–American expedition struck inland from the Arctic ports of Murmansk and Archangelsk, the French landed at Odessa, on the Black Sea coast.

Mixed Motives

No pussyfooting around with the revolutionary regime, then. At this historical distance, though, it's easy to oversimplify the complex

> **'The world has been made safe for democracy. But democracy has not yet made the world safe against irrational revolution.'**
>
> *President Woodrow Wilson, 1923*

The October Revolution reverberated far beyond Russia itself, inspiring workers and horrifying governments in the West.

MANUAL OF CIVIL DEFENCE: Vol. I

PAMPHLET No. 1

Nuclear Weapons

IA/III/129

12 September 1957

U.K. EYES ONLY

Copy No 3 of 5

BLUE PEACOCK

RESISTANCE TO COUNTERMEASURES TRIAL

PROOF TRIAL No. A6

INTRODUCTION

1. BLUE PEACOCK is the Atomic Mine based on the RAF BLUE DANUBE weapon. The War Office Specification includes the following Major Characteristics:-

"The design must incorporate measures to eliminate the possibility of a complete and exploded weapon, which has not been initiated due to failure of the firing circuits, falling intact into the hands of the enemy". A self-destruction unit has been developed to meet this clause of the specification.

The anti-handling specification is as follows:-

"Anti-handling devices are required to prevent either removal of the weapon, or its neutralisation. These devices shall be self-locking, i.e. once set they cannot be made safe. In the event of a change in the tactical situation after the mine has been armed it must be possible to prevent the mine functioning by fission (An explosion, with the resulting contamination, is acceptable). It is desirable that the anti-handling devices be such that the mine functioning be obtained only by a secret method. In the event of enemy interference, full fission should result". Various anti-handling devices have been incorporated in the weapon with a view to meeting the specification. Details of these are given at Annex 'A' (Not issued to all addressees).

AIM

2. The Aim of the trial is:-

(a) To assess the difficulty and probable delay in neutralising BLUE PEACOCK.

(b) To compare the effectiveness of the individual types of anti-handling devices fitted.

METHOD

Personnel

3. The trial will be carried out by a security cleared team from U.G.S.R. ... who will have NO previous knowledge of BLUE PEACOCK. Mr. G.L.V. Crawford (Project Engineer) and Major D.G. Hascham R.E. (Trials officer) will be available to supervise the trial.

The instructions given to the Trials Team are at Annex 'B'.

Phasing

4. The trial will take place in three phases. Phase 1 will commence in Building G.14, ARDE, Fort Halstead on Monday 28 October 1957, to be immediately followed by Phase 2. Phase 3 will be staged at a later date at a place to be decided by U.G.S.R. Trials Team.

Preparation of BLUE PEACOCK

5. To state of readiness to which BLUE PEACOCK must be prepared during the trial is given at Annex 'C' (Not to all addressees).

D.G. Hascham

Major R.E.
(D. G. Hascham)

'A' to 70/Engrs/168 GS (W)2 of 12 Nov 54

Dwight D. Eisenhower Library
Eisenhower: Papers, 1953-61
(Ann Whitman file)

Downgraded To Secret
By Authority Of NSC 7/154
By LAO   NLE Date 6/14/96

MEMORANDUM

SUBJECT: Discussion at the 387th Meeting of the National Security Council, Thursday, November 20, 1958

Present at the 387th Meeting of the National Security Council were the President of the United States, presiding; the Secretary of State; the Secretary of Defense; and the Director, Office of Civil and Defense Mobilization. Also present and participating in the Council actions below were the Secretary of the Treasury; the Attorney General; the Director, Bureau of the Budget; and the Chairman, Atomic Energy Commission; also attending the meeting were the U.S. Ambassador to NATO; the Director of Central Intelligence; the Deputy Secretary of Defense; the Secretary of the Army; the Secretary of the Navy; the Secretary of the Air Force; the Chairman, Joint Chiefs of Staff; the Acting Chief of Staff, U.S. Army; the Chief of Naval Operations; the Chief of Staff, U.S. Air Force; the Director, International Cooperation Agency; the Acting Director, International Cooperation Administration; the Chairman, Interdepartmental Intelligence Conference; members of the Net Evaluation Subcommittee Staff also attending this meeting: General Gerald C. Thomas, Director; Lt. General Thomas F. Hickey, Deputy Director; Lt. General ... Granger, USMC, ...; Colonel Charles L. ..., USA, Colonel ... Designate; Colonel William H. Calhoun, USN, Colonel Kenneth ... USAF; Colonel ... Dashiell, USN, and Colonel ...; Captain Edward L. ... J. Smith, CIA, and Colonel ... USAF. Also attending the meeting were the Special Assistants to the President for National Security Affairs and for Science and Technology; Major John Eisenhower for the White House Staff Secretary; the Executive Secretary, NSC; and the Deputy Executive Secretary, NSC.

There follows a summary of the discussion at the meeting and the main points taken.

1.   REPORT BY THE NET EVALUATION SUBCOMMITTEE
     (NSC Actions Nos. 1260, 1330, 1430, 1463, 1532, 1641 and 1815; NSC 5816)

Mr. Gordon Gray introduced General Thomas, the Director of the Net Evaluation Subcommittee Staff, and explained the general purpose

DECLASSIFIED
Authority NLE 95-... Doc!
By ...   NARA, Date 8/9/96

Increases in the capability of Soviet Forces in Central Europe

	1968	1976	% increase
...ks	7,250	9,500	31
...llery	3,200	4,000	25
...ured Personnel ...ters (including ...nnaissance and ...and variants)	5,300	9,450	78
...al Aircraft	1,655	1,975	20

- 9 -

CONFIDENTIAL

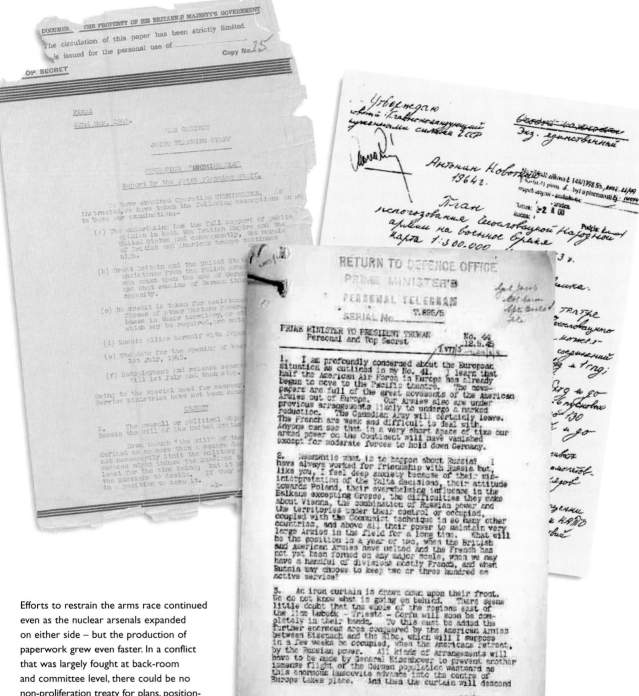

Efforts to restrain the arms race continued
even as the nuclear arsenals expanded
on either side – but the production of
paperwork grew even faster. In a conflict
that was largely fought at back-room
and committee level, there could be no
non-proliferation treaty for plans, position-
papers, feasibility studies and surveys –
which now endure, the residue of a
virtual war.

motives that prompted this intervention. In the first instance, at least, the Allies' concern was not so much ideological as strategic: Russia's Revolution had deprived their war with Germany of its second, Eastern Front.

What we now think of as World War I was a conflict between capitalists, Russia's new rulers argued; one in which the workers of the West were nothing more than cannon-fodder and one in which the workers' state that was the Soviet Union could have no interest. By restoring some sort of monarchy, the Western Allies hoped they'd be able to rebuild the Triple Entente, which, since 1907, had united Britain, France and Russia against Germany. A newcomer to the conflict (its first troops arrived in the trenches that same summer), the United States shared the same objectives.

Best of Enemies

Once World War I was won, the Allies were able to devote more men and resources to the fighting in Russia – but their incentive had largely gone, and enthusiasm quickly waned. The Reds now firmly in charge, the two sides settled down into a routine of rhetorical denunciation and mutual suspicion, but with no sign of serious aggression on either part. Lenin's death in 1924 eased relations a little: Western rulers were reassured when Stalin rejected Marx's internationalist stance and the previous plans of his Russian comrades for world revolution, and instead proclaimed his doctrine to be 'Socialism in One Country'.

That he was doing his best to turn that one country into a hell on earth was regrettable, of course, but it wasn't their

problem. Western governments were relieved that this 'Red Tsar' was reverting to introverted type. Historically, Russia had always been paranoid about its own security – and to this end taken chunks of Lithuania and Poland – but it had never threatened to expand into western Europe.

It was to guarantee the Soviet Union's security that, increasingly through the 1930s, Stalin reached out from his isolation towards the West. Not that he felt any affection towards the nations that had striven so hard to stamp out his country's revolution, but he'd recognized that capitalists who were content to stay at home and leave Russia alone were preferable to a Nazi Germany led by a madman (it took one to know one . . .) who was bent on world (or at least European) domination. Whatever their faults, they didn't froth at the mouth about 'Judeo-Bolshevism' the way the Nazis did. Neither did they make a virtue of militarism, talk of war as some sort of spiritual fulfilment or speak unabashedly of the need for national *lebensraum* – territorial 'living space'. Little as he liked the way they did things, Stalin had no hesitation picking out the Western powers as the lesser of two evils.

It wasn't a judgement he made on ethical grounds, of course – more on a cold consideration of the dangers that he faced. Hence his (increasingly frantic) overtures

Stalin (front right) and Molotov (front centre) review Soviet forces from the balcony of Lenin's Mausoleum in Red Square.

British Foreign Secretary John Simon (centre) meets Maxim Litvinov (to his right).

to the Western powers through Foreign Minister Maxim Litvinov in the 1930s, in his hope that they might join him in an anti-fascist alliance. And then, when all his advances were rejected, came his unceremonious dumping of the (Jewish) Litvinov and the negotiations that eventually led to the Nazi–Soviet Pact.

Worst of Friends

Signed on the very eve of war by Germany's Foreign Minister Joachim von Ribbentrop and his Russian opposite number Vyacheslav Molotov, the Pact wasn't quite a friendship agreement, or even a partnership arrangement pledging mutual support. It committed both sides to staying neutral in the event

that one was attacked by a third country. Even so, Stalin's willingness to do a deal with Hitler has been roundly condemned by historians since. As a 'non-aggression' pact it seemed particularly cynical given that it green-lighted immediate acts of aggression by both signatories – in Poland, in Germany's case; in the Baltic states in the Soviet Union's.

Slammed by Western historians, and long quietly suppressed by chroniclers of the Soviet camp, the Nazi–Soviet Pact prompted an exodus of members from the Communist parties of western Europe at the time. Other commentators in the Western democracies were just as disgusted, if less personally affected. But the

great Bolshevik-baby-strangler Winston Churchill had no difficulty in understanding Stalin's actions. As far as he was concerned, in what was clearly an impossible situation, the Soviet leader had done the only thing he could. It might have been repugnant morally, but the right thing pragmatically.

Just as it was the right thing for Britain to make common cause with the Soviet Union when the Pact fell apart with Operation Barbarossa. 'If Hitler invaded hell,' Churchill – now Prime Minister – admitted, 'I would make at least a favourable mention of the devil in the House of Commons.' That didn't make their relationship any easier, : personalities apart, Stalin's strategic priorities differed significantly from those of the other Allied leaders. They chafed at his incessant clamour for the opening of a 'Second Front', which would take some of the pressure off his forces.

More profoundly, even as the Eastern and Western Allies advanced towards and then through Germany in the 'Race to the Rhine', they felt gloomy about the demands Stalin was making for influence in the postwar era over Eastern and Central Europe – demands they felt in no real position to refuse. The establishment of Soviet dominance in East Germany, Czechoslovakia, Hungary, Yugoslavia, Romania and Bulgaria was, Churchill wrote to his Foreign Secretary Anthony Eden in April 1945, 'one of the most melancholy events' in the continent's history, 'and one to which there is no parallel'.

Chapter One

The War That Nearly Was

If conflict with the Soviet Union at some point was – as seemed to be the case – an inevitability, why not simply push ahead and have it now?

Five years' fear, anxiety and stress were all released at once, in an explosion of relief: 'VE Day' (Victory in Europe Day, 8 May 1945) saw general jubilation. Impromptu parties broke out in workplaces, pubs and social centres, spilling out into the streets to make what was ordinarily an industrious capital an enormous singing, dancing, drinking carnival. South London swayed and strutted to the Lambeth Walk, conga lines wound their way down Piccadilly. By early afternoon, the crowd collecting in Trafalgar Square had surged up the Mall to Buckingham Palace. From the palace's balcony, King George VI and Queen Elizabeth waved while the young princesses looked on. Beside them, beaming cheerfully, stood the man who had done more than anything else to bring Britain through its darkest hour. Winston Churchill was in a celebratory mood. He had earned his moment of cheer, inspiring the people of his country when all seemed lost: no one had done more than him to bring the present triumph.

Flanked by his country's King and Queen, Churchill smiles – as well he might – in the moment of victory. Already, though, he was preoccupied with the conflict yet to come.

Operation Unthinkable

Was real peace with the Soviets possible? Or should the Allies attack them now, perhaps pre-empting problems in the years to come?

An Uneasy Peace

All wasn't quite the way it seemed, however. While Britain gave itself up to revelry, the Prime Minister stayed sober; the hangover had already come for him. Not that any of the Allied leaders could think of relaxing while war raged on in the Pacific, but there were dangers much closer to home, Churchill believed. The German enemy had been defeated – but what about the Soviets, the Allies' 'friend in need'? Without them, the war would surely not have been won, but glad and even grateful as Churchill was, the 'peace' in prospect looked like being profoundly problematic.

Western propagandists had done their best to stir up enthusiasm for the alliance with the Soviets for as long as the war went on, but no one had been under too many illusions about a relationship that had always been very much a marriage of convenience. The ideological gulf between the Nazis and the Soviet Communists was, of course, ostensibly enormous, but there had been little to choose between their two forms of totalitarianism. Hitler had represented the most immediate danger – so some sort of understanding with the Soviet

Harry S. Truman came to the presidency with much to learn.

Union had been necessary; but that didn't diminish the menace represented by the USSR now.

Allied Anxieties

Almost a month before, on 12 May, the British premier had signalled his concerns in a telegram to Truman:

I have always worked for friendship with Russia but, like you, I feel deep anxiety because of their misinterpretation of the Yalta decisions, their attitude towards Poland, their overwhelming influence in the Balkans excepting Greece, the difficulties they make about Vienna, the combination of

Russian power and the territories under their control or occupied . . .

That 'like you' was wishful thinking – or, more likely, an attempt to push the President towards his own way of reasoning. Truman doesn't actually seem to have felt any such thing. No enthusiast for the Russian Communist way, he was still strikingly pragmatic in his diplomatic posture; and almost warm in his praise for the Soviet leader. 'I can deal with Stalin. He is honest,' he was to opine soon afterwards (conceding, however, that he was 'smart as hell').

If Harry S. Truman had a 'deep anxiety', it did not relate to a rampant Russia but to the responsibilities the United States might find itself racking up in Europe. Would there be no end to the demands of both Churchill and Stalin? Not a day went by, he confided in his journal, without his having yet again to try to get through to them that 'so far as this President is concerned Santa Claus is dead and that my first interest is [the] USA'.

World War II had jolted America out of its longstanding isolationism, but its instinct now was to revert immediately to type. Eventually, however, the 'Truman Doctrine' would tie the United States in to rivalries and conflicts

'The idea is, of course, fantastic and the chance of success quite impossible. There is no doubt that, from now on, Russia is all-powerful in Europe.'

Sir Alan Brooke, Chief of the Imperial Staff, on 'Unthinkable'. Journal entry for 24 May 1945

Churchill's authority was immense – but Truman was US President. He wouldn't let himself be patronized for long.

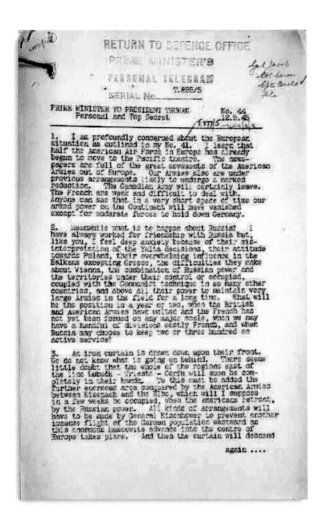

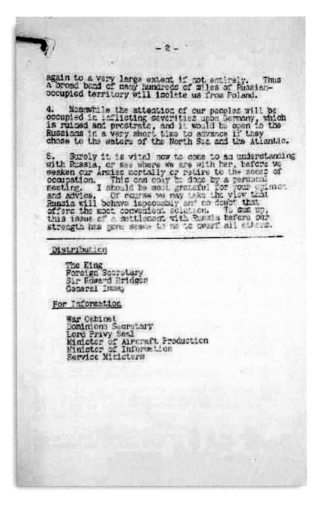

around the world, becoming the cornerstone of Cold War foreign policy. Its formulation lay some way in the future, though: for the moment, the new President's own instincts were isolationist. An all-American homeboy, he was ill-equipped to be anything else. He had neither the education nor the experience to cut a dash on the diplomatic stage.

Training Up Truman

Churchill's telegram can be read as his (more or less tactful)

attempt to coach the US President in his own way of thinking. Patronizing, perhaps, and yet his concerns don't seem unjustified in hindsight. They boil down to the difference between the democracies, for whom the default position is peace, and a strongly militarized communist state: Western inertia will leave the Soviets in possession of the Central European field, he fears.

What will be the position in a year or two, when the British and American Armies have melted

and the French have a handful of divisions, mostly French, and when Russia may choose to keep two or three hundred on active service?

In the democratic nations, the Prime Minister recognized, the pressure was already on for the armed forces to be demobilized; there was no corresponding urgency in the Soviet Union. There, regimentation was the rule, the citizen always at the bidding of the state; military service an unquestioned duty – emergency

TRANSCRIPT OF KEY PARAGRAPHS

Copy of telegram dated 12 May 1945 from Prime Minister Winston Churchill to President Harry Truman.

(Left) 3. An iron curtain is drawn down upon their front. We do not know what is going on behind. There is little doubt that the whole of the region east of the line Lübeck – Trieste – Corfu will soon be completely in their hands. To this must be added the further enormous area conquered by the American Armies between Eisenach and the Elbe, which will I suppose in a few weeks be occupied, when the Americans retreat, by the Russian power.

All kinds of arrangements will have to be made by General Eisenhower to prevent another immense flight of the German population westward as this enormous Muscovite advance into the centre of Europe takes place. And then the curtain will descend again . . .

. . . Thus a broad band of many hundred of miles of Russian-occupied territory will isolate us from Poland.

or not. The Soviet system approached peace as if it were war, attacking social and economic challenges as if they were enemies, the nation rallying in defence of the communist cause. Whatever the situation in Europe, the Red Army was still very much in the field – neither the soldiers nor their families expected them to be standing down any time soon. But Americans were anxious to wrap up the war with Japan and get on with the peace, making the danger twofold in Churchill's view. Almost as worrying as the direct threat from the Soviet Union was the prospect of abandonment by the United States. It seemed only natural that American forces would now 'melt' away, their work in Europe apparently complete. Yet this disastrous outcome had to be avoided at any cost.

In his eagerness to win the President round, the Prime Minister gives him the benefit not just of his strategic wisdom but his historic rhetoric, predicting the establishment of an 'iron curtain . . . drawn down upon their front. We do not know what is going on behind.' Churchill's first recorded use of this famous image comes almost a year before its famous outing at Westminster College, Missouri, on 5 March 1946. He was clearly 'talking up' the Red Peril – but just as clearly felt that he had to: he was well used to the role of Cassandra, after all.

Thinking the Unthinkable

His telegram to Truman sent, Churchill didn't simply settle down and wait – that wasn't his way. Rather, he asked his staff to explore the options for a pre-emptive attack on the Soviet Union – a project for which he himself seems to have chosen the title 'Operation Unthinkable'. Working together under the supervision of the Army's Field Marshal Alan Brooke, Admiral of the Fleet Andrew Cunningham and Air Chief Marshall Douglas Evill, the Joint Planning Staff (G. Grantham, G.S. Thompson and W.L. Dawson) had presented their final report on 22 May. Churchill's Chief Military Assistant, Hastings Ismay, delivered it to Churchill; the document was called 'Russia: Threat to Western Civilization'.

The apocalyptic tone of the title wasn't what would normally have been expected. Inside, though, all seemed measured and precise. Carefully, the report set out some basic assumptions, before moving on to the 'object' of the operation ('to impose upon Russia the will of the United States and the British Empire'). It then considered the expected Soviet response and the stages through which such a conflict (scheduled to begin on 1 July 1945) might be expected to proceed. The chiefs were anything but gung-ho. Indeed, they could hardly have spelled out the dangers of the operation more exactly:

A quick success might induce the Russians to submit to our will at least for the time being; but it might not. That is for the Russians to decide. If they want total war, they are in a position to have it.

Churchill's 'Iron Curtain' speech set out the new realities in the starkest terms.

And what were the chances of that 'quick success'? As we read on, we find just about every sentence underlining quite how unthinkable an operation 'Operation Unthinkable' is.

Outrageous Assumptions

If, as we've seen, the language of the report itself is bland after the portentous poetry of its title, that blandness soon starts to seem a wild extravagance in itself. What are we to make of the aplomb with which the chiefs set out such 'assumptions' as 'The undertaking has the full support of public opinion in both the British Empire and the United States and consequently, the morale of British and American troops remains high'? After five

years of World War II, the Western public is going to jump at the chance of waging World War III – that, surely, was an assumption-and-a-half?

It would be an exaggeration to claim that ordinary men and women in the West were eager to enfold their Soviet counterparts in a fraternal embrace, but most were conscious of the contribution – and the sacrifices – they had made. In Britain, especially, that was so. The British had looked on the Russians, fighting far away, as an unproblematic ally – unlike the Americans, notoriously 'overpaid, oversexed and over here'. And if Conservative attempts to brand Britain's Labour Party as standing for Red Revolution were only too plainly hyperbolic, that July's

TRANSCRIPT OF KEY PARAGRAPHS

Operation Unthinkable, May 1945

. . . We have taken the following assumptions to base our examination: –

(a) The undertaking has the full support of public opinion in both the British Empire and the United States and consequently, the morale of British and American troops continues high.

(b) Great Britain and the United States have full assistance from the Polish armed forces and can count upon the use of German manpower and what remains of German industrial capacity.

(c) No credit is taken for assistance from the forces of other Western Powers . .

(d) Russia allies herself with Japan.

(e) The date for the opening of hostilities is 1st July, 1945.

2. The overall or political object is to impose upon Russia the will of the United States and British Empire.

DOCUMENT THE PROPERTY OF HIS BRITANNIC MAJESTY'S GOVERNMENT

The circulation of this paper has been strictly limited.

It is issued for the personal use of ....

TOP SECRET Copy No. 15

Final

22nd May, 1945.

WAR CABINET

JOINT PLANNING STAFF

OPERATION "UNTHINKABLE"

Report by the Joint Planning Staff.

We have examined Operation UNTHINKABLE. As instructed, we have taken the following assumptions on which to base our examination:-

(a) The undertaking has the full support of public opinion in both the British Empire and the United States and consequently, the morale of British and American troops continues high.

(b) Great Britain and the United States have full assistance from the Polish armed forces and can count upon the use of German manpower and what remains of German industrial capacity.

(c) No credit is taken for assistance from the forces of other Western Powers, although any bases in their territory, or other facilities which may be required, are made available.

(d) Russia allies herself with Japan.

(e) The date for the opening of hostilities is 1st July, 1945.

(f) Redeployment and release schemes continue till 1st July and then stop.

Owing to the special need for secrecy, the normal staffs in Service Ministries have not been consulted.

OBJECT

2. The overall or political object is to impose upon Russia the will of the United States and British Empire.

Even though "the will" of these two countries may be defined as no more than a square deal for Poland, that does not necessarily limit the military commitment. A quick success might induce the Russians to submit to our will at least for the time being; but it might not. That is for the Russians to decide. If they want total war, they are in a position to have it.

election made it abundantly clear that the voters would not be spooked. The experience of the Blitz, rationing and combat had made the recent conflict seem very much a 'people's war': ordinary men and women felt great pride in what they had achieved. That didn't make them communists – at the same time, though, they didn't recoil from the idea in horror as just a few years later they surely would. Anti-communism may indeed have been strongly embedded in American public opinion, but so too was a strong resistance to the idea of involvement in other people's wars. The notion that either population was straining at the leash to embark on a further war with the Soviet Union strains credulity pretty much to breaking-point.

Then there's the 'assumption' that the plan will involve, not just the recruitment of 100,000 Poles unhappy at their country's subjection to the Soviets, but 'the re-equipment and re-organization of German manpower'. Having been mortal enemies through a fierce and protracted war, the *Wehrmacht* and the armies of Britain and America will now, it seems, embrace one another as comrades-in-arms to go into battle against the Soviets.

It's hard to know now how far 'assumptions' like these were assumptions that the authors of the report actually made themselves – or even thought for a moment could be made. Were they just saying 'for the plan to have any hope of success, these are prerequisites'? The most important assumption, perhaps, is the implicit one – that Churchill needed 'handling'. Could it be that, swallowing any scepticism they themselves might feel, the chiefs were reporting on 'Unthinkable' as though it were any other – completely credible – operation, while discreetly pointing up the difficulties it would involve?

Winston Churchill stood on his war record in the election campaign of 1945. Britain felt warm gratitude – but voted Labour.

TRANSCRIPT OF KEY PARAGRAPHS

4. Apart from the chances of revolution in the U.S.S.R. and the political collapse of the present regime – on which we are not competent to express an opinion – the elimination of Russia could only be achieved as a result of: –

(a) The occupation of such areas of metropolitan Russia that the war making capacity of the country would be reduced to a point at which further resistance became impossible.

(b) Such a decisive defeat of the Russian forces in the field as to render it impossible for the U.S.S.R. to continue the war.

5. The situation might develop in such a way that the Russians succeeded in withdrawing without suffering a decisive defeat. They would then presumably adopt the tactics which they employed so successfully against the Germans and in previous wars of making use of the immense distances with which their territory provides them.

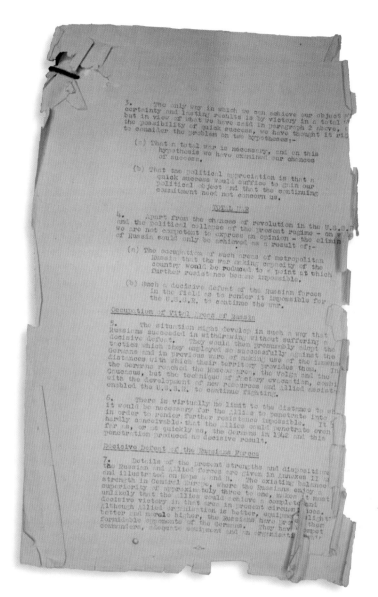

How Much is Enough?

One of the greatest of these difficulties was that of getting any accurate sense of the scale or shape of the challenge. The Soviets were a real enemy – but a curiously amorphous one. The chiefs anticipated that, as in the months after Germany's invasion in June 1941, the Soviets would pursue a policy of tactical retreat, 'making use of the immense distances with which their territory provides them.'

Just how much of the Soviet Union would you have to occupy before you could really feel you were an occupying force? This question was addressed in a section entitled 'Occupation of Vital Areas of Russia'. What were those areas, though? The answer

Mission accomplished for a Soviet air crew, but were they now facing war with the West?

'The war between the Russians and the democracies is approaching and indeed has already begun, and Germany will be invited to participate.'

British Intelligence Officer Goronwy Rees, July 1945

to that question should have been straightforward – yet it was anything but, a point revealed by recent history. 'In 1942', the chiefs pointed out, 'the Germans reached the Moscow area, the Volga and the Caucasus, but the technique of factory evacuation, combined with the development of new resources and Allied assistance, enabled the USSR to continue fighting.'

There is virtually no limit to the distance to which it would be necessary for the Allies to penetrate into Russia in order to render further resistance impossible. It is hardly conceivable that the Allies could penetrate even as far as, or as quickly as, the Germans in 1942 and this penetration produced no decisive result.

You could win, and still not win, in other words.

Numbers Game

The next section of the report rejoiced under the title 'Decisive Defeat of the Russian Forces', but this apparently upbeat heading only introduced more doom and gloom. A 'decisive victory' seemed unlikely, the report concluded, given that a Soviet superiority in overall numbers of more than 2:1 became as much as 3:1 in Central Europe. More detailed breakdowns of strength and deployment were given in extensive annexes to the report.

Forty-seven divisions were to be deployed in the western assault, 14 of them armoured. The Soviets, it was anticipated, would send out a force equivalent in strength to 170 Allied divisions, 30 of them armoured. 'We should therefore be facing odds of the order of two to one in armour and four to one in infantry.' And that was just the direct response: the Red Army was in position in strength in a line from the Baltic to the Black Sea; it might mount counterattacks anywhere from Austria to Turkey. It could further be expected to create what trouble it could for the Allies elsewhere, from the Middle East to India – and, of course, throw in its lot with Japan, opening a terrible new chapter in the Pacific War.

There *was* good news to be had, and Grantham, Thompson and Dawson were industrious in ferreting it out: 'The Allies could, of course, achieve dominating superiority at sea', for instance. But they didn't elaborate on this truth, which (no doubt rightly) they held to be self-evident, but instead passed quickly on. For, although control of the Baltic and Black Sea and their approaches was worth having, in the last analysis ruling the waves was neither here nor there. Dry land was the overwhelming issue: almost 3 million square miles of it in European Russia alone; more than twice as much again beyond the Urals.

Naval power was not without some significance, though: it seems to have swayed the planners in their view that the Allies should attack the Soviet Union in the northeast. That way, as they pushed their way into Russia, they'd have logistical and artillery support on their left flank – at least in the early days of their invasion. Two attacking thrusts were envisaged: a northern one 'on the axis Stettin – Schneidemuhl – Bydgoszcz' and a southern one 'on the axis Leipzig – Gottbus – Poznan and Breslau'. Of course, the further the invaders advanced into Soviet territory, the further they'd leave behind their naval back-up. Could they look instead to reinforcement from the air?

Up to a point, it seemed. Though it too was at a numerical disadvantage, the RAF enjoyed clear 'superiority' in the air. Or, at least, it would until the wear-and-tear of combat took its toll.

An Elusive Enemy

But in the air, as on the ground, there was that strange nebulousness which the Soviet Union presented to its would-be attackers – an enormous target it might be, but the Soviet bear was hard to hit.

As regards Strategic Air Forces, our superiority in numbers and technique would be to some extent discounted by the absence of

Soviet and Polish troops roll into Berlin aboard a T-34 tank, in May 1945. The end of the war … and the beginning of a new confrontation.

strategical targets compared with those which existed in Germany.

This was a delicate way of making the point that, as a result of Operation Barbarossa's initial onslaught and the Red forces' fightback in the years since, western Russia was now so much scorched earth. Industrial production was so 'dispersed' – centres so small and scattered, after years of destruction and upheaval – that it didn't present many suitable targets for Allied air attack.

And while opportunities were to be seen in the lengthy supply-lines the Soviets would have to maintain between industrial centres east of Moscow and the frontline action, Allied air power would be more stretched-out than the chiefs would like. Though it was true that 'ownership' of western Europe now gave the Allies an abundance of staging posts for refuelling, 'the elaborate ground organization of the bomber force' (the facilities for maintaining, arming, loading and directing large flights of aircraft) was to be had only in Britain. Moreover, the most vulnerable points in the Soviet Union were well out of the range of UK-based bombers: either raids would have to be mounted by small groups established in continental bases or stops would have to be made at staging airfields.

The findings of Grantham, Thompson and Dawson were distilled into three pages in a further report of 8 June, signed by their commanders, Brooke, Cunningham and Evill. Again, to the non-military mind there's an odd mismatch between the crispness of the language, the terseness with which the facts are laid out and – in the last analysis

TRANSCRIPT OF KEY PARAGRAPHS

The following is our estimate of the total forces in Europe on 1st July: –

<u>Land Forces</u>
U.S.: 64 divisions, British and Dominion: 35 divisions, Polish: 4 divisions.
Total: 103 divisions (including 23 armoured)

Russian: 264 divisions (including 36 armoured)

<u>Air Forces</u>
. . . The preponderance in numbers of Russian aircraft would for a time be off-set by the vastly superior handling and efficiency of the Allied Air Forces, especially the Strategic Air Forces. After a period of operations, however, our lack of replacement aircraft and air crews would seriously impair our air strength.

<u>Naval Forces</u>
The Allies could, of course, achieve dominating superiority at sea.

I.

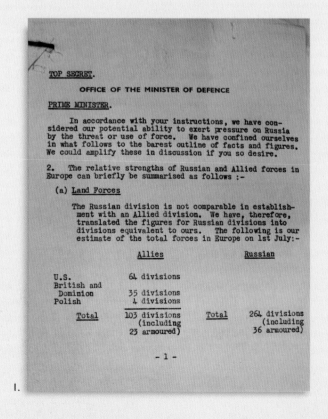

– the vagueness of the import, but really this is just the discipline of officers determined to confine themselves to the task they have been set. As they say at the start: 'We have confined ourselves . . . to the barest outline of facts and figures. We could amplify these in discussion if you so desire.' Not that they really need to; those 'facts and figures' speak for themselves. As does the warning note in their conclusion:

Our view is, therefore, that once hostilities began, it would be beyond our power to win a quick but limited success and we should

be committed to a protracted war against heavy odds. These odds, moreover, would become fanciful if the Americans grew weary and indifferent and began to be drawn away by the magnet of the Pacific War.

Unthinkable Rethought
Churchill took on board the implications of the report.

On 10 June he sent a minute to General Ismay asking the chiefs to consider a more defensively minded operation to be mounted in the event of a US withdrawal and a consequent Soviet invasion

of western Europe. They should give thought to the desirability of keeping hold of Denmark as an outpost controlling access to the Baltic and of other continental bridgeheads that might help them keep the Soviets at bay. The 'Unthinkable' title should be kept, he says, to underline the fact that 'this remains a precautionary study of what I hope, is still a highly improbable event'. Not quite so improbable as all that, however. Looking over the minute after it had been typed up, he made a handwritten correction, changing that conclusion to 'of

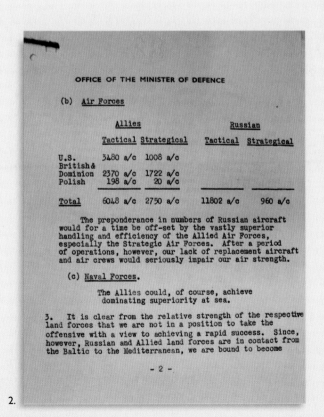

2.

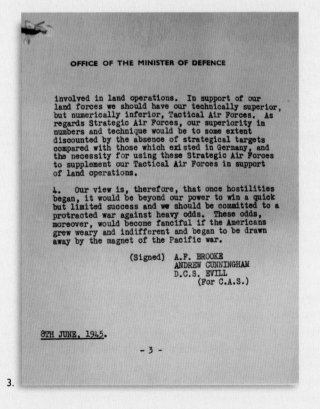

3.

what, I hope, is still a purely hypothetical contingency'.

'Improbable', 'hypothetical' or whatever it was, the chiefs took Churchill's request extremely seriously: it was a month before they reported back to him, and when they did, it was with a full and frank assessment of the likely threat. Overall, they were reassuring: whatever their strengths, Soviet forces lacked the experience or expertise to mount the massive amphibious assault that would be needed for an island like Great Britain to be taken. The Red Army's heroics on steppe and tundra were no

G. R.

TOP SECRET

DRAFT

GENERAL ISMAY
C.O.S. COMMITTEE

I have read the Chiefs of Staff note on "UNTHINKABLE" dated 8th June, which shows Russian preponderance of 2-1 on land.

2.   If the Americans withdraw to their zone and move the bulk of their forces back to the United States and to the Pacific, the Russians have the power to advance to the North Sea and the Atlantic. Pray have a study made of how then we could defend our Island, assuming that France and the Low Countries were powerless to resist the Russian advance to the sea. What Naval forces should we need and where would they be based? What would be the strength of the Army required, and how should it be disposed? How much Air Force would be needed and where would the main air-fields be located? Possession of airfields in Denmark would give us great advantage and keep open the sea passage to the Baltic where the Navy could operate. The possession of bridgeheads in the Low Countries or France should also be considered.

3.   By retaining the codeword "UNTHINKABLE" the Staffs will realise that this remains a precautionary study of what, I hope, is still a ~~highly improbable~~ event. purely hypothetical contingency.

TRANSCRIPT OF KEY PARAGRAPHS

Winston Churchill's minute to General Ismay, his chief military assistant. 10 June 1945.

If the Americans withdraw to their zone and move the bulk of their forces back to the United States and to the Pacific, the Russians have the power to advance to the North Sea and the Atlantic. Pray have a study made of how then we could defend our Island, assuming that France and the Low Countries were powerless to resist the Russian advance to the sea.

What Naval forces should we need and where would they be based? What would be the strength of the Army required, and how should it be disposed? How much Air Force would be needed and where would the main airfields be located?

Possession of airfields in Denmark would give us great advantage and keep open the sea passage to the Baltic where the Navy could operate. The possession of bridgeheads in the Low Countries or France should also be considered.

Germany's V2 became the model for the intercontinental ballistic missile (ICBM) of the Cold War era.

preparation for the logistical challenge of such a large-scale seaborne assault – and even if they had been, the operation would have been way beyond the Soviet navy. Granted, the Soviet air force was formidable, its pilots proven in months of heavy fighting over Europe – but so, of course, were the 'Few' of the RAF. Britain, they believed, would be best off relying on its traditional defence, the deep blue sea: Churchill's beloved bridgeheads would not be needed. Neither were they desirable, it was argued: these were an open invitation to the enemy, offering 'a well defined, compact target'; the need to defend them would 'impose a heavy and continuous drain on our resources'.

The main threat, as far as the chiefs were concerned, was now going to come from the new generation of rocket and pilotless-aircraft weapons. These had, of course, been developed by the Germans in the final months of the war: the V1 and V2 had been deployed, to devastating effect, and the Soviets were known to have taken these projects further. The chiefs were frank in their admission that

. . . We must expect a far heavier scale of attack than the Germans were able to develop, and we do not at present see any method of effectively reducing this.

Neither, though, did they see the likelihood of the Soviet Union being able to launch a serious attack on Britain without 'a period of preparation which must last some years'.

History moved on, and though it is certainly true that relations between the Western Allies and the Soviets did not improve, 'Operation Unthinkable' was overtaken by non-events. Even as the opposition between the two sides hardened, the logic of the Cold War began to exert its hold and fears of an immediate military conflict started to subside.

Chapter Two

If Things Turned Hot

The nuclear stand-off between the West and the Soviet bloc was to keep the peace for half a century · but only because both sides geared up seriously for war.

Three months after VE Day, on 15 August 1945, 'VJ Day' (Victory in Japan Day) dawned to ecstatic celebrations. In New York, in London, in Sydney and in liberated Paris, the people partied raucously, thrilled to think that the nightmare was over; that the war was definitively at an end. The official smiles were thin, though, concealing real concern: the war might be over, but there was little prospect of real peace. No one was under any illusions about ongoing relations with the Soviet Union, even if any plans for an immediate attack, discreetly mooted, had been quietly shelved.

In Moscow, the mood was altogether less rapturous – even on the streets. The Pacific War hadn't really gripped the public imagination here. Behind the scenes, in the Kremlin, the USSR's political masters had a clearer appreciation of VJ Day's significance. Here too, however, the response was distinctly muted. Indeed, it would be better described as downright grim.

Times Square is a scene of jubilation as New Yorkers turn out in their thousands to celebrate VJ Day and the end of World War II.

Atomic Weapons

The atom bomb changed everything. The rules of warfare were clearly now going to have to be rewritten. As yet, though, no one knew exactly how.

Bombshell

The bombings of Hiroshima and Nagasaki had blasted the confidence of the Communist leaders. Not that they hadn't had an inkling of what was about to happen. Soviet technicians were already at work on a weapon of their own. In fact, they had been for some years. Like the rest of the scientifically developed world, the Soviet Union had been pursuing research into nuclear physics since the 1930s. And, like the rest of the scientifically developed world, Soviet experts had been well aware of the potential military applications. Spies within the American establishment had warned them of US efforts in this area as early as 1942.

But while it was one thing to be fully up to speed with researches into atomic explosive power, it was quite another to comprehend the impact it could have. The Americans themselves had been taken aback by the dreadful destructive force they found they had set off at that summer's successful Trinity Test.

The first-ever nuclear explosion brought the Trinity Test to a close, opening a new strategic era.

'The lighting effects beggared description', recalled one observer, Brigadier General Thomas F. Farrell:

The whole country was lighted by a searing light with the intensity many times that of the midday sun. It was golden, purple, violet, gray and blue.

It lighted every peak, crevasse and ridge of the nearby mountain range with a clarity and beauty that cannot be described but must be seen to be imagined.

Physicist Kenneth Bainbridge, the test's director, had found a (brutal) clarity of his own as he watched the eruption:

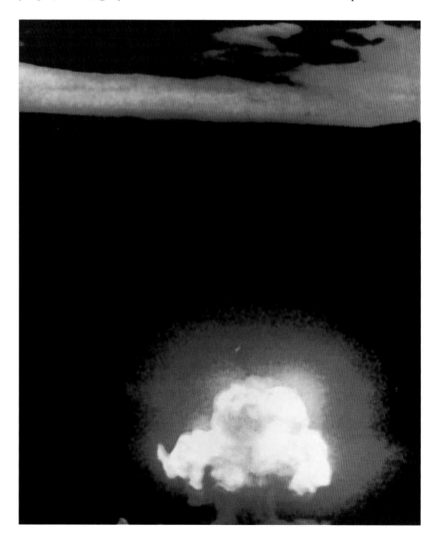

Kenneth Bainbridge (far left) and J. Robert Oppenheimer (third from left) stand with their fellow scientists at the test site.

Atomic Inequalities

Everyone was taking stock – and, to some extent, reviewing their positions week by week. These were confusing times for world leaders. In the immediate aftermath of VE Day, with Japan still to be beaten and every likelihood of astronomical casualties still to be sustained, the Americans had been eager to lock the Soviets in to their continuing alliance against the Axis. Scarcely had they secured Stalin's guarantees, however, than success of the Trinity Test had transformed the situation: the balance of power had abruptly shifted in America's favour. 'Had we known what the Atomic Bomb would do,' President Truman was afterwards to observe, 'we'd have never wanted the Bear in the picture.' The Soviets knew full well that they were *de trop*.

'Now we are all sons of bitches,' he had said.

Back on the Defensive

Having worked so hard to develop their weapon, the Americans were naturally going to deploy it. This could hardly have been a surprise to the Soviets, but it was still a shock. Scarcely had they completed their victory over the biggest and most lethally equipped invasion force in history than their hard-won aura of invincibility had been blown away. Foreign Minister Viacheslav Molotov went so far as to suggest that Little Boy and Fat Man had actually been aimed at the Soviet Union, not at Japan.

He didn't mean it literally, of course, but he meant it absolutely seriously. Nor could it be said that he was entirely wrong. While the attacks had clearly been primarily intended to bring about Japan's defeat after a long and shockingly costly war, they certainly *had* sent

a shot across Soviet bows. As so often, Winston Churchill was quick to sense what this might mean, specifically for the West's relations with the Soviets: 'It may make them a little more humble', he wrote.

Stalin didn't do humble. The news from Japan just hardened his determination to get even; to urge on the researchers he had working to build the Soviet bomb. In time, of course, they were to be successful – with a little help from communist friends in the American scientific establishment, like David Greenglass, his sister Ethel and her husband Julius Rosenberg. For the moment, though, the Soviet Union was completely adrift: if there was an 'arms race' in the summer of 1945, the Soviets were stuck firmly at the starting line.

Ethel and Julius Rosenberg passed atomic secrets to the Soviets.

The first Soviet atomic test ('First Lightning') was held on 29 August 1949.

'What a terrible thing we have made. The only thing we should bother about is to forbid all this and exclude nuclear war.'

Soviet scientist Igor Kurchatov on 'First Lightning', 1949

might not have been granted a few months later. His most pressing priority was to secure his sphere of influence in Eastern Europe – and to work for nuclear parity behind the scenes.

Britain Bereft

The Soviet Union was not, of course, the only country to have been left behind. Britain's bomb too lay some years in the future. This in part explains Churchill's earlier eagerness to pursue Operation Unthinkable. While there was clearly an argument for dealing with the USSR before it could arm itself with nuclear weapons, that wasn't the Prime Minister's sole concern. At least as important, from his point of view, was the need to secure the best possible settlement in Europe before the United States lost interest and disengaged.

Almost from the moment he took office, Truman had been signalling his desire to set a distance between America and Europe, to make it clear that Uncle Sam was not going to play Santa Claus.

The advent of the atomic bomb might have made an invasion of the Soviet Union not just unthinkable but unnecessary, but that wasn't necessarily a comforting thought as far as Churchill was concerned. Reliance on American protection in the new era was going to mean client status for the United Kingdom – quite a comedown for what was still a proud imperial nation.

Britain had won honour in the recent war – and a permanent seat

To be frozen out by their erstwhile Allies was neither a surprise nor a major blow, of course, to the Soviets; they weren't sentimental about their relationship with the West. The connection had been made only in a situation of the utmost peril, had been entered into with the utmost reluctance on both sides and characterized throughout by mutual mistrust. Stalin was conscious too (as Churchill bitterly complained) that he'd won out at Yalta, gaining concessions that

on the Security Council of the United Nations. And its atomic weapons programme, begun in 1940, was well advanced. By October 1952, Britain was to be a nuclear power, having conducted its first atomic weapons test in the Monte Bello Islands, off Australia's northwest coast. But prestige came at a price, and in the years that followed an economically exhausted Britain was to struggle to continue as a leading player on the world stage.

Bypassing the Public

There was no going back, however: what was really 'unthinkable' now was a world without the atomic bomb, for it could not now be uninvented. Though conventional warfare

Stalin (right) did well out of the Yalta Conference, February 1945, securing key concessions from his Western Allies.

was still going to have a place, it was clear that the ultimate power was going to lie with the nation that possessed superior strength in the nuclear sphere. More than this, though, the atomic bomb ensured that, within the nation itself, the ultimate power was going to lie – perhaps now more than ever before in the modern, democratic era – with a small political and military elite.

Churchill himself was later, famously, to remark that democracy was 'the worst form of government except all those other forms that have been tried'. He spoke with feeling, having been turned out of office in the autumn of 1945 by an electorate who revered him as a hero, but still didn't want him as prime minister. Whatever his impulsive drive or his waywardness, he had no desire for dictatorial power. At the same time, though, he was acutely conscious of democracy's besetting sins: indecision, delay and – sometimes grubby – compromise. For better or for worse, moreover, democratic rule had to be determined by the public mood – which, as of this moment, wanted an end to all the fighting.

If Operation Unthinkable had turned out to be just that, a war-weary western public had played its part. Granted, the scale of suffering in Britain and America could hardly compare with that in German-occupied western Europe, let alone that in Germany itself or the Soviet Union. Even so, the public in America felt – with justification – that it had been

Britain joined the nuclear club in 1952, testing its bomb in the Monte Bello Islands.

through a dangerous and difficult ordeal. Even those who had not fought themselves had suffered on account of loved ones away in Europe or the Pacific; many had known the pain of bereavement, or had to welcome home damaged or traumatized sons or husbands. Britain's civilians, as well as having relations abroad to worry about, had found themselves in the front line in Hitler's 'Blitz'. In neither country would there have been much enthusiasm for the idea of breaking off celebrations to start the fight all over again, however unsettling the threat from the Soviets.

But then why involve them at all? The 'beauty' of the atomic bomb, from the strategic thinker's point of view, was that it made war so much less 'labour intensive' than it had been before. Twelve men had crewed the B-29 *Enola Gay* for its attacking flight to Hiroshima, as against the 400,000 or more earmarked earlier for Operation Downfall, the projected invasion of the Japanese home islands by air and sea. No longer did the decision to go to war mean mass-mobilization: life could go on while a handful of politicians, technocrats and professional servicemen took care of things.

Right: Pilot Colonel Paul W. Tibbets, Jr, waves from his cockpit before taking off for Hiroshima on 9 August 1945.

Above: Queuing for coke in a United Kingdom in which most essentials were strictly rationed: frequently, the British did not feel like victors.

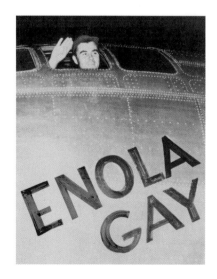

Attack Plans

US strategists made detailed plans for the complete and utter immolation of the Soviet enemy. Only by doing so, they reasoned, could they hope to achieve peace.

From Totality to Dropshot

One thing America's leaders did was to draw up plans for an all-out nuclear attack on the Soviet Union: Plan Totality was hatched in February 1947. On the orders of President Truman, Dwight D. Eisenhower directed the planners – and it's easy to see why he later came to worry about the problem of 'overkill'. For, by subsequent standards, Plan Totality seems anything but total. Indeed, in hindsight it could be seen as an almost laughably small-scale effort, involving the dropping of no more than 30 bombs on 20 Soviet cities, from Moscow and Leningrad to Tashkent, Tbilisi and Novosibirsk. Yet each one of those bombs would have dealt untold destruction to its target city, causing unimaginable misery and suffering on a scale not seen in history.

Plan Totality had been hastily formed in the heat of the moment after World War II. As time went on (and the US nuclear arsenal grew), more ambitious operations were worked out. Amidst mounting fears of Sino–Soviet attempts to expand into western Europe and eastern Asia, Operation Dropshot was drawn up as early as 1949, though no major communist attack was

Above: A victor for America in Europe, Dwight D. Eisenhower was the obvious person to oversee strategic planning.

Below: Winter snow was going to be the least of Moscow's worries if any of America's attack plans of the 1950s went ahead.

Many thousands of lives were lost on both sides in the Korean War.

'The son of a bitch isn't going to resign on me. I want him fired.'

President Truman, after MacArthur's nuclear threats, 11 April 1951

expected before the beginning of 1957. The Soviet Union and China were still close at this point, though as far as the Americans were concerned, the Soviets were very much the senior partner in the alliance – and, accordingly, the chief target of any US response. Up to 300 atomic bombs – and almost 30,000 conventional ones – were to be dropped on scores of Soviet cities and airbases, dealing a devastating blow to the USSR's capacity to wage war and maintain morale.

In the event, of course, communist expansion came rather earlier than anticipated – in 1950, in Korea – and the resulting conflict remained on a (relatively) small scale. US troops from Japan and Allied reinforcements went in to repel the North Korean force that had invaded South Korea. With the Western forces on the back foot for a while, General MacArthur mused aloud about the possible need to resort to atomic weapons – to the horror of America's allies and the embarrassment of President Truman. Though he did make

If Korea didn't spark nuclear war, it was no thanks to General Douglas MacArthur, who did everything he could to raise the stakes.

the threat to use the atomic bomb, his instinct was to keep America's powder dry – and avoid an attack that would just about inevitably have brought the Soviets into an all-out nuclear war.

Arm's-Length Enmity

The concentration of till now undreamt-of destructive power in the hands of a tiny political leadership was to transform the whole experience of enmity in the Cold War. The threat overhanging

the human race was without any precedent, but few felt much actual disquiet day by day; the sense of personal involvement was in inverse proportion to the actual stakes.

Old-fashioned wars – featuring armed forces – were still to be fought, of course. Those in Korea and Vietnam were significant conflicts by any standards. Allies of the superpowers engaged in 'proxy-wars' around the world; and enormous armies still faced

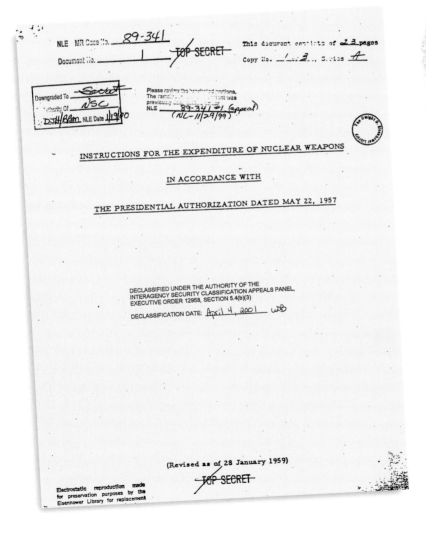

TRANSCRIPT OF KEY PARAGRAPHS

Instructions For The Expenditure Of Nuclear Weapons In Accordance With The Presidential Authorization, Dated May 22, 1957

(Right)
Operational Limitations
. . . The authority to expend nuclear weapons in the event urgency of time and circumstances clearly does not permit a specific decision by the President, or other person empowered to act in his stead, in an emergency measure necessitated by recognition of the fact that communications may be disrupted by the attack.

It is mandatory to insure that such authority is not assumed through accident or misinformation.

The authorization to expend nuclear weapons should be regarded as an authorization effective only until it is possible, in light of time and circumstances, to communicate with the President, or other person empowered to act in his stead.

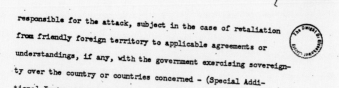

responsible for the attack, subject in the case of retaliation from friendly foreign territory to applicable agreements or understandings, if any, with the government exercising sovereignty over the country or countries concerned - (Special Additional Instructions in Section "C" below).

5. OPERATIONAL LIMITATIONS. Because of the serious international implications of the use of nuclear weapons by U. S. military forces, it is essential that particularly strict command control and supervision be exercised, and that the use of nuclear weapons be limited to circumstances of grave necessity. The authority to expend nuclear weapons in the event urgency of time and circumstances clearly does not permit a specific decision by the President, or other person empowered to act in his stead, is an emergency measure necessitated by recognition of the fact that communications may be disrupted by the attack. It is mandatory to insure that such authority is not assumed through accident or misinformation. The authorization to expend nuclear weapons should be regarded as an authorization effective only until it is possible, in light of time and circumstances, to communicate with the President, or other person empowered to act in his stead. In the expenditure of nuclear weapons pursuant to these instructions,

7

(Revised as of May 12, 1960)

quickly sets about exploring such legalistic – indeed, all but philosophical – questions as what exactly is meant by the 'United States', or by 'nuclear weapons' ('The term . . . includes all types of weapons and devices which release atomic energy.'). The document also considers – given the US position that nuclear bombs and missiles were maintained primarily as a deterrence, and only secondarily as defensive weapons – what would be deemed to constitute an 'attack':

The term 'attack' refers to a major hostile assault of such magnitude and against such areas or forces as to constitute an immediate and vital military threat to the security of the United States or to Major U.S. forces . . .

Who Gives the Order?
The key concern, however, is to establish a clear chain of command – understandable, given the power potentially to be unleashed. Previous conflicts had been the sum of many thousands of individual decisions by generals, officers and others on the ground (or at sea or in the air). A nuclear war between the Cold War superpowers would not only cause devastation on a scale as yet unimagined: it would do so effectively on the say-so of two men, in Moscow and Washington.

What if there wasn't time to go through channels? The writers' position is pragmatic:

When the urgency of time and circumstances clearly does not permit a specific decision by the President, or other person

each other east of the Rhine – for the ordinary citizen, East or West, the cold war seemed somehow unreal.

Battle of the Bureaucrats
There's an extraordinary air of detachment about the documentation that's become available from this time. Granted, a military plan isn't supposed to

be sensationalist. Even so, the bloodless way in which America's ideas for atomic war are officially laid out can seem quite startling, half a century on. Take, for example, the 'Instructions for the Expenditure of Nuclear Weapons' (22 May 1957; Revised January 1959). 'Expenditure' here means 'firing' – though you'd hardly know it. The mandarin prose

The B-29 did sterling service for America throughout the 1950s.

empowered to act in his stead, the Armed Forces of the United States are authorized by the President to expend nuclear weapons in the following circumstances in conformity with these instructions.

Scarcely have they ceded this power, though, than they seem to start rowing back:

Operational Limitations. Because of the serious international implications of the use of nuclear weapons by U.S. military forces, it is essential that particularly strict command control and supervision be exercised, and that the use of nuclear weapons be limited to circumstances of grave necessity.

It's a genuine dilemma, apparently, because the writers promptly reiterate the point that authority is to be delegated to Armed Forces commanders; yet this still seems to have been a

sticking-point. Handwritten revisions of May 1960 suggest that there was some thought of this clause being deleted. It actually *is* cut – scrawled through by hand – where it reappears a couple of pages later, along with further stipulations (that action

by the Authorizing Commander take place only where the damage of an attack would constitute 'an immediate and vital threat to the security of the United States'; and that it should remain as limited as the circumstances allowed).

Nuclear Options
The authors' thoughts on the rules of engagement reflect the growing diversity of means available for delivering nuclear weapons: by now, we've come a long way from the days of *Enola Gay*. The authors allow explicitly for attack by 'submarine or surface craft' against the US itself, its territories or possessions; a 'Sino–Soviet' assault on a major US force on the high seas or in foreign territory, whether by missile-launch, bombing, strafing or air-to-air attack; and ground assault

Launched in 1954, the USS *Nautilus* was the world's first nuclear submarine.

on areas of foreign territory under occupation by US forces.

The B-29 remained the bomber of choice for the Americans right through the 1950s. Its Soviet equivalent was the Tupolev Tu-95. Both sides had been hard at work designing ICBMs (Intercontinental Ballistic Missiles), building on the work of the Germans during World War II. Both the Soviet R-7 and the American Atlas D were recognizably descendants of the German V2. The former, which had a range of about 8850km (5500 miles), was introduced in 1957; the latter was not in service until two years later but had a range of 14,480km (9000 miles). Flying at up to 10 times the speed of sound (and so approximately 20 times as fast as a heavy bomber), ICBMs allowed either side to attack the other's homeland at short notice.

At sea, the submarine had markedly increased the possibilities – especially since the launch of the USS *Nautilus* in 1954. The world's first 'nuclear submarine', SSN-571 was 'nuclear' in two senses: firstly, that it was armed with Regulus I nuclear-capable cruise missiles and, secondly, that it was propelled and lit by atomic power. New 'inertial guidance' systems tracked the *Nautilus*'s every shift in position from the moment it left port, so it didn't have to surface to establish where it was. It did have to emerge from the deep, however, to replenish its air supply. It would also have to surface to fire off its missiles – another area of vulnerability. Since the Regulus I's effective range was only about 805km (500 miles), the *Nautilus* would have to come to the surface under the nose of the Soviets, a sitting target for Soviet planes and shore-based missiles. However, Polaris, in development from 1956 and in

The Soviet TU-95 strategic bomber came into service in 1956. It is used by the Russian Air Force to this day.

service (in version A-3) by 1950, had two solid-fuel stages, giving it a range of almost 4838km (3000 miles). A submarine could fire its missiles from far beyond the continental shelf – without surfacing and betraying its position. Since the technology had by now been developed to extract oxygen from sea water by electrolysis, it could lurk in the depths for months on end.

Meanwhile, the development of smaller, lighter (and, gradually, more securely stable) atomic bombs made possible the arming of faster, more manoeuvrable fighter-bombers. In the game of shadow-boxing that was deterrence, the peace was kept by both sides' consciousness that the other really *could* mount an effective attack if it so desired.

Single Integrated Operational Plan (SIOP)

As nuclear arsenals grew, so did the challenge of coordinating their deployment in the case of war. Careful planning was going to be required.

Fantasy Fighting

The fact that Armageddon did not break out, while obviously welcome, was problematic too: how were the Americans to test their defences, their capacity for waging war? They had no alternatives but to try out different scenarios as games. Extremely serious games, as becomes clear when we consider the 'Discussion at the 387th Meeting of the National Security Council, Thursday, November 20, 1958'. President Eisenhower had called the meeting, asking members in advance to consider a hypothetical case study: that of a surprise attack by Soviet nuclear bombers to take place in the middle of 1961. The tortuousness of the exercise is underlined by the artificiality of reporting as a past-tense completed action an event that's supposed to 'have' taken place in two years' time.

There isn't the least hint of playfulness or tongue-in-cheek about the tone, however:

Colonel William Calhoun described the Soviet attack on the continental U.S. Captain Edward L. Dashiell, USN, subsequently described the U.S. retaliatory attack on the Soviet Union as well as the U.S. military posture after the attack on the U.S. by the Soviet Union.

Colonel Calhoun next expounded the estimate of the damage inflicted on the U.S. by the Soviet attack and Captain Dashiell described the damage

TRANSCRIPT OF KEY PARAGRAPHS

November 1958
National Security Council
Meeting

(Left) . . . Mr Gray presented a recommendation in substantially the following language:

"The presentation you have just heard has concluded that a substantial reduction of the capability of the USSR to recover would be accomplished by the concentration of a U.S. retaliatory effort against a combined military-urban industrial target system as opposed to a strictly military target system,. The conclusion also was that such an effort would destroy the Soviet nuclear offensive capability.

"A central aim of our policy is to deter the Communists from use of their military power, remaining prepared to fight general war should one be forced upon the U.S. There has been no suggestion from any quarter as to a change in this basic policy. However, as you know, NSC 5410/1, the so-called 'war objectives' paper is in the process of review.

inflicted on the Soviet Union by the U.S. retaliatory attack.

Scary stuff – though perhaps more frightening still was the sense of how impossible everything was to predict, a fact underlined by General Gerald C. Thomas, Chairman of the Net Evaluation Subcommittee, in his summing-up:

There were obviously many uncertainties with respect to the military capabilities of the U.S. at a period as distant as mid-1961 and of course even more uncertainty as to the military capabilities of the Soviet Union at the same time.

That said, Thomas stressed his belief that the scenario they had come up was broadly realistic; that it represented an approximation of what might actually happen.

Hitting Where it Hurts

As the meeting moved on to discuss America's response in greater detail, National Security Advisor Gordon Gray addressed what was becoming a key question for US nuclear defence. The growing strength of America's nuclear arsenal had brought with it a new challenge: that of deciding where these different weapons should be aimed. The earlier view that they should be targeted exclusively at the Soviet Unions's own nuclear forces had gradually been giving ground to a feeling that – while the overall defensive character of America's weapons should not be forgotten – the US should do whatever it took to protect itself. What

analysts were already calling 'megadeath' might be morally justifiable if it ultimately saved comparable numbers of US lives.

Hence President Eisenhower's request, in Gray's report,

that the exercise concern itself with the retaliatory objective of immediately paralyzing the Russian nation, rather than concentrating on targets of a military character although not entirely ruling out particular military targets.

Determined Deterrence

The basic intentions of the Americans were clear, and continued substantially unchanged:

A central aim of our policy is to deter the Communists from use of their military power, remaining prepared to fight general war should one be forced upon the U.S.

Specific approaches were up for discussion, however. Gray was going to ask the President to consider

. . . an appraisal of the relative merits, from the point of view of effective deterrence, of retaliatory efforts directed toward:

1. Primarily a military target system, or

2. What might be felt to be the optimum mix of a combined military-urban industrial target system.

What was the point of pounding away at the Soviet Union's nuclear sites if you weren't also going to attack the communists' will to pursue the war? It was all very well to shun 'civilian' targets, but if public morale was allowed to remain high and industrial production to continue, wouldn't you really just be dragging out the conflict and (in the longer run) increasing casualties? On the other hand, as Secretary of State McElroy warned, it was no use simply flattening Soviet cities and hoping that the Soviets would lose the will to fight, given the dispersal of the USSR's hardened ICBM bases:

Even if we succeeded in destroying the cities and urban centers of the Soviet Union, these missile sites would still enable the Soviet Union to retain an add-on capability with their long-range missiles.

Eisenhower himself considered a reappraisal of targeting to be essential, if only on account of the sheer number of targets that had been identified. These included, he noted, 'every city in the U.S.S.R. with a population of over 25,000 people.'

In view of this very large number of urban targets, the President believed that we must get back to the formulation of the series of targets in the Soviet Union destruction of which would most economically paralyze the Russian nation . . .

Overkill?

This thought took discussion to the question of quite how much destruction was necessary. Did the USSR's military capability really *have* to be destroyed completely, Eisenhower asked:

We are trying to destroy the will of the Soviet Union to fight.

If in the first thirty hours of the nuclear exchange the U.S. succeeded in accomplishing the degree of devastation in the Soviet Union that had been outlined in this morning's presentation, we would already have accomplished our purpose of destroying the will of the Soviet Union to fight. One could not go on to argue that we must require a 100 per cent pulverization of the Soviet Union. There was obviously a limit – a human limit – to the devastation which human beings could endure.

Eisenhower is known to have been ambivalent about the mushrooming growth of what he himself would subsequently (in 1961) christen the 'military-industrial complex'; is some of that concern to be detected here? If that's so, it seems fair to say that, along with any ethical anxieties, we can discern too a seasoned general's unease about a vast and spreading system that shows every sign of getting out of control.

Communicate, Coordinate . . . And Automate?

That this unease was justified is clear from a memo sent by Nathan F. Twining, as Chairman of the Joint Chiefs of Staff on 17 August 1959, under the heading 'Target Coordination and Associated Problems'. Acknowledging that America's growing strength in nuclear arms has brought with it certain 'weaknesses', he insists that coordination is the key:

Before 1952 there were so few atomic weapons in the stockpile

"Such appraisal should also take into account the requirements of a counter-force capacity which might conceivably be called upon in the case of unequivocal strategic warning of impending Soviet attack on the U.S. The question here might be whether the character and composition of such a force would be adequate to the purposes of 1 or 2 above, and vice versa.

"These matters have been under intensive study in the Department of Defense. If it is agreeable to you I shall be glad to work with Mr. McElroy and General Twining to determine the best way to accomplish such an appraisal, relating it as necessary to the review of the so-called War Objectives paper, bearing in mind that the knowledge and views of the State Department and other Federal agencies would be importantly involved."

When Mr. Gray had concluded his suggested Council action, the President said he was convinced that what Mr. Gray proposed to have done was essential for the obvious reason that in today's presentation of the U.S. retaliatory attack on the Soviet Union, the U.S. had as targets every city in the U.S.S.R. with a population of over 25,000 people. In view of this very large number of urban targets, the President believed that we must get back to the formulation of the series of targets in the Soviet Union destruction of which would most economically paralyze the Russian nation. Turning to General Twining and addressing him and other members of the Joint Chiefs of Staff, the President said that he could remember well when the military used to have no more than 70 targets in the Soviet Union and believed that destruction of these 70 targets would be sufficient. Now, however, a great many more targets had been added. He accordingly expressed his approval of the suggested action by Mr. Gray.

Secretary McElroy expressed his view that the dispersal of the hardened Soviet ICBM bases introduced a new element in the picture because even if we succeeded in destroying the cities and urban centers of the Soviet Union, these missile sites would still enable the Soviet Union to retain an add-on capability with their long-range missiles.

In response to Secretary McElroy's point, the President commented that in this morning's presentation the Soviets delivered all of their ICBM's in the first two hours of their attack on the U.S. Secretary McElroy agreed that this was the case but said that there was some doubt as to whether this was a sound assumption as to the Soviet use of their ICBM's. The President replied that the presentation assumed that we are trying to destroy the will of the Soviet Union to fight. If in the first thirty hours of the nuclear exchange *and such limited capability outside the Air Force that coordination presented no significant difficulties. Early in 1952, as the stockpile became larger, and delivery capability of other than Air Force forces increased, the Joint Chiefs of Staff set up machinery to coordinate atomic targeting . . .*

Though the Chiefs had required their commanders to 'develop and dove-tail' their strike plans together, the results to date had been 'somewhat spotty'. Indeed, Twining went on: 'Out of a total of about 2,400 targets, something over 300, or about 13%, have been labelled "duplications."' Some degree of overlap was inevitable – necessary, even, given the need to ensure that a key target was taken out. In such cases it should be possible to cancel the second 'duplicating' attack if the first one was known to have succeeded. For this to work,

---

Dwight D. Eisenhower Library
Eisenhower: Papers, 1953-61
(Ann Whitman file)

the U.S. succeeded in accomplishing the degree of devastation in the Soviet Union that had been outlined in this morning's presentation, we would already have accomplished our purpose of destroying the will of the Soviet Union to fight. One could not go on to argue that we must require a 100 per cent pulverization of the Soviet Union. There was obviously a limit - a human limit - to the devastation which human beings could endure.

Secretary McElroy expressed his agreement to the action recommended by Mr. Gray and the President brought the meeting to a conclusion with an expression of warm congratulations to General Thomas and his associates and also a welcome to General Hickey who would be taking over henceforth from General Thomas.

The National Security Council:

a. Noted and discussed the Annual Report for 1958 of the Net Evaluation Subcommittee, pursuant to NSC 5816, as presented orally by the Director and other members of the Subcommittee Staff.

b. Noted the President's request for an appraisal of the relative merits, from the point of view of effective deterrence, of alternative retaliatory efforts directed toward: (1) Primarily a military target system, or (2) an optimum mix of a combined military-urban industrial target system. Such an appraisal is to take into account the requirements of a counter-force capacity and whether such a counter-force capacity would be adequate for (1) or (2) above and vice versa. The Secretary of Defense, the Chairman, Joint Chiefs of Staff, and the Special Assistant to the President for National Security Affairs are to determine the best means of defining and accomplishing such an appraisal, relating it as necessary to the current review of NSC 5410/1 and the interests of the Department of State and other Executive agencies.

NOTE: The action in b above, as approved by the President, subsequently transmitted to the Secretary of Defense, the Chairman, Joint Chiefs of Staff, and the Special Assistant to the President for National Security Affairs for appropriate implementation.

S. Everett Gleason

S. EVERETT GLEASON

5.

TRANSCRIPT OF KEY PARAGRAPHS

November 1958
National Security Council
Meeting (ctd.)

One could not go on to argue that we must require a 100 per cent pulverization of the Soviet Union. There was obviously a limit - a human limit - to the devastation which human beings could endure.

The National Security Council noted the President's request for an appraisal of the relative merits, from the point of view of effective deterrence, of alternative retaliatory efforts directed toward:
(1) Primarily a military target system, or (2) an optimum mix of a combined military-urban industrial target system.

Such an appraisal is to take into account the requirements of a counter-force capacity and whether such a counter-force capacity would be adequate for (1) and (2) above and vice versa.

S. Everett Gleason

however, good communications were essential. That was far from being the case at the time, though, as 'maneuvers and exercises' had shown; wouldn't it be worse in actual combat conditions?

The answer was organization: the nuclear 'button' should start a single, well-oiled machine.

Atomic operations must be pre-planned for automatic execution to the maximum extent possible and with minimum reliance on post-H-hour communications.

There are obvious advantages in having a system so well planned it could take care of itself in all the chaos and confusion of conflict – but, just as obviously, reducing the human element reduces the element of choice. Was this really going to be the first war in history in which an ability to improvise, to adapt to changing realities, would not be needed?

Twining too worried away at the targeting question: 'How many and what kind of targets should be destroyed?' Even among the experts, he noted, the disagreement was 'exceedingly wide'. On the one hand, striking at cities might be seen as a strategy of despair, rooted in the fear of not being able to find the Soviet ICBM bases. On the other, there was the argument that it was

. . . easier to destroy a missile before it is launched than after; that the Soviets will not be able to launch anything like 100% of their missiles in the first salvo; that, in any case, we must destroy the Soviet capability to re-attack in order to minimize damage to the United States . . .

All in all, he concludes, the response to the Soviets has to be overwhelming:

Soviet military doctrine is based on the Principle of Mass, and I believe that the Soviets will respect only a very powerful force.

An SAC Stranglehold?
Who better to deliver a crushing response than the planes of the United States Air Force?

We have developed a strategic capacity to launch, under good to optimum conditions, possibly 2,000 to 4,000 strategic weapons with manned aircraft, and we have, thus far, deterred general war.

Twining's service loyalties are easily recognized, a cynic might say. Rival service chiefs had in fact already grown frustrated at the stranglehold the Strategic Air Command, or SAC, now held over nuclear policy. It's easy to forget the early impact of the atom bomb: Hiroshima and Nagasaki had not just crushed Japanese resistance but had awed the wider world – including those charged with the defence of the United States. Truman and his colleagues believed that they'd seen the future, that the new weapon offered a silver-bullet solution to all America's foreign-policy problems. Indeed, they weren't far off wondering whether the US needed a navy, an army or other such antiquities at all.

The feelings of the other service chiefs aren't hard to imagine. There wasn't too much love lost at the best of times. An indispensable element in thriller

US Air Force General Nathan Farragut Twining took charge as Chairman of the Joint Chiefs of Staff in 1957. Some resented what they saw as his pro-Air Force bias.

'The central question is whether or not we have the ability to destroy anyone who attacks us, because the biggest thing today is to provide a deterrent for war.'

President Eisenhower, 1959

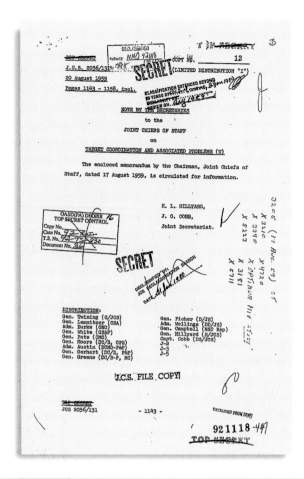

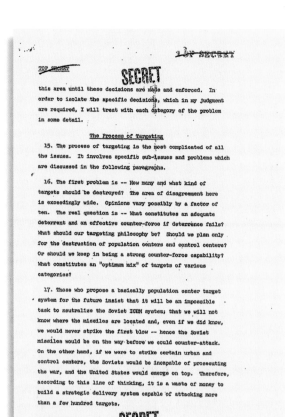

Joint Chiefs of Staff Memorandum – Target Coordination, 17 August 1959

16. The first problem is -- How many and what kind of targets should be destroyed? The area of disagreement here is exceedingly wide. Opinions vary possibly by a factor of ten. The real question is -- What constitutes an adequate deterrent and an effective counter-force if deterrence fails? What should our targeting philosophy be? Should we plan only for the destruction of population centers and control centers?

17. Those who propose a basically population center target system for the future insist that it will be an impossible task to neutralize the Soviet ICBM [intercontinental ballistic missile] system; that we will not know where the missiles are located and, even if we did know, we would never strike the first blow – hence the Soviet missiles would be on the way before we could counter-attack.

On the other hand, if we were to strike certain urban and control centers, the Soviets would be incapable of prosecuting the war, and the United States would emerge on top. Therefore, according to this line of thinking, it is a waste of money to build a strategic delivery system capable of attacking more than a few hundred targets.

novels and films, inter-service rivalry in the US military can easily be exaggerated, but that doesn't mean that it doesn't exist or that it isn't sometimes damaging. To take just one example, Project Danny, a plan in 1944 to attack the silos in which V1 rockets were being housed, had to be abandoned because senior Army officers were unwilling to work with their counterparts in the Marines. Things between the service chiefs hadn't quite come to this all-but-mutinous pass by the end of the 1950s, but the Navy especially

was chafing under the SAC's authority. (This was perhaps inevitable, given the extent to which advances in submarine and missile technology had enhanced the Navy's ability to contribute – even while it remained, to all intents and purposes, outside the strategic loop.)

Tom Trips Up

As a case in point, we might consider a conversation between Chief of Naval Operations Admiral Arleigh Burke and William B. Franke, the Secretary of the Navy. Held on 12 August

1960, it's tonally a world away from the brisk and businesslike manner of the memos and reports we've seen so far. Admiral Burke strikes a plaintive note from the very start: 'I have had a rough time in the last couple of days', he tells his boss. He then explains that, as far as he sees it, the SAC has mounted an air-force coup, convincing Defense Secretary Thomas S. Gates to give it control of the target lists for

Inter-service rivalry had caused Project Danny to be aborted in 1944, spoiling a chance of stopping Germany's V1 programme.

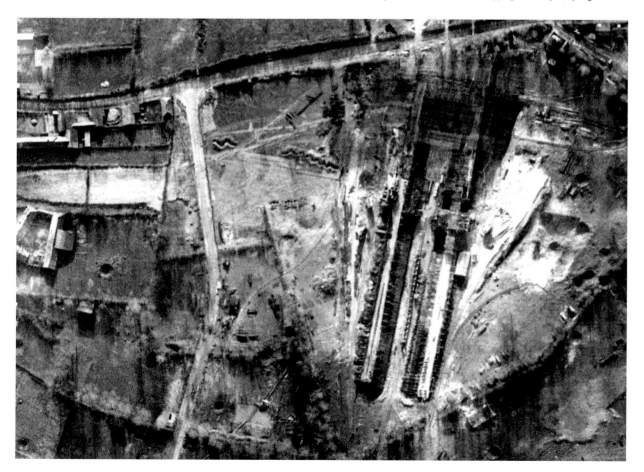

Admiral Arleigh Burke felt his US Navy was a service under siege.

nuclear strikes. In theory, collective responsibility will be taken – but, believes Admiral Burke, 'Tom' Gates has made the gravest of errors:

He is ignoring the fundamental thing – what SAC has done in the past. They have never followed through with the Joint Chiefs policies. He says well they ought to. Well, sure they ought to. But the Joint Chiefs and the Secretary of Defense himself have not made SAC amenable to control.

'We Will Wreck This Country'

There's a lot at stake, says Burke:

If SAC gets control of this thing, the number of atomic weapons will be tremendous and they will be the wrong kind of atomic weapons . . . They will control the budget. They will control everything, and they will wreck – I am sure they will wreck everything in the rest of it if they can.

They'll set to work making the changes irreversible: 'In a year of this stuff – you can never undig it,' he adds.

The systems will be laid. The grooves will be dug. And the power will be there because the money will be there. The electronic industry and all of those things.

The 'military-industrial complex', in other words. And if we let it win, 'We will wreck this country,' Burke concludes.

Arleigh Burke had form for this sort of complaint, of course. Over

a decade earlier he had been a key conspirator in what came to be known as the 'Revolt of the Admirals', encouraging superior officers to make a stand against what they saw as the neglect of naval strength in favour of the bomber force. In the years that followed, he'd backed Admiral Hyman Rickover in his drive to build the world's first 'nuclear navy' for the United States.

A Concerted Response

The Admiral was right that decisions being made now were going to shape the approach to nuclear defence for the foreseeable future. SIOP-62 was being finalized at this point. The title is confusing in that this, the first of a series of progressively refined strategic blueprints, was put together in 1960 and introduced in 1961. Made in response to concerns about effective organization, coordination and targeting, this 'Single Integrated Operational Plan' gave detailed instructions on the part to be played by each government office and armed service in the event of nuclear emergency, and the exact procedures to be followed should the fighting start.

Years of lobbying on Burke's part had not been in vain, however: SIOP-62 gave the Navy and its submarines a major role. Where Burke – and allies in the Army – had been less successful was in calling for a more measured, graduated approach of a sort that would not only suit those services better but be more appropriate to an ever-evolving

TRANSCRIPT OF KEY PARAGRAPHS

General Power, in his capacity as DSTP, was guided by the National Strategic Targeting and Attack Policy (NSTAP), a JCS document which formed the core of this nation's strategic strike planning. Specific objectives of this policy were to destroy or neutralize Sino-Soviet Bloc strategic strike forces and major military and government control centers, and to strike urban-industrial centers to achieve the level of destruction indicated in Study 2009. These objectives were to be accomplished by integrating strategic forces and directing them against a minimum list of targets.

The first task of the JSTPS after its organization was to determine what targets were to be attacked. On 18 August General Power directed his Directorate of Intelligence to prepare a preliminary target list. At the initial meeting of the Staff six days later Intelligence presented a working list, known as the National Strategic Target Data Base (NSTDS) of about 4,000 targets.

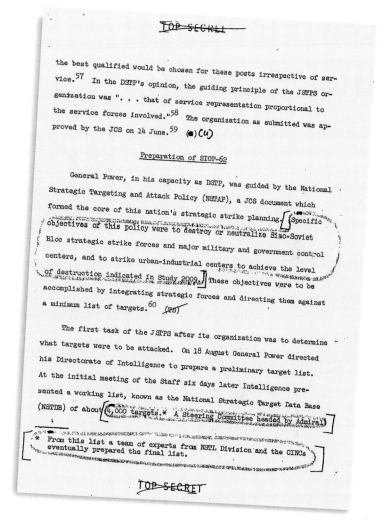

world-situation. SIOP-62 was a nuclear sledgehammer. More than 3000 warheads were designated for a pre-set list of targets – not just missile sites and airfields but cities and industrial centres too.

The plan also made no distinction between the Soviet Union and the People's Republic of China. Comradeship between the two powers had never been entirely easy. Mao's brand of Marxism-Leninism had been idiosyncratic, to say the least.

Moreover, the two had very different histories and regional interests, and were at markedly different stages of industrial development. Indeed, by 1960, relations had broken down more or less completely.

Later versions of SIOP recognized this new reality. Subsequent versions were issued annually thereafter, named for the relevant fiscal year (SIOP-63, SIOP-64 . . .), and took into account political changes.

British Plans and Blue Streak

An also-ran in the Arms Race, Britain was nevertheless a nuclear contender: possession of the bomb brought prestige to an imperial power in decline.

Poor Relation

After 1945, Britain was having an uncomfortable time confronting difficult realities in a very different world: the overriding problem, it's often been argued, of postwar life. The country had to cut its strategic coat according to its economic cloth: there were humiliating sacrifices to be made. The Defence Estimates for 1950–51 warn of the loss of political authority, economic influence and security likely to result from any 'discarding of responsibilities' in Western Europe, the Far and Middle East or Africa. Yet the expense of maintaining a convincing presence in these regions was bound to be immense – even allowing for the massive scaling-down of the armed services since the war.

TRANSCRIPT OF KEY PARAGRAPHS

<u>Memorandum by the British Prime Minister, 8th December 1949</u>

2. The report . . . showed that the effect of reducing the defence budget to anything in the neighbourhood of £700 million could not fail [but be] . . . equivalent in the political field to a major disaster in the "cold war."

4. (i) Emphasis is placed on winning the "cold war," the underlying thought being that if we succeed in this we may avoid being called upon to fight any other kind of war;

(ii) The three main pillars of our strategy are defined, as in earlier studies, as the defence of the United Kingdom, of our sea communications, and of our position in the Middle East;

---

cwd 8/7/49 @ 5.15 pm (Special)

THIS DOCUMENT IS THE PROPERTY OF HIS BRITANNIC MAJESTY'S GOVERNMENT

386

Printed for the Cabinet. December 1949

The circulation of this paper has been strictly limited. It is issued for the personal use of *Sir Norman Brook*

TOP SECRET

Copy No. 31

C.P. (49) 245
8th December, 1949

CABINET

DEFENCE ESTIMATES, 1950–51

MEMORANDUM BY THE PRIME MINISTER

The size of the defence budget for 1950–51 has recently been investigated by the Defence Committee and I now bring before the Cabinet the upshot of their discussions.

2. My colleagues will recall that when, on 24th January, we approved a total of £760 million for the defence estimates 1949–50 (C.M. (49) 6th Conclusions, Minute 1) it was agreed that the Minister of Defence should in due course bring before the Defence Committee a fully co-ordinated plan for the future defence of the country. By arrangement with the Minister, the Chiefs of Staff entrusted the first stage of this study to an inter-Service Working Party, who were invited to consider how an annual defence budget limited to £700 million for the three years beginning April 1950, could best be distributed and what the effects on the fighting strength of the Forces would be. The report suggested many useful economies, but showed that the effect of reducing the defence budget to anything in the neighbourhood of £700 million* could not fail to be of a most serious character, necessitating major withdrawals all over the world, and equivalent in the political field to a major disaster in the " cold war."

3. A new start was required and the Minister of Defence, assisted by the Service Ministers and the Chiefs of Staff, proceeded to work out new proposals for the three years 1950–51, 1951–52 and 1952–53, designed to avoid the worst of these difficulties. These proposals, which for the first time took the form of a properly co-ordinated plan, aimed at mitigating or eliminating the most damaging reductions inevitable under the inter-Service working party's proposals; and at avoiding default on our obligations under Western Union and the Atlantic Pact without placing an intolerable burden on the Exchequer.

4. The main features of the Minister's proposals, set out at Annex A, are as follows :—

(i) Emphasis is placed on winning the " cold war," the underlying thought being that if we succeed in this we may avoid being called upon to fight any other kind of war;

(ii) The three main pillars of our strategy are defined, as in earlier studies, as the defence of the United Kingdom, of our sea communications, and of our position in the Middle East;

* Subsequent detailed examination of the report showed that the Committee's proposals would cost about £50 million more than their initial estimate.

37978

The test site at Spadeadam Rocket Establishment in Cumberland, England with the Blue Streak Rocket on the left.

An annex explains the problem neatly in terms of 'teeth and tail': a modern fighting force, with its specialized equipment and complex organization, requires considerable administrative and logistical support.

Radar alone has introduced a new and very exacting requirement in the Services. The modern heavy bomber does not merely need a bigger crew to operate it, but also makes a very much heavier demand on the ground staff than its predecessor. The modern destroyer requires a crew about one-third stronger than her pre-war counterpart of comparable main armament.

National Service might offer an expensive way of maintaining an army – one that was mediocre at best – but it couldn't yet be dispensed with, the Defence Chiefs warned. Britain's current responsibilities were simply too extensive – and, indeed, geographically too far flung. Moreover, as of 1947, there was no Indian Army to be called on any more. 'While the cost of this Army to the United Kingdom was relatively small, it was a definite factor in our military strength.'

The answer? This had largely been dictated by the signature (in 1948) of the Atlantic Pact: priority had to be given to the Cold War. As the document disarmingly puts it:

The keynote of the plan is the emphasis it places on the Cold War with the underlying thought that if this is done we may hope not to be called to fight any other kind of war.

A compromise would have to be made. According to the authors:

The forces we shall have, if the plan is approved . . . are not as large as those which the Chiefs of Staff consider necessary on purely military grounds, but equally, they are not so small as to lead to the frustration, if not the abandonment of some of the major objects of our foreign policy . . .

The Chiefs of Staff clearly understood the risks of putting all their eggs in the Cold War basket. Should a military threat arise from any other source than the Soviet Bloc, Britain might find itself badly caught short. Their answer, then, was the development of a 'substantial arms export trade to enable us to maintain the industrial war potential on which we can call and, if necessary, rapidly expand in emergency.'

Anglo-Saxon Allies

NATO was supposedly an equal alliance of democratic nations, but no one really doubted America's pre-eminence among the partners. Unproblematic as this might be for most, it was difficult for former imperial powers like Britain and France to accept.

The first 'British bomb' had been tested in 1952; four years later, a series of tests established that the country had its own viable hydrogen bomb. In the meantime, development had begun on the 'Blue Streak' – an intermediate-range ballistic missile (IRBM). Britain was a serious atomic power. This meant that the partnership inaugurated by the US–UK Mutual Defence Agreement of 1958 wasn't as obviously unequal as it might otherwise have been. (Indeed, France's feeling that it was losing out in the jostling competition with Britain for second-among-equals status within NATO led to its withdrawal from the alliance later that same year.) The June 1958 'Report to the President and Prime Minister' sets out the procedures Her Majesty's armed forces – and US forces stationed in the United Kingdom – would follow in the event of a communist attack.

Critics on the Left were to sneer that Britain was meekly surrendering its sovereignty; that Shakespeare's 'sceptred isle' had become an 'unsinkable aircraft carrier' for the United States. Perhaps. It's certainly difficult to dispute that the country allowed its freedom of action to be

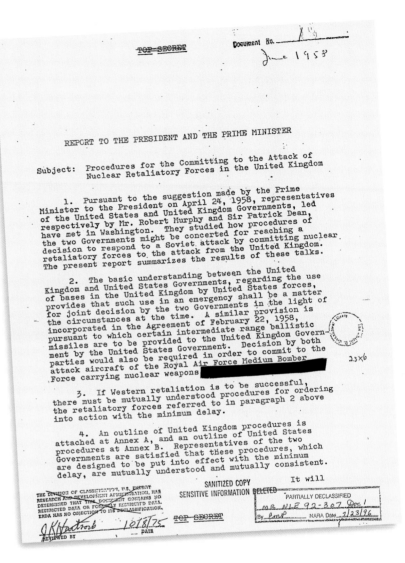

circumscribed by its agreements with America. That said, however, successive governments – and the general public, for the most part – looked eastward to the Iron Curtain, where freedom wasn't to be found in any meaningful sense at all. And, while cynics might dismiss it as an empty show, politicians and officials on both sides of the Atlantic went to strenuous lengths to underline

the autonomy of Britain, its 'ownership' of its own nuclear deterrent and its continuing right to be consulted over the use of American bases on its soil.

Fortunately, the bombs weren't dropped; the ICBs went unlaunched; the subs continued their cruises without ever firing off their missiles to start the nuclear holocaust. Did the threat of Mutually Assured Destruction

TRANSCRIPT OF KEY PARAGRAPHS

UK–US plans for launching US nuclear missiles from the UK following a Soviet nuclear attack, 1958

Left) The basic understanding between the United Kingdom and United States Governments, regarding the use of bases in the United Kingdom by United States forces, provides that such use in an emergency shall be a matter for joint decision by the two Governments in the light of the circumstances at the time.

(Right) The categories of retaliatory forces to which the attached procedures apply are as follows:

(a) Aircraft of the Royal Air Force Medium Bomber Force which would carry nuclear weapons

(b) Royal Air Force IRBM [intermediate range ballistic missiles] to be created pursuant to the Agreement of February 22 1958;

(c) Units of the United States Strategic Air Command located in the United Kingdom.

('MAD') keep the peace? That's still debated. Certainly, there's a case to be made for the claim – even if there's also quite clearly a case for the suggestion that Western governments 'talked up' the extent and imminence of the Soviet threat. Even if this were so, however, it doesn't alter the fact that real weapons – and cataclysmically destructive ones – faced off across Europe and the Atlantic for over 40 years. The acronym 'MAD' seemed, to most people, bleakly appropriate not just in terms of the prospect of an eruption of violence that destroyed the world but also to the sense of nuclear war as something that was unthinkable; something that couldn't actually take place. That said, both sides did mean business: they couldn't afford not to. These were no pretences, no shadow plays: these were real plans.

-2-

It will be seen that the "joint decision" required by the basic understanding between the two Governments would be taken by the President and the Prime Minister, who would speak personally with each other.

5. It should also be noted that the attached procedures relate only to the committing to the attack of retaliatory forces referred to in sub-paragraphs (a), (b) and (c) of paragraph 6 below. They do not deal with the employment of United States retaliatory forces located outside the United Kingdom or with the employment of United Kingdom retaliatory forces other than those specified in sub-paragraphs (a) and (b) of paragraph 6. The United States Government, of course, retains the right in accordance with normal procedures to withdraw from their United Kingdom bases United States Air Force units deployed in the United Kingdom, and to redeploy such units elsewhere.

6. The categories of retaliatory forces to which the attached procedures apply are as follows:

(a) Aircraft of the Royal Air Force Medium Bomber Force which would carry nuclear weapons ███████████████   25×6

(b) Royal Air Force IRBM force to be created pursuant to the Agreement of February 22, 1958;

(c) Units of the United States Strategic Air Command located in the United Kingdom.

In addition, there are also located in the United Kingdom certain United Kingdom and United States tactical bomber units committed to SACEUR and having a nuclear retaliatory capability. The use of the bases in the United Kingdom on which United States tactical bomber units are located falls under the basic understanding referred to in paragraph 2 above. Some adaptation of the attached procedures may be required to make them applicable to the NATO-committed tactical bomber units referred to earlier in this paragraph. Accordingly, the two Governments have agreed that they will respectively review as soon as possible their procedures covering such units. After consultation with SACEUR, they will make any additions and/or modifications to the attached procedures that may prove necessary in order to make such procedures applicable to all categories of retaliatory forces, including tactical bomber units, located in the United Kingdom.

Robert Murphy

Washington, June 7, 1958.

P. Dean.

Patrick Dean

Chapter Three

In Case of Attack

Elaborate plans were set in place so that
NATO countries would be able to cope in
the event of an attack with atomic weapons.
Thankfully, these never had to be carried out.

The prevention of a nuclear attack would be so infinitely better than the cure that it hardly bore thinking about, but think about it the Western allies absolutely had to do. The more clearly the consequences of an atomic explosion were understood – the blast, the burns, the radiation, the long-term atmospheric and environmental contamination – the more desperate they became to avoid an all-out war. In the early days, civil defence preparations were arguably undertaken out of sheer naivety, based on the innocent assumption that the death, the destruction and enduring damage could be contained. As time went on, and the realities were more clearly understood, an element of cynicism perhaps entered into official calculations: civil defence work was a way of raising and maintaining morale, of encouraging a 'can-do' spirit in a population that, if it clearly understood the dangers facing it, would just despair. Thus the people were encouraged to involve themselves in their own defence.

Soldiers bussed in for the US Nevada tests felt privileged to be witnessing the greatest show on earth. But these 'observers' were being observed themselves – monitored for radiation damage. Many would suffer severely in the years to come.

Duck and Cover

Civil Defence started with the young in the United States: it was vital that they be protected – and they were easily reached by central government through the school system.

It was just after 2 p.m. on a cloudless summer's afternoon – the sun could hardly have been brighter. Even so, the sudden strident light lit up the sky. As though it had been captured in a camera's flash, the entire class was frozen in the instant: no one moved a muscle; no one made a sound as time stood still.

Only for a moment, though. The silence was broken as abruptly as it had taken hold by a clamour of scraping chairs and creaking desks. Teacher and students scrambled to the floor, moving automatically now as a well-drilled procedure restored a sense of purpose they'd briefly been robbed of by the shock. Crouching down and pushing their way underneath their desks head first, they curled up tightly in a foetal position, their faces covered by their hands, and waited, braced for the blast they knew must come. Turtle Bert's efforts had not been wasted: within a few seconds the class had withdrawn into its collective shell; shielded – touch wood – from the worst of the coming fury.

That, at any rate, was how things were supposed to work when the Cold War went hot and

Children drilled so they could scramble under their desks at a moment's notice.

the bomb fell, perhaps without warning: America's children responding with resource and discipline to protect themselves. Could a school desk keep Armageddon at bay? Would a wall keep radiation out? We never had to find out, fortunately. From 1951, though, in schools across the United States, the 'Duck and Cover' campaign kept up its relentless barrage of upbeat encouragement and advice. A film funded by the Federal Civil Defense Administration was central to the scheme.

'Why not let your children teach you what they have learned at school about protective measures?'

From a draft letter for parents offered to all schools by the US Office of Civil and Defense Mobilization, 1952

As with all good public-information drives, the values of 'Duck and Cover' were summed up in an engaging cartoon character, who was supposed to take on a talismanic status for the nation's children. Bert the Turtle had his own celebratory song:

There was a turtle by the name
*   of Bert*
And Bert the turtle was very alert.
When danger threatened him he
*   never got hurt*
He knew just what to do.
He ducked . . .
And covered . . .

Bert was in some ways a confusing symbol: carrying his own shell round with him, he was naturally self-reliant. America's children were less fortunate. 'He's smart,' the posters warned, 'but *he* has his shelter on his back. You must learn to find shelter.'

The counsel was sensible enough, as far as it went, but

Bert the Turtle walked a fine line between warning and reassurance.

the best that can be said for it in hindsight is probably that it made a very little scope for genuine action go an awfully long way. If the sirens went, an atomic attack was obviously imminent; the good news was that the authorities were aware and taking what measures they could in your defence. Hearing sirens also meant, by definition, a (short) safe period: you could seek out the special public shelters that had been opened in every town.

If, without prior notice, you just saw the flash, there was no time to lose: rather than crowding round the window to see what was happening (and thus get caught in the lacerating deluge that would follow the impact of the shockwave), you should 'duck' down, and dive for whatever 'cover' there was to be had. That might be a table, a door, a wall – you curled up as small as you

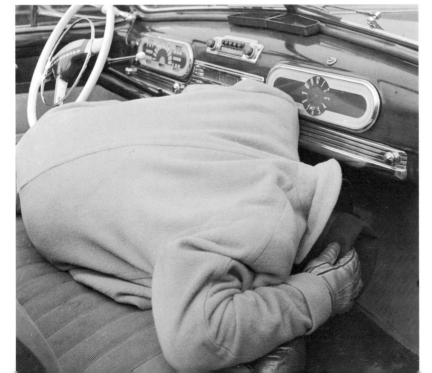

The hope was that lessons learned in school would (quite literally) be brought home to America's adults.

could, facing inward, away from the blast and any flying débris, clutching the back of your neck with your hand to increase the protection.

Atomic Optimism

Without for a second saying that nuclear war was fun, 'Duck and Cover' was relentlessly – indeed, wildly – optimistic in its assumptions. It didn't dwell on the likelihood that the wall you were

crouched behind would be blown away, and you along with it. Or that, if you were within even several miles of the site of the explosion, you'd be vapourized by temperatures measuring in the thousands of degrees.

Nor did it address the problem that, even many miles away from the impact, terrible burns could be expected – and radiation sickness in the days and weeks that followed. These would, like as

not, give way to terrible cancers in the longer term. In Japan, a generation not yet born when the bombs fell on Hiroshima and Nagasaki was to suffer sicknesses for decades – even into the twenty-first century.

In fairness, it should be borne in mind that the Nuclear Era was still young and the dangers of 'fallout' not yet fully understood. The longer-term consequences of the Japanese attacks would – by definition – reveal themselves only in the longer term, while US tests had not yet highlighted this problem. (Those conducting the atomic tests at Bikini Atoll in 1946 were notoriously cavalier in their regard for their own safety, scorning protective clothing and drinking contaminated water.) For the moment, the assumption was that an atomic blast differed from a conventional explosion in degree only – not that it was different *in kind*.

Even so, 'Duck and Cover' didn't explicitly deny the possibility of more serious consequences: it simply avoided them – ducked them, it might be said. Few children were sophisticated enough in their awareness of the issues to question what they were told. Few adults were actually any better informed. By and large, ordinary Americans were content to take these things on trust. Besides, no outright lies were told. Though Bert the Turtle, the song said, 'never got hurt', no

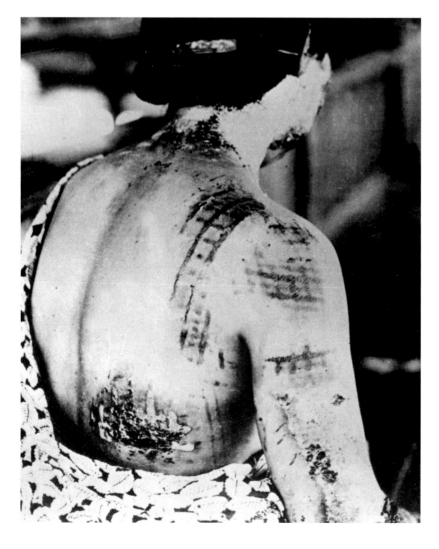

A Japanese victim of the atomic bombs shows her scars. Few Americans had any sense of the horror of nuclear war.

At the Bikini Atoll tests, a gung-ho recklessness prevailed.

such commitment was ever offered to the public: these precautions would keep you 'safer', it was suggested – never 'safe'.

Relaxed Attitudes

While it's often been suggested that the best form of defence is attack, a PR offensive never protected anyone. What had the US authorities actually been doing to defend the civilian population – apart from threatening the enemy with destruction? Not as much as might be imagined, as it turns out. It had been clear from the outset that America's nuclear monopoly could not last for ever, but the consciousness of having a headstart had inevitably fostered some complacency.

Up to a point, America *had* remained alert: many of the civil defence measures that had been introduced to bring the nation through World War II were widely maintained throughout the late 1940s. Created in 1947, the National Security Resources Board (NSRB) had overseen these efforts. First responders had been kept up to speed with evacuation and first-aid procedures and volunteer fire crews kept in training. The vigilance of Coastguard and Border Patrol was also maintained. The public remained prepared.

That was the theory, at any rate. The reality had been that, in the absence of any obvious immediate threat, it had been harder to keep the wider population motivated. There had been a significant scaling down in the number of public air-raid drills. And if the public didn't want to turn out for drills for their own defence, they weren't wild about the idea of paying for civil defence measures either. While it wasn't difficult to justify expenditure on the Army, Navy and Air Force – high-profile services of proven value – civil defence was another story. People didn't feel afraid. Not since Pearl Harbor had an external enemy

Air-raid warning systems were installed in cities like New York. This one is on the RCA (now GE) Building.

successfully mounted an attack on US soil (and, to most Americans, Hawaii seemed geographically remote). Civil defence had been a 'grudge purchase', then, its benefits unclear to the taxpayer – and to beleaguered politicians and officials on the lookout for painless cuts.

But on 29 August 1949, much sooner than anyone in the West had been expecting, the Soviet Union tested an atomic bomb. A badly jolted America was immediately galvanized: nobody disputed the necessity of some response. Even so, the wheels of government cranked into action only very slowly. In September 1950, the NSRB 'Blue Book' of 1950 called for the foundation of a new system of civil defence appropriate to the Cold War era; a new Federal Civil Defense Administration was to be created with far-reaching powers. That the FCDA's chief administrator was to be a civilian reflected fears that the military might be tempted to exceed its authority in a rapidly rearming America, but it also underlined the desire to make civil defence relevant to ordinary US citizens.

Ideological Issues

Superficially, the civil-defence idea might be expected to appeal to a nation of self-sufficient settlers, who had come together to throw out their English colonial masters. As historian Laura McEnaney has shown, however, the civil-defence programme had proven problematic – dividing opinions even in the obvious emergency of World War II.

McEnaney identifies two competing (and, on occasion, actually hostile) strands. One was a broadly conservative commitment to a sort of 'macho' vigilanteism (neighbourhood militias, air-raid patrols, volunteer firefighters . . .). The other – 'softer', more feminine friendly – emphasized such things as soup kitchens, refuges for families and other socially based support. Ideally, of course, a civil defence programme would allow for both these sides, but the reality was that their advocates pulled in

The first successful Soviet test of 1949 was unwelcome news.

different directions. At the same time, there were the old American ideological struggles between federal and local government on the one hand, and between state and private funding on the other. A question of great national importance for which the answers had to be found at grassroots level, civil defence was always going to be a problem. And it didn't help that the large-scale construction of shelters and the establishment and administration of supply stockpiles were projects

that seemed much better suited to federal provision.

In the end, the suspicion of government action won out over the fear of what still seemed a distant danger: self-help, it was decided, was the American way. People would make their own provision – or take their chances. Conceived as just the start of a mass mobilization, 'Duck and Cover' ended up as pretty much its high point, though the film was constantly re-shown and schoolchildren were routinely drilled. America at large paid little heed, though. After a brief initial flurry of enthusiasm, organized civil defence activities were for the most part confined to the government-run sector – schools, hospitals, federal offices. Despite the publicity, despite the endless exhortations of Bert the Turtle, little substantive action was ever taken. So much so that it's possible to see America's civil-defence programme as just another Cold War 'operation that never happened'.

New Yorkers assemble in a subway station for an air-raid drill.

250M–10-51 ― 114

City of New York
Office of Civil Defense

THIS IS A
TEST AIR RAID DRILL
PLEASE LEAVE THE BUS AND
TAKE SHELTER IN BUILDINGS

On the "All Clear" Signal
Return to the Bus Promptly
and Show This to the Driver

THIS IS A
TEST AIR RAID DRILL

PLEASE COOPERATE

ARTHUR M. WALLANDER
Director, Civil Defense

Above: Air-raid drills were organized for
a variety of different situations.

Right: US households had to prepare to live
for a time as nuclear Crusoes.

The Defence Deception?

If civil defence 'didn't happen', the media offensive assuredly did. Millions saw Turtle Bert and heard his message. They may not have responded to it by carrying out drills and preparing themselves, but they heeded its warnings of war and went out to vote for politicians who in their turn voted for massive rises in military expenditure. They also allowed themselves to be buoyed in the belief that such a war, though grave, was ultimately survivable – so they shouldn't be pursuing a policy of peace at any cost. That, some cynics would

'Civil Defense, like
charity, begins at home.'

*Millard Caldwell, Director of the Federal Civil
Defense Association (FCDA), 1951*

SHELTER SUPPLIES

Not every item on this chart is vital to life. (The most essential ones are outlined in color.) But even though you might be able to leave your shelter briefly after a day or two, you should prepare to be *completely* self-sustaining for at least two weeks.

EATING UTENSILS AND FOOD

EATING UTENSILS · CUPS · NAPKINS · BOTTLE OPENER · CAN OPENER · POCKET KNIFE · MEASURING CUP · PAPER PLATES · PAN · WATER · FOOD AND CONTAINERS

CLOTHING AND BEDDING

SEWING KIT · SLEEPING BAGS · BLANKETS · EXTRA CLOTHING

SANITATION AND MEDICAL SUPPLIES

FIRST AID KIT · DISINFECTANT · GARBAGE CAN · PAPER TOWELS · SANITARY NAPKINS · EMERGENCY TOILET · TOILET PAPER · HUMAN WASTE · NEWSPAPERS · SOAP · PLASTIC AND PAPER BAGS

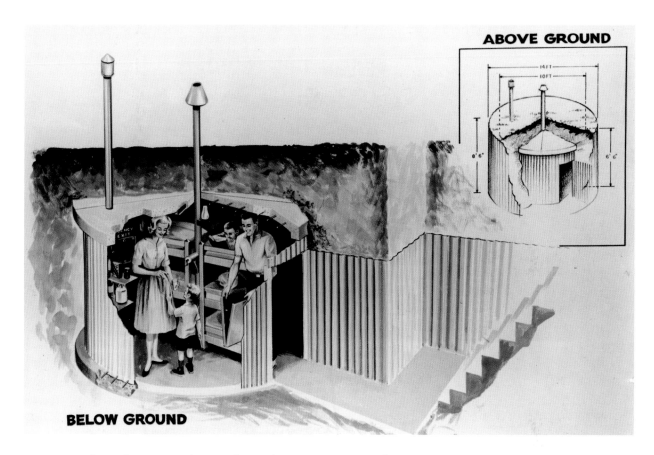

ABOVE GROUND

BELOW GROUND

argue, was the real purpose of 'Duck and Cover': it mobilized public opinion in support of their military masters. That so little effort was actually put into practical measures for civil defence just shows successive administrations knew perfectly well that the threat of attack by the Soviets was an empty one.

A justified criticism? That's difficult to say . . . perhaps a little bit around the edges. There are good grounds for judging that, if the US Government failed to mobilize the masses, it wasn't for want of trying. It's hard to see the historical realities clearly, given the well-attested exaggerations of

later administrations. President Eisenhower would struggle unavailingly to scotch the idea – increasingly influential among more hawkish opinion-formers – that a 'missile gap' was opening up in the Russians' favour. John F. Kennedy himself was subsequently to refer to this notion as a 'myth', while admitting that, 'patriotic and misguided', he'd helped to foster it. (He was being overmodest: in the course of his campaign for the presidency, he and his aides had horrified key officials of the Eisenhower administration with their blood-curdling claims of the Soviets' superiority in intercontinental ballistic missiles.)

Some 260,000 of these leaflets were circulated in the Chicago area – but only 19 permit applications were received.

In truth, though, even with the intelligence resources at America's disposal, it was hard to reach a reliable estimation of the real threat. And there were obvious reasons for erring on the side of caution. No president, no official, no military officer wanted to be the one who allowed complacency to get the better of his vigilance. In the early 1950s especially, with the shock of the Soviets' acquisition of the atomic bomb still new, the cost of underestimating the enemy was all too clear.

The UK Home Office 'War Book'

The Home Office is a government department responsible for security and order. It made preparations for nuclear attack with impressive thoroughness and set out strict procedures for all its officials.

In Britain, resistance to the civil-defence philosophy wasn't quite so strong. Not that the military and official elite necessarily shared the popular collectivizing spirit that had seen Clement Attlee's Labour government elected by a landslide. There was generally less suspicion of government's centralizing impulses, however – while the sense that the nation had survived World War II by 'pulling together' was felt at just about every level of society. Geography must have had a bearing too. Britain was so much closer to the Soviet Union than was the main homeland of the United States: it might quite easily have found itself in the line of nuclear fire.

There was no question here, then, of civil defence being a mere show put on for propaganda purposes: indeed, many of the plans that were set in place were

kept strictly secret. The preparations that were going to be needed were carefully thought through, and all laid out, in extraordinary detail, in the 'War Book'. 'The purpose of the Home Office War Book', this remarkable volume began,

 . . . *is to summarise the action to be taken by the Department in a period of transition from peace*

to war; to record the allocation within the Office of responsibility for taking action; and to provide a summary of home defence plans of which this action forms part.

The book began with the assumption that there would be at least a few days' warning of any nuclear attack; that the outbreak of war would be to some extent predictable:

The assumption is that the Government would be able to foresee the possibility of war and would be able to institute a 'Precautionary Stage' (which would not be made public) during which measures could be taken to improve national preparedness against nuclear attack. For planning purposes, it is assumed that not more than seven days would intervene between the institution of a precautionary stage and the outbreak of hostilities.

News of nuclear war would first of all trigger a burst of back-room activity rather than a rush to battle-stations on the ground. Indeed, no specific civil or military measures would be spurred by the declaration of a Precautionary Stage:

War Book codewords

1. To protect key points against sabotage. **DOMINION**

2. To take Emergency Powers. **DORCAS**

6. To appoint Regional Commissioners and Deputy Regional Commissioners. **EARTHQUAKE**

7. To instruct oil, gas, coal and electricity industries to set up their emergency headquarters. **EGGSHELL**

10. To put the police on a war footing. **EPIGRAM**

13. To institute Emergency Feeding Organisation **FLANK**

15. To evacuate the major ports and activate the Regional Port and Shipping Organisation. **FORGIVE**

16. To instruct oil industry, the three nationalised fuel industries and the coal distribution trade to assume emergency operational control. **FRAUD**

17. To implement emergency plans for water supply **GLUM**

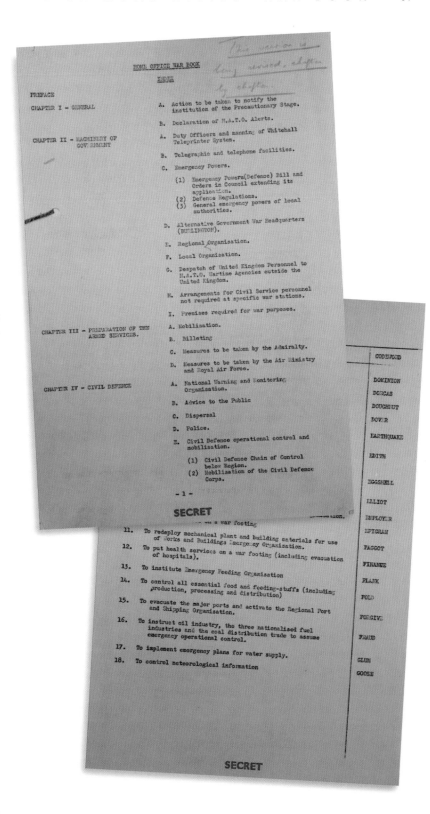

Generally speaking, it would amount to an instruction to all Departments to mount a twenty-four-hour watch and bring up to date urgently their plans for the transition to war.

It would also prompt the creation of the 'Transition to War Committee'. Rightly (if,

perhaps, not very excitingly), the mandarins' number one priority was to establish an unambiguous administrative hierarchy; a clear line of command.

The plan was a thing of bureaucratic beauty: the 'index' page (really, what we'd normally describe as a table of contents)

APPENDIX F

CODEWORDS TO BE USED IN TRANSMITTING WAR BOOK
MESSAGES AND CABINET DECISIONS TO REGIONAL DIRECTORS OF CIVIL DEFENCE

A. FOR ACTION

MESSAGE	CODEWORD
1. A Precautionary Stage has been declared	SHAME
2. All Press notices to be issued through Chief Regional Officer of the Central Office of Information.	ARMAND
3. Complete plans for the collection and distribution of radiac instruments.	ATTEMPT
4. Complete plans for the collection and distribution of civil defence operational stores.	BANKRUPT
5. Prepare to requisition non-load carrying vehicles to meet Regional Headquarters requirements	BANSTEAD
6. Inform local authorities of arrangements for the control of POL supplies.	BAYTOWN
7. Prepare to activate regional seats of government	BETROTHAL
8. Complete activation of regional seats of government	BITE
9. Instruct Corps Authorities to mobile the Corps	CONNIE
10. Instruct Corps Authorities to request managements with industrial civil defence units to put them on a war footing; and managements of other firms to take such action as Corps Authorities think appropriate.	CORDAGE
11. Put into operation plans for collection and distribution of radiac instruments	COSY
12. Put into operation plans for collection and distribution of civil defence operational stores.	CROCK
13. Authorise Corps Authorities to secure by local purchase sufficient operational stores to bring supply up to war duty establishment.	CULPRIT
14. Arrange for collection of training vehicles by Corps Authorities.	CUTE
15.(a)Inform Clerks to Authorities and Regional Fire Commanders that the requisitioning of load-carrying and non-load carrying vehicles can begin.	DIRECTION
(b)Requisition non-load carrying vehicles to meet Regional Headquarters requirements.	
16. Inform Regional Police Commanders that the requisitioning of load-carrying and non-load carrying vehicles can begin.	DISCOURAGE
17. Central Government control has now been transferred from Whitehall to an emergency relocation site.	BELPER

SECRET

TRANSCRIPT OF KEY PARAGRAPHS

War Book codewords

1. A Precautionary Stage has been declared. **SHAME**

2. All Press notices to be issued through Chief Regional Officer of the Central Office of Information. **ARMAND**

9. Instruct Corps Authorities to mobile the Corps. **CONNIE**

11. Put into operation plans for collection and distribution of radiac instruments. **COSY**

13. Authorise Corps Authorities to secure by local purchase sufficient operational stores to bring supply up to war duty establishment. **CULPRIT**

15 (a) Inform Clerks to Authorities and Regional Fire Commanders that the requisitioning of load-carrying and non-load carrying vehicles can begin. **DIRECTION**

17. Central Government control has now been transferred from Whitehall to an emergency relocation site. **BELPER**

The Operations and Status Room in Gravesend Civil Defence Bunker, Region 6.

gives a sense of how carefully things had been thought through, how elegantly everything had been brought together into a single, integrated plan: instructions to NATO partners and to the public; liaison with air and admiralty chiefs and with local police forces; and arrangements for communications and for commandeering premises as required. Thought had even been given to what was to be done with those civil servants who weren't needed for the precautionary preparations.

To leaf further through the 'War Book' is simply to marvel at the meticulousness with which it's all laid out: the mandarins who compiled this blueprint for Britain's defence really do appear to have thought of everything. How communities would be policed when panic reigned; how justice would be administered; how food and drugs would be moved about the country; how essential industries would be kept in production and ports open . . . There were even coldly worked-out plans for the rounding-up of

'You can't be certain. You can be prepared.'

Slogan promoted by Britain's Central Office of Information (COI)

Members of the Civil Defence Corps tried to prepare for every conceivable eventuality.

subversives – and the introduction of censorship for people's private mail. The officials even established procedures for the evacuation of major artworks and archaeological treasures from London's great museums – what, after all, would Britain be without its cultural heritage? A list of codewords gives a wonderfully serendipitous sense of the range of concerns addressed in the document: these range from DOMINION ('To protect key points from sabotage') to GOOSE ('To control meteorological information').

Concrete Measures

It wasn't all theoretical. Massive bunkers were being built, buried deep in the ground and strengthened with concrete, in secret out-of-town locations across the country. These were to be the command posts for Britain's defensive operations in the event of an atomic attack – and its administration in the weeks and months thereafter. By the 1960s, a network of Regional War Rooms included centres in Scotland, Newcastle, Leeds, Nottingham, Manchester, Reading, Bristol, Cardiff, Cambridge and Tunbridge Wells.

A cabinet minister was to be assigned to each: assisted by a judge, a local police chief, a military officer and a handpicked teams of civil servants, he would make sure the life of the country could continue, even if the capital had been hit. (He would also, incidentally, wield all-but-dictatorial power in what was now to all intents and purposes a sovereign state.)

Local authorities had their own smaller bunkers so that the work of government could go on at grassroots level even while nuclear war was raging all around. Vital though they were, however, military direction and civil administration weren't the only things that had to be considered. The nation's infrastructure – its power and communications – had to be protected. Special secret depots were also created to house the sort of equipment and materials that were going to be needed to carry out repairs to high-tension cables and telephone lines. Reinforced pumping stations for drinking water were established, so that a beleaguered country wouldn't run dry under enemy attack. Step-by-step instructions were issued, identifying crucial tasks and allocating codenames to each, so that smooth running and secrecy alike could be assured.

Government members, officials and military high-ups were kept on their toes by regular rehearsals every year. These featured mock Cabinet meetings – even news bulletins describing scenes of terror, destruction and disorder

The need for Civil Defence is greater than ever

JOIN THE AMBULANCE SECTION C.D. CORPS

ASK AT YOUR COUNCIL OFFICES

Anyone could make a contribution, the posters urged.

along with more mundane challenges like workplace absenteeism and food-queues.

Organization on the Ground
At community level, real steps were being taken to organize

the people. In 1949, a force of uniformed volunteers – the Civil Defence Corps (CDC) – was established. The response was good, among a population most of whose adults had either served in the armed forces and imbibed their values or toiled courageously on the 'home front' in the recent war. To an extent that is easily forgotten now, wartime conditions still prevailed. Rationing, far from ending with the war, had actually been extended to cover key provisions such as bread and potatoes; other, earlier, restrictions were mostly still in force. Britons didn't generally question their duty to serve. While the 'Dunkirk Spirit' is easily exaggerated, it shouldn't be underestimated. The public believed that World War II had indeed been (as Churchill put it) 'their finest hour'; it had brought Britons together in a common purpose.

Of those men who hadn't seen active service abroad during that war, many had performed specific civil-defence roles – in everything from the Sky Watch (looking out for enemy bombers) to auxiliary fire services and ambulance corps. Women had been no less busy, acting as nurses, counsellors, firefighters, drivers or as searchers – excavating collapsed buildings to recover the dead or injured. Some 53,000 members of the Women's Royal Voluntary Service (WRVS) enlisted in the CDC *en masse* in 1949. Anyone who'd been through the Blitz had acquired a certain skill-set that lent itself to the disciplines of civil defence and a cast of mind that was comparatively receptive to calls to public action.

By 1956, the Corps had getting on for 330,000 members. A further 200,000 had joined the Industrial Civil Defence Corps – 20,000 of these in the coal mines.

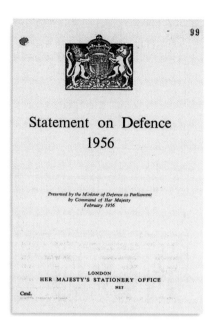

The 1956 Defence Statement addressed the question of fallout for the first time.

A branch of this more specialized corps could be set up at any workplace with over 200 staff. This would most obviously be a factory, a steelworks, shipyard or some other industrial concern – but it could as easily be a commercial premises like an office building or department store. Its wardens – employees at the site themselves – could bring their first-hand knowledge and experience to bear to optimize plans for evacuating workers and visitors, administering first aid, fighting fires and, as far as possible, safeguarding buildings and equipment so that – ideally – production might resume. The Civil Defence Corps had its own training schools: the one at Falfield, Gloucestershire, was probably the largest – it had its own mock-up of a bombed-out

street, so members could practise rescue work.

In the end, though, in the absence of a nuclear attack (or, people were coming to conclude, any real threat of one) enthusiasm for the CDC began to wane. Members felt they were 'all dressed up, with nowhere to go.' So, real though the Corps clearly was, its activities were starting to smack as much of make-believe as those of Bert the Turtle in the US public information campaign. Meanwhile, a growing understanding of the likely consequences of a nuclear war meant that people were less inclined to volunteer, and tending to become fatalistic instead.

Fallout Fears

They had good reason. The British Defence Statement for 1956, published by Anthony Eden's Conservative government in the February of that year, is fully alive to the question of fallout. True, you have to be alert to pick up the sense of impending cataclysm in bland references to 'extensive problems of welfare for those who have left their homes', and to 'large-scale movements of people' in the aftermath of an attack. There's something unmistakably frightening in the thought of 'the revolutionary implications of the threat of persistent contamination from radioactive fall-out over very wide areas':

. . . in contaminated areas, severe restrictions for some days of movement out of doors would be called for. For purposes of

TRANSCRIPT OF KEY PARAGRAPHS

<u>British Statement on Defence, 1956</u>

To give full protection to everyone from sickness or death from the hazard of radioactivity alone would involve physical preparations on a vast scale and to make such preparations against all the hazards of a thermo-nuclear attack on this country would place a crippling burden on the national resources.

Whatever the preparations made, an attack on this country would involve loss of life and destruction on an unparalleled scale.

Unduly heavy expenditure now on purely defensive measures, by weakening our economic strength and reducing the resources available for building up the strength of the deterrent, might very well work against the primary objective of ensuring that global war itself is prevented.

Nevertheless . . . the Government's aim will be to take the precautions without which, should the worst happen, ordered society could not survive.

survival under such conditions the household becomes the basic unit. So general and widespread a danger will need to be met primarily by each household acting on guidance and instructions from the central and local authorities both before the event and after.

Government would do what it could, in other words, but there was no way round the fact that, for 'some days' after the explosion, every household would essentially be on its own. It's introduced prosaically and understatedly here, but this is the sort of scenario that was to become familiar in ever more lurid versions presented by science-fiction novels and films: that of society breaking down into a sort of pre-civilized anarchy.

---

23   **110**

105.   The reshaping of home defence plans has to have special regard to the revolutionary implications of the threat of persistent contamination from radioactive fall-out over very wide areas.   Sufficient is already known, from information made public by the United States Atomic Energy Commission in February, 1955, and from other information available to the Government, to establish the nature and extent of this threat; in contaminated areas severe restrictions for some days on movement out of doors would be called for. For purposes of survival under such conditions the household becomes the basic unit.   So general and widespread a danger will need to be met primarily by each household acting on guidance and instructions from the central and local authorities both before the event and after.   Measures to inform the public of the nature of the danger and of the measures they can take to counter it in their own homes will accordingly occupy a place in the forefront of the Government's plans for home defence.

106.   To give full protection to everyone from sickness or death from the hazard of radioactivity alone would involve physical preparations on a vast scale and to make such preparations against all the hazards of a thermo-nuclear attack on this country would place a crippling burden on the national resources.   Whatever the preparations made, an attack on this country would involve loss of life and destruction on an unparalleled scale.   Unduly heavy expenditure now on purely defensive measures, by weakening our economic strength and reducing the resources available for building up the strength of the deterrent, might very well work against the primary objective of ensuring that global war itself is prevented.

107.   Nevertheless, within the proportion of our resources that can be made available for home defence, the Government's aim will be to take the precautions without which, should the worst happen, ordered society could not survive.   The emphasis will be on plans and preparations to establish a system of warning and monitoring of radioactive fall-out and an adequate scheme of control, through the organs of central and local government, and to ensure the availability of the necessary communications; to build up local and national services, trained and equipped to deal with casualties and to mitigate the other effects of thermo-nuclear attack; to revise evacuation plans; to secure the continued functioning of essential public services; and to inform the public fully, both as to the dangers involved and the steps that can be taken to meet them.

Research and Development

108.   One task of the first importance is to continue and expand research into the problems of nuclear warfare, and into the most effective and practical methods of dealing with them.   Many factors of fundamental importance remain obscure; and the danger of misdirected effort is considerable. Research, both basic and applied, will accordingly be pressed forward to the limit of resources available.

Civil Defence Services

109.   The training of members of the Civil Defence Corps and the Industrial Civil Defence Service has continued under revised syllabuses with an increased emphasis on practical methods, and local authorities have

Monitoring the Menace

The death and destruction that a nuclear blast brought were just the beginning, the authorities were realizing: ways were needed of dealing with the fallout.

The fallout threat was something entirely new in either the field of war or civil defence. No official agency was obviously equipped to handle it. The most natural fit seemed to be with the work of the Royal Observer Corps (ROC), a uniformed civilian service whose volunteers had been training to watch out for air raids since soon after World War I. World War II had seen them come of age: they were skilled not just in spotting and identifying enemy planes but in assessing their numbers and tracking raiders as they went. While their humanitarian contribution had unquestionably been immeasurable, saving untold lives in air raids on major population centres, they had also helped coordinate the armed response from RAF fighters in

The activities of the UK's Royal Observer Corps (ROC) were coordinated from its Watford headquarters.

the air and from anti-aircraft defences on the ground.

The ROC was disbanded at the end of the war – but for only a very brief time. It soon became clear that the aerial threat to Britain was set to continue. Granted, much had changed: so devastating was the power of the atom bomb that the first air raid to reach UK shores was likely to be the last. But this only made the ROC's skills more vital. There were other changes too: while heavy bombers still reigned, it was already evident that the future might well belong to the ballistic missile. But the Observers had gained some experience in this area when attempting to track the V-1s and V-2s in the final months of World War II – they at least understood the difficulty of the challenge they were going to face.

A disciplined force, with developed skills in observation and a relatively high degree of technical know-how, the ROC seemed the obvious agency to take charge of the task of tracking and measuring fallout in the aftermath of an atomic explosion – it was going to be vital, in organizing rescue efforts and in marshalling further resistance and retaliation, to know where the worst and least badly affected areas in the country were. Thousands were equipped with Geiger counters and given training in their use. First invented in 1908, in the earliest days of atomic research, the 'Geiger-Müller tube' detected radiation by registering (with an audible clicking sound) when it ionized

a gas in a sealed canister around which a strong electric field was maintained. Such equipment was very much designed for use in the laboratory – the only place where atomic radiation was to be found in those days. Obviously, though, the dropping of the bomb on Hiroshima had ushered in another era; these new realities brought with them new demands.

The 1950s saw the introduction of the first portable Geiger counters, specially designed to be

ROC wardens operated out of blast-protected bunkers.

'The widespread damage and immobilisation caused by 'fall-out' call for a radical reshaping of our plans for the defence of the home front.'

William Strath's Report to the British Cabinet, 1954

carried by an individual and operated in the field. Headphones allowed the clicks of the counter to be heard even in the sort of noise that was likely to prevail in the panic after a nuclear attack – though in later designs these were replaced by visual dials. Britain's Contamination Meter No. 1, introduced in 1953, was quickly surpassed by the more reliable Radiac Survey Meter No. 2, though both models remained in use for many years.

As time went on and strategic emphases changed, this sort of work became the main focus of the ROC. From 1957, its members doubled as members of the United Kingdom Warning and Monitoring Organisation (UKWMO). A handful of full-time officers organized a network of weekend volunteers – most of whom were themselves science professionals (teachers, technicians and engineers).

A HANDEL on the Situation
Initially, the ROC, as we've seen, had been primarily responsible for warning of impending air raids; that role continued to be recognized in the 'Warning' part of the title of the UKWMO. But the function was increasingly becoming secondary – partly because of sophisticated radar tracking systems that were now in development (and up and running by the early 1960s),

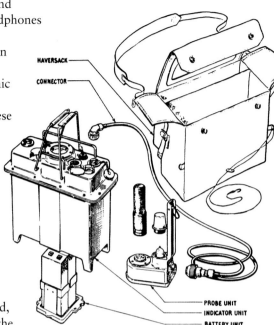

HAVERSACK

CONNECTOR

PROBE UNIT
INDICATOR UNIT
BATTERY UNIT

The 'Contamination Meter' was crude, and became quickly outdated – though it remained in use.

but partly too because the length of any warning period was likely to be so short. The idea of the 'four-minute warning' chilled a generation when it was first proposed by the British Government in the 1950s: few knew that it was, if anything, on the optimistic side.

What was supposed to happen in the event of nuclear attack was that local sirens were to sound, and the people were to seek such shelter as they could find. Some guidance had been issued on preparing home and workplace fall-out shelters, but the authorities had taken a decision not to undertake their construction on any scale. The

The 'Radiac Survey Meter' became the mainstay of ROC monitoring on the ground.

costs would have been prohibitive, official publications acknowledged. (They didn't add, though the implication hovered in the air, that the significant benefits would have been uncertain, to say the least.)

But UKWMO's warning role became secondary also because the timeliness and reliability of any warning had become far too important to be left to local officials and police forces in the regions. Nuclear war was an all-or-nothing affair, with absolutely no room for error. You couldn't afford to drop the ball once the country was under attack – miss a message, lose communication, get the codes confused. It might also be just as dangerous to go off half-cocked: a false alarm that set off defensive actions on the ground might send the signal to the Soviets that an attack by the West was about to start – and

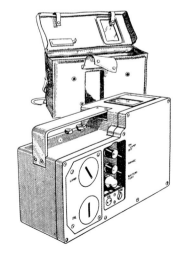

invite a 'retaliatory' first strike.

Hence the introduction of 'HANDEL' in 1962. This centralized (and to a considerable extent automated) the issuing of warnings around the country. To reduce the risks of getting wires crossed, a single staffer sat at the HANDEL console, ready to receive any alert as it came in (though he had a duplicate phone and alarm button in case of equipment failure). The procedure was (dramatically) simple: by pressing and holding down a red button, he transmitted a signal that set off the local air-raid sirens and mobilized police forces and other agencies up and down Britain. This signal was transmitted via the national telephone system, then run by the General Post Office (GPO), while as a back-up it used the cables normally allocated to the speaking clock.

A Counsel of Despair?

Despite all these measures (on the face of it impressive) and this air of resolution and organization on the part of the authorities, there's a whiff of defeatism about the various civil-defence initiatives taken by Britain. Or, at the very least, there is the tacit suggestion that civil defence was not really the way to ensure national survival. Perhaps it's just in hindsight that these various measures seem woefully inadequate, elaborate and expensive, as they undoubtedly

Could there really be civil defence against nuclear weapons? People were beginning to have their doubts.

were, but there are also signs of half-heartedness in official rhetoric as well.

The 1956 Defence Statement very clearly discounted the possibility of providing 'full protection . . . from sickness or death'. Whatever the government did, nuclear attack would mean 'loss of life and destruction on an unparalleled scale'. The authors, it might even be argued, came close to questioning the very

basis of civil defence:

Unduly heavy expenditure now on purely defensive measures, by weakening our economic strength and reducing the resources available for building up the strength of the deterrent, might very well work against the primary object of ensuring that global war itself is prevented.

If safety was to be achieved only by frightening the enemy, what was the point of civil

MANUAL OF CIVIL DEFENCE: Vol. I

PAMPHLET No. 1

Nuclear Weapons

CIVIL
CD
DEFENCE

PUBLISHED FOR THE HOME OFFICE
AND SCOTTISH HOME DEPARTMENT BY
HER MAJESTY'S STATIONERY OFFICE
1956

PRICE 2s. 6d. NET

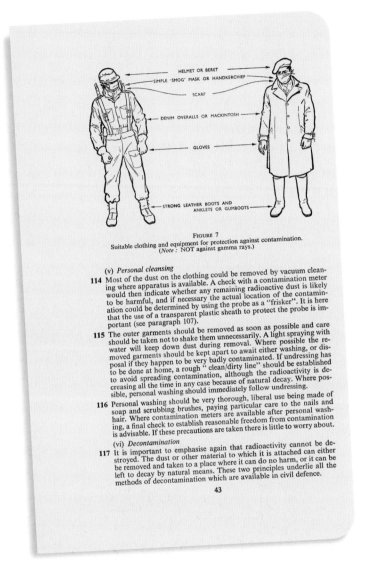

FIGURE 7

Suitable clothing and equipment for protection against contamination.
(Note : NOT against gamma rays.)

HELMET OR BERET
SIMPLE 'SMOG' MASK OR HANDKERCHIEF
SCARF
DENIM OVERALLS OR MACKINTOSH
GLOVES
STRONG LEATHER BOOTS AND ANKLETS OR GUMBOOTS

(v) *Personal cleansing*

114 Most of the dust on the clothing could be removed by vacuum cleaning where apparatus is available. A check with a contamination meter would then indicate whether any remaining radioactive dust is likely to be harmful, and if necessary the actual location of the contamination could be determined by using the probe as a "frisker". It is here that the use of a transparent plastic sheath to protect the probe is important (see paragraph 107).

115 The outer garments should be removed as soon as possible and care should be taken not to shake them unnecessarily. A light spraying with water will keep down dust during removal. Where possible the removed garments should be kept apart to await either washing, or disposal if they happen to be very badly contaminated. If undressing has to be done at home, a rough "clean/dirty line" should be established to avoid spreading contamination, although the radioactivity is decreasing all the time in any case because of natural decay. Where possible, personal washing should immediately follow undressing.

116 Personal washing should be very thorough, liberal use being made of soap and scrubbing brushes, paying particular care to the nails and hair. Where contamination meters are available after personal washing, a final check to establish reasonable freedom from contamination is advisable. If these precautions are taken there is little to worry about.

(vi) *Decontamination*

117 It is important to emphasise again that radioactivity cannot be destroyed. The dust or other material to which it is attached can either be removed and taken to a place where it can do no harm, or it can be left to decay by natural means. These two principles underlie all the methods of decontamination which are available in civil defence.

43

defence? In reality, how much more was it than a show of action and purpose aimed at maintaining public morale?

Stopping Subversion

One thing it might conceivably have been was a pretext for attacking civil liberties, an excuse for persecuting critics of the political status quo. Britain had historically been tolerant of dissent. Even – despite the comfortable conservatism of the British political establishment – dissent of the revolutionary socialist sort. A hundred years before, Karl Marx himself had come to live in London as an exile; a steady stream of foreign radicals had found a refuge in Britain since. More recently, Vladimir Ilyich Lenin and Leon Trotsky had actually met one another in London, where they'd worked together editing the leftist paper *Iskra*.

The eruption of McCarthyism in the United States at the end of the 1940s left Britain bemused, therefore – and this was true not only of an easygoing public, but also of the political classes, including the crustier Tories. That said, the country had just come through a major war in which the necessity for democracy to be tempered with discretion had been only too apparent. No one doubted that the Soviets would do all they could to spy and sabotage in Britain. Likewise, it was only rational to expect that British Communists would cooperate with their Iron Curtain comrades. They and their sympathizers in the labour and trade union movement could potentially bring strategic industries to a standstill at vital times; and disrupt wartime preparations by acts of sabotage.

They might work more subtly as well, shaping the public consciousness over the longer term. In 1949, the counter-espionage agency MI5 informed the Foreign Office that, boasting of its representation in key economic sectors, the Communist Party of Great Britain (CPGB) claimed 775 teachers among its 38,000-odd members. 'That education is considered not only as an important field for exploitation but also as analogous to an industry, is not perhaps without significance' came the reply.

The authorities reserved special powers for themselves to arrest known or suspected 'subversives' or restrict their movements. If it was ironic to think of ancient liberties being set aside by the state in the service of democracy, it was no more so, most people in the country felt, than using democratic freedoms to plot democracy's overthrow.

War on the Peaceniks

The authorities were in murkier waters when it came to pacifist

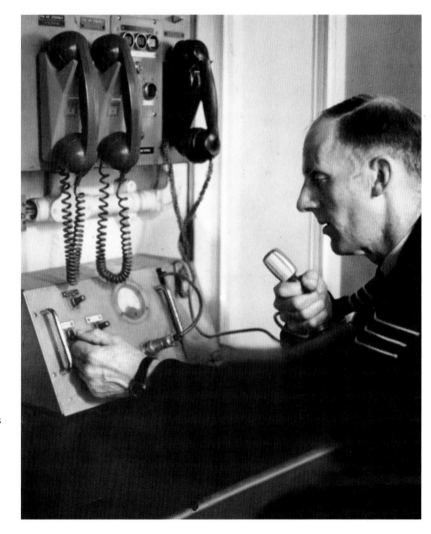

HANDEL was the lynchpin of the UK's early-warning system.

groups. Since the 1930s, British intellectuals had been drifting into the Peace Pledge Union (PPU), making common cause with influential churchmen. From 1958, the PPU was increasingly marginalized by the growth of the Campaign for Nuclear Disarmament (CND). While groups of this sort did not pose any threat of violence, their demonstrations could chip away at public confidence, potentially undermining national resolve. Their apocalyptic prophecies of death and destruction – however accurate they might be – weren't going to boost the British public's support for the nuclear deterrent. Nor was the suggestion made by some campaigners that the Cold War divide was nothing more than the self-serving strategy of

Joseph McCarthy's campaign against communism sowed suspicion and paranoia in the United States.

MARCH FROM
LONDON
FROM
ALDERMASTON

Clerics, communists and liberals marched together behind the banners of the Campaign for Nuclear Disarmament (CND).

communist and capitalist elites; that no quarrel existed between the 'people' on either side.

Such rhetoric had a particular appeal to the young and highly educated – the elite of the next generation. Among the peace campaigners, along with leading clerics (including several bishops), were high-profile personalities such as philosopher Bertrand Russell, composer Benjamin Britten, actresses Peggy Ashcroft and Edith Evans, writers E.M. Forster and J.B. Priestley, the artist Patrick Heron and the sculptors Barbara Hepworth and Henry Moore.

A who's who of British artistic and intellectual life; and who knew what the impact of their thinking might be on British attitudes in the longer term? The authorities were not taking any chances. As far as they were concerned, the peace campaigners were with the enemy. They were at best to be viewed with suspicion – and if, when the nuclear crunch came, their activities were seen to be hampering the country's efforts to defend itself, they would be stopped with whatever force

'Is all this to end in horror because so few are able to think of Man rather than of this or that group of men?'

Philosopher Bertrand Russell, 1956

Paranoia and PROFUNC

In defence of democratic freedom, fundamental freedoms had to be suspended. Thus, at any rate, was the conclusion of a Canada in the grip of Cold War fears.

In September, 1945, an obscure clerk at the Soviet Embassy in Ottawa defected. Some see Igor Gouzenko as the man who began the Cold War. He certainly had some arresting revelations to make – and brought highly sensitive codebooks and logs and other papers with him. Leading communists in Canada, he alleged, had been helping out the Soviets with information – on the West's atomic weapons programme, among other things. He revealed other things as well, including the now-clichéd craft of Cold War espionage – the sleeper agents and dead drops, the stuff of a thousand films. In 1945, though, such details were unfamiliar to the general public: so much so that it's said that, when Gouzenko first presented himself at a police station to hand himself over, he was sent packing by the disbelieving officers at the desk.

Once examined, the revelations caused considerable disquiet. If the Soviets had been so busy in Canada – not, after all, the most militarily or diplomatically important of the NATO partners – what had they been up to in the United States or Britain? While agents in those countries scurried off to search for spies, Canada tried to get its own house in order.

Canadian Police Chief Stuart Taylor Wood.

Canada has a reputation as an easygoing sort of place, socially liberal and politically moderate. It's a measure of the shock the 'Gouzenko Affair' delivered to the political establishment that the PROFUNC plan was considered – let alone that it was developed in great detail. The brainchild of Stuart Taylor Wood, Chief of the Royal Canadian Mountain Police (RCMP), PROFUNC was a plan to round up enemies of the state in the event of crisis: its name referred to the 'PRO-minent FUNC-tionaries of the Communist Party' against which it was aimed.

Red Round-up
On M-Day (mobilization day), the police would swoop and round up suspects, who would then be

What else was being concealed? Igor Gouzenko's revelations stunned Canadians.

TRANSCRIPT OF KEY PARAGRAPHS

<u>Commissioner Wood, Chief of the Royal Canadian Mountain Police, to Stuart S. Garson, Minister of Justice, Ottawa, Ontario, 15 February 1950</u>

In negotiations with the provinces as to the responsibility for guarding those vital points which are provincially owned or controlled, I recommend:

a) that the Provincial Government provide guard forces and physical security measures;

b) that the Federal Government assist financially on an agreed basis and subject to maintenance of satisfactory security standards;

The Federal payments might be based on:

a) a straight percentage of cost; or

b) the difference between the cost of maintaining normal peacetime security and that of meeting expanded wartime needs.

I favor the first alternative on the ground of administrative simplicity.

taken to reception centres. Existing installations would be used for this: some – as might be expected – were military camps or colleges, but Toronto's Casa Loma Country Club and Saskatchewan's Regina Exhibition Park (now Evraz Place) were also earmarked. After processing, internees would be moved to prisons or camps to be held in the longer term.

The scale of the scheme was staggering. A memo of February 1950 from Commissioner Wood to the Minister of Justice Stuart Carson illustrates the kind of administrative headaches entailed by so ambitious an internment plan. While, from this historical distance, the startling thing is to see the confinement of thousands of Canadian citizens to camps

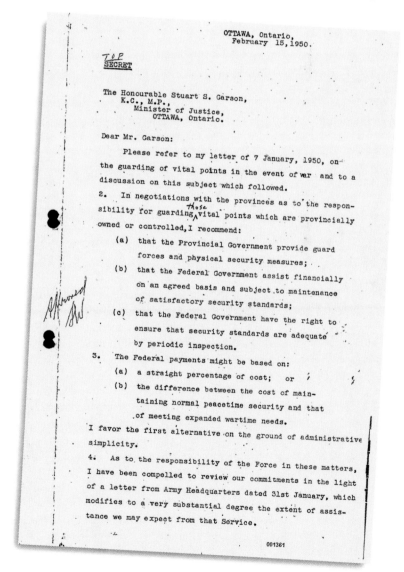

envisaged (some 16,000 party members, writes Wood, and in excess of 50,000 'sympathizers'), he and his superiors seem to have been preoccupied mainly with the logistical challenge. And with the questions of how financial and administrative responsibility should be divided between the Federal and Provincial authorities and of which agency (Army or RCMP) should have to provide the manpower for the initial round-up and for guarding the camps thereafter.

Iron Fist, Velvet Glove

Careful records were kept and regularly updated so that the authorities knew exactly who they were watching and who was going to be picked up when the moment came. Figures were kept meticulously and 'apprehension orders' issued and completed for each one: seldom can so high-handed an action have been so conscientious in the planning. The camps themselves were to show the same ironic interplay of cavalier high-handedness and correctness. Tough rules were to be enforced – and inmates might be shot if they attempted to escape. At the same time, the authorities were almost comically caring in the rigorousness with which they set out all the arrangements they planned to make for their prisoners' welfare.

A copy of the Regulations shows how provision was made for the election of 'camp spokesmen' to represent internees in their dealings with the authorities; with the creation of a 'camp bank' to

safeguard money confiscated from them when they were brought in. The 11-page document outlines procedures for camp life, including admission and release and transfer from one camp to another. The duties of the Commandant, and his powers, are set down; stipulations are made for the provision of canteens and medical facilities, the enforcement of camp rules and penalties for their infraction. There is even a scrupulous section governing the provision of religious chaplains – not, presumably, a priority for the committed communist!

It's extraordinary, in hindsight, that so big and elaborately organized a programme could have continued unknown to the mass of the Canadian population. It remained in place, though, with its records maintained and its procedures practised in regular exercises, until its eventual abolition in 1983. By that time, the Cold War was still far from over, and subversion continued to be as potentially problematic as ever, but officials felt a more flexible approach might be more successful. Not until a decade after the Cold War's end did the first inklings of PROFUNC make it into the Canadian press; only in 2010 did fuller details emerge in an exposé by the CBC TV programme *The Fifth Estate*. While for many an old leftist the revelations can't have come as much of a surprise, several well-meaning liberals were genuinely flabbergasted to find the plans their government had been making with them in mind.

TRANSCRIPT OF KEY PARAGRAPHS

Memorandum to Canadian Area Commanders, 16 June 1983.

As a result of recent discussions between the Solicitor General and the Security Service concerning all aspects of the PROFUNC program, the Minister directed that all activity relative to the program be stopped immediately and that no new programs are to be implemented.

. . . This system is not to be used in mock-up exercises or for any other purpose relating to Security Service possible implication in contingency planning.

. . . The Security Service has, for a number of years, been attempting to have the PROFUNC program replaced by a more flexible system, specifically the Special Identification Program. While the Minister's decision regarding PROFUNC is most welcome, we cannot afford to lose sight of the fact that a replacement system is required if we are to meet our responsibilities during times of crises.

M E M O R A N D U M

83 JUN 16 A10: 30

S E C R E T

FILE 6270-2-2
DOSSIER Our Ref.: IP 282

1983 May 27

TO: AREA COMMANDERS - SECURITY SERVICE -
      ALBERTA AREA - B.C. AREA - MANITOBA AREA -
      ATLANTIC AREA - ONTARIO AREA - QUEBEC AREA -
      SASKATCHEWAN AREA - SOUTHWESTERN ONTARIO AREA

INFO: - Officer i/c "F" Operations
      - Security Service Audit Unit

      - Police & Security Branch
        Ministry of the Solicitor General
          Attention: Mr. J.A.L. Cloutier

      - Director, Protective Policing,
        "P" Directorate

FROM: Officer i/c "D" Operations

RE: PROFUNC

       This should be read in conjunction with our letter
       of 1982 SEP 20 on this file.

       As a result of recent discussions between the
       Solicitor General and the Security Service concerning
       all aspects of the PROFUNC program, the Minister
       directed that all activity relative to the program
       be stopped immediately and that no new programs are
       to be implemented.

       Correspondence from the Director General dated
       1983 APR 27 reads:

       "The Solicitor General ... has instructed that we
       abandon all activity with the current system."

       In a memorandum dated 1982 MAY 02, the Deputy Director
       General (Operations) states:

                                              2

000001

S E C R E T

ral's instructions,
ctivities pertaining
system is not to be
for any other purpose
possible implication

sider the Profunc
hich no alterations
l further notice."

is to be no further
he PROFUNC program.
ing is to take place
system, however, no
of fulfilling
ROFUNC program.

curity Service has,
pting to have the
e flexible system,
cation Program.
arding PROFUNC is
lose sight of the
required if we are
g times of crises.
ure developments in

000002

Chapter Four

Europe in the Firing Line

No one in Europe took too much comfort from the protective presence of the 'nuclear umbrella'. If war broke out, the continent would be the battlefield.

President Eisenhower's policy of 'Massive Retaliation' was, quite consciously and unabashedly, disproportionate; a threat to use a sledgehammer to crack a nut. As long as the Soviets believed the threat, though, the world would be a safer place. It would be in no one's interests to start a fight. But, while the thought of Mutually Assured Destruction (MAD) maintained a precarious peace, both sides cast around for means by which it might be circumvented; by which they might gain the upper hand in some sort of less-than-nuclear war.

So cataclysmic would be the consequences of all-out atomic conflict that it was possible to imagine the enemy going to almost any lengths to avoid that outcome. That, paradoxically, could be seen as a spur to aggression. Hence the rash of 'proxy wars' that broke out around the world during the Cold War and allowed the two sides to jab and spar without actually attempting a knockout blow.

American troops trudge down a German street in 1945. As the victorious Allies took charge, the map of Central Europe was radically redrawn.

German Plans

After 1945, Germany was no longer in any position to start a war – but, as the Cold War foes squared off, the country itself had every chance of becoming a battlefield.

Although allies of convenience during World War II, the (capitalist) West and the Soviet Union soon refound their earlier mutual antipathy. Churchill had expressed anxiety in 1945 that the Red Army would not actually be stood down, despite its victory. Those fears had proven all too

14 May 1955: Eastern European leaders gather together for the ceremonial signing of the Warsaw Pact.

justified. What, from 1946, was to be known as the 'Soviet Army' was believed to number more than 500 divisions – substantially more than five million men.

By no means all were based in Central Europe: relations with China were increasingly fraught and there were trouble spots to the south in the Caucasus and Central Asia. But between what was left of the Soviet force and those of its Eastern European satellites – formally brought together by the Warsaw Pact of 1955 – there were plenty of troops to maintain a threatening presence. By that time, they had already shown their aggressive – if not, perhaps, expansionist

– intent by blockading Berlin (prompting the airlift of 1948). They'd also intervened in that same city to put down the anti-Soviet uprising of 1953; three years later, it was to be the Hungarians' turn to have their hopes for freedom cruelly suppressed.

What of the West? Was democracy there in danger? It was hard to say, though it seemed only prudent to prepare for the worst. At any moment, analysts feared, the Iron Curtain might abruptly be drawn and Soviet and satellite forces come pouring through the Fulda Gap from East Germany into West Germany. Streaming across the Netherlands, Belgium, France

Only a frantic airlift saved Berlin for the West in 1948.

'No nation has ever been successful in avoiding the terrors of war by refusing to defend its rights.'

President Eisenhower, broadcast to Americans, 1959

and Spain, they might easily be in Lisbon within three days.

Calculated Risks

Such, at least, was the doomsday scenario. Should it come to pass, the West would, of course, have the option of unleashing atomic Armageddon – but would that irrevocable step seem justified when the moment came? Might it not seem to the Soviets that a conventional attack was a risk worth taking? A way of recovering the initiative it appeared to have lost?

For, while the Soviet Union was a nuclear power now – and had been since 1949, indeed – the Americans had clearly got an all-important headstart in the 'Arms Race'. Quite how big an arsenal the Soviets had assembled by the early 1950s, no one knew. The competition really only intensified

in the years that followed, both sides lining up bombs and missiles as quickly as they could. Even then, though, it was far from clear that the USSR was catching up – despite the doom-and-gloom from Washington hawks.

West Berlin was divided into separate British, French and American sectors.

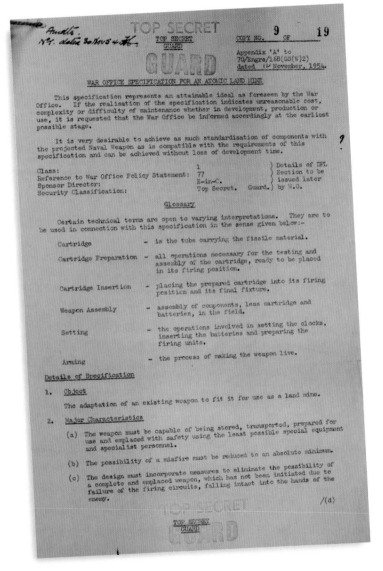

TRANSCRIPT OF KEY PARAGRAPHS

UK War Office Specification For An Atomic Land Mine, November 1954.

This specification represents an attainable ideal as foreseen by the War Office. If the realisation of the specification indicates unreasonable cost, complexity or difficulty of maintenance whether in development, production or use, it is requested that the War Office be informed accordingly . . .

It is very desirable to achieve as much standardisation of components with the projected Naval Weapon as is compatible with the requirements of this specification and can be achieved without loss of development time.

Glossary
Certain technical terms are open to interpretations.

Cartridge – is the tube carrying the missile material.

Setting – the operation involved in setting the clocks, inserting the batteries and preparing the rifling units.

Yet if, as some were starting to suspect, the much-vaunted 'Missile Gap' was actually in America's favour, wasn't that all the more reason for the Soviets to make use of their battalions on the ground?

Outnumbered
The NATO powers knew that they had to prepare, not just for nuclear bombs and missiles but for an invasion of the more old-fashioned sort. Yet this was easier said than done: the Western armies had gone home in good faith at the end of World War II; it was going to be quite a task to mobilize the men required and ready democratic Europe's eastern frontier – especially in the absence of any *immediate* threat. They did

their best: by the mid-1950s, around 50,000 soldiers were serving in the British Army of the Rhine (BAOR) while the United States had somewhere in the region of half a million infantry and over 100,000 airmen in Europe. This was an astonishing number to be stationed so far from home and in a time of (admittedly uneasy) peace, but still far fewer than those arrayed against them on the other side.

The hope was that Western troops were better trained and equipped than their Warsaw Pact equivalents. As far as it went, it was well grounded. There's no doubt that NATO's forces would have 'punched above their weight'; but they were massively outnumbered, and it seemed all too likely that, despite their superlative discipline, their weapons and their fighting skills, in the event of an invasion, they would be overwhelmed.

Atomic Landmines

The obvious answer for the West – given that it still held a stronger hand in atomic capability – was to make sure that any conventional war became atomic by default. A line of what amounted to atomic landmines arrayed along the frontier of West Germany, to be set off remotely at a distance or with a time-fuse, would wipe out the communists' advantage at a stroke. Granted, it would also wipe out a sizeable tranche of Germany as well, but if the

alternative was going to be Red rule in western Europe . . .?

By the standards of atomic-weapons design, this should have been a relatively straightforward task: there was no need for any delivery vehicle more sophisticated than a heavy lorry. No advanced rocketry, in other words: no fine-tuning of fuel use, aerodynamics or guidance systems. But there were other factors that had to be considered, as the War Office made clear in the top secret specifications it produced for the project in 1954. To be of use in the sort of situation that was realistically likely to arise, such a mine would have to be not just workable but foolproof:

The weapon must be capable of being stored, transported, prepared for use and emplaced with safety using the least possible special equipment and specialist personnel.

The authors then went on to add, with masterly *sang froid*, that 'the possibility of a misfire must be reduced to an absolute

minimum'. No matter how simple the technology, this challenge becomes all but insurmountable when the tolerance for error is precisely nil.

If accidental self-detonation was to be avoided at all costs, a failure to go off at all might if anything be worse. The War Office was adamant about the need to build in safety features to eliminate the possibility of

. . . a complete and emplaced weapon, which has not been initiated due to failure of the firing circuits, falling intact into the hands of the enemy.

Bertha, Bunnies, Peacocks . . . and Chickens

Work began on Big Bertha that same year. The weapon was soon renamed Brown Bunny; then, in 1955, when it was adapted to accommodate a different explosive device based on the Blue Danube atomic bomb, Blue Bunny.

Blue Danube weighed 7 tonnes (7.7 tons) but it had a 'yield' of 20kt. By the time a special casing

Britain's Blue Danube bomb had a yield of 20 kilotons.

'The weapon must be capable of being stored, transported, prepared for use and emplaced with safety. . .'

Brown Bunny specifications briefing, 1954

The landmine project went through repeated reviews and re-reviews.

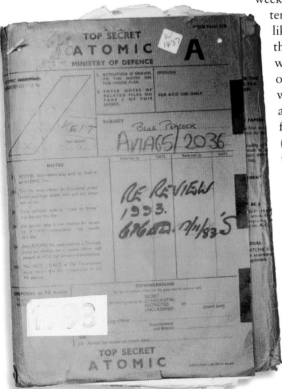

had been designed for it (and tested at an abandoned gravel pit outside Sevenoaks, Kent), the finished mine weighed around 10 tonnes (11 tons). In 1957, it reached its most refined form. Owing to fears that the name Blue Bunny had been compromised, it was renamed yet again, this time Blue Peacock.

The succession of codenames given to what in fact remained substantially the same project attests to the difficulties it posed, as well as the developers' reluctance to let it go. Many of these problems related to the need to maintain a steady temperature for a device that was to be sunk deep into the ground before being left – perhaps for days or even weeks. The winter temperatures were likely to be so low that the electronic systems were impeded. A range of different measures were mooted to address this problem, from the obvious (insulating lagging) to the outlandish. One – quite serious – proposal involved live chickens being placed inside the casing with a few days' food and water: their body heat would help to keep the wiring warm. To monitor fluctuations in temperature, thermometers were fitted to the Blue

Peacock mines and heat loss studied in careful 'climatic trials'. Precautions had also to be taken to ensure that, once in position, the mines could not be sabotaged by agents on the ground. These precautions had to be tested in their turn.

Nothing was to be left to chance: 'Generally speaking', a document of 1957 insisted,

. . . design and development trials are built up from a base of component trials, leading to assembly trials, leading in turn to complete weapon trials. The schedule of trials is always under review.

Each part was to be tested separately before being incorporated into the whole and then carefully monitored so that nothing could conceivably go wrong when Blue Peacock came into use.

In the end, their efforts were wasted: Blue Peacock was cancelled at the beginning of 1958. Some of the reasons for this were banal, though they might arguably have been thought of sooner. The immediate cause of cancellation appears to have been the difficulty of carrying so heavy a weapon to a site that would be suitably remote; no lorry that was big enough could go far enough off-road. Then there was the question of how to ensure that the damage caused was limited as far as possible to the enemy: how, while destroying the Warsaw Pact attackers, was NATO going to contain the destruction and the subsequent fallout in what was, after all, an allied country?

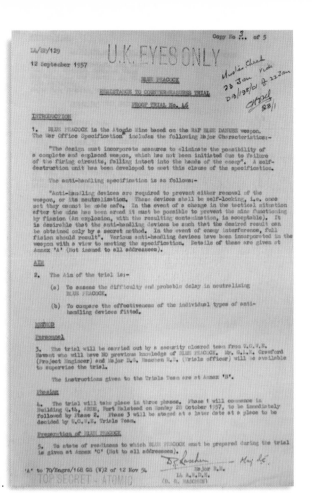

1.

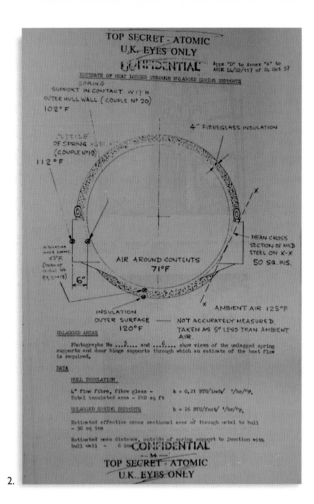

2.

TRANSCRIPT OF KEY PARAGRAPHS

<u>Blue Peacock – Resistance To Countermeasures Trial, September 1957</u>

Blue Peacock is the Atomic Mine based on the RAF Blue Danube weapon. The War Office Specification includes the following Characteristics:

"The design must incorporate measures to eliminate the possibility of a complete and emplaced weapon, which has not been initiated due to failure of the firing circuits, falling intact into the hands of the enemy". A self-destruction unit has been developed to meet this clause of the specification.

"Anti-handling devices are required to prevent either removal of the weapon, or its neutralisation. These devices shall be self-locking, i.e. once set they cannot be made safe. In the event of a change in tactical situation after the mine has been armed it must be possible to prevent the mine functioning by fission (An explosion, with the resulting contamination, is acceptable). It is desirable that the anti-handling devices be such that the desired result can be obtained only by a secret method. In the event of enemy interference, full fission should result."

The trial will be carried out by a security cleared team from U.C.W.E. Havant who will have NO previous knowledge of Blue Peacock.

Warsaw Pact

The stand-off between East and West appeared static, yet with the foes forever rethinking their strategy and reconfiguring their forces, it was actually fluid.

A Philosophical Quandary

The British planners of the Blue Peacock weapon found themselves facing what was to be a major dilemma of the period: the quasi-philosophical problem that the idea of the 'tactical nuclear weapon' is almost a contradiction in terms. The whole point of an atomic blast is that it's big: why would you want to make it smaller? Except that, without some way of doing that, you'd hardly be able to fight with it at all.

Had the atomic bomb made its swansong simultaneously with its triumphant debut over Japan? Since 1945 – and certainly since the Soviets had developed their own atomic weapons to cancel out their advantage – it had not proven to be quite the trump card the Americans had hoped. On the contrary, it had been a card that could not be played: paradoxically, if atomic bombs and warheads kept the peace, it was because they more or less made themselves redundant because they were too powerful to be used.

Arming for Peace

But then this was a thoroughly paradoxical age, both sides happy to heed the injunction of the

President John F. Kennedy moved America to a posture of 'Flexible Response'.

ancient Roman writer Vegetius: 'whosoever should wish for peace, let him prepare for war'. It was paradoxical too in the sense that, while all the anxious talk was of nuclear holocaust, both sides were building up their conventional forces on the ground. President John F. Kennedy had fired the starting gun in this phase of the Arms Race when, in 1961, he replaced Eisenhower's doctrine of 'Massive Retaliation' with a new one of 'Flexible Response'.

Where Eisenhower had locked the United States and its allies into an all-or-nothing logic of nuclear deterrence, Kennedy allowed for a more calibrated – and ultimately, the President reasoned, more convincing – reaction to Soviet actions in Europe, in the North Atlantic and around the world.

TRANSCRIPT OF KEY PARAGRAPHS

Statement on the Defence Estimates. British Ministry of defence 31st Jan 1977

Negotiations on the mutual and balanced reduction of forces in central Europe (MBFR) are now in their fourth year but progress has been disappointingly slow. The agreed aim of the negotiations is to contribute to a more stable relationship in the area at a lower level of forces, without damaging the security of East or West.

The Allied proposals for mutual reductions to a common collective ceiling on the ground and air manpower of the Warsaw Pact and of NATO, and for the withdrawal of a Soviet tank army, are designed to redress the major destabilising imbalances between the two sides.

The additional Western proposals of December 1975, including an offer to withdraw from the reductions area significant numbers of American nuclear weapons, represent a reasonable compromise between the initial demands of both sides.

have continued their negotiations on the detailed provisions of a new comprehensive agreement on strategic offensive weapons. The British Government is kept informed of progress by the United States in the North Atlantic Council and looks forward with keen interest to a successful conclusion of these negotiations, since strategic stability is essential for the further development of détente in East/West relations.

Force Reductions in Central Europe

110.   Negotiations on the mutual and balanced reduction of forces in central Europe (MBFR) are now in their fourth year but progress has been disappointingly slow. The agreed aim of the negotiations is to contribute to a more stable relationship in the area at a lower level of forces, without damaging the security of East or West. The Allied proposals for mutual reductions to a common collective ceiling on the ground and air manpower of the Warsaw Pact and of NATO, and for the withdrawal of a Soviet tank army, are designed to redress the major de-stabilising imbalances between the two sides. The additional Western proposals of December 1975, including an offer to withdraw from the reductions area significant numbers of American nuclear weapons, represent a reasonable compromise between the initial demands of both sides. By contrast the Eastern proposals, involving a mixture of equal percentage and equal numerical reductions, have not been significantly modified and would merely serve to give permanent status to the existing imbalances at a lower level of forces.

111.   At the outset of the negotiations in November 1973 the West

- 4 -

The 1977 British Ministry of Defence estimates on the increases of Soviet armed forces.

In Europe specifically, though, it involved a full-scale overhaul and reinforcement of NATO conventional forces so that they could provide a credible deterrence to Soviet invasion in themselves. It might seem in some ways a backward step, a bid by the West to undermine its own nuclear deterrent, but it offered a greater range of options in the longer run.

However, it caught the West in a second stand-off on the ground in Germany and made permanent what had seemed a temporary (if alarmingly protracted) postwar confrontation with the Soviets. Over time, it became a way of life, continuing through the rest of the 1960s and beyond. While the mid-1970s brought *détente* (the easing of relations), the relaxation was only relative, as the Draft Statement on the Defence Estimates, issued by the UK's Ministry of Defence in 1977, makes clear. Talks on 'Mutually Balanced Force Reductions' (MBFR), which had set out to allow both sides to step back a little from the confrontation in Germany, had only given them more to disagree about. As the report notes: 'Progress during the year has been disappointing.'

Numbers Games

A lack of progress between East and West was hardly surprising, perhaps, when they couldn't agree on the most basic facts and figures. The MoD officials spoke with exasperation of:

. . . significant discrepancies between the figures put forward by the East and Western assessments of Warsaw Pact force levels in the area.

Whilst the Warsaw Pact had disputed NATO's claims (tabled in 1973) that their ground forces outnumbered those of the West 'by 150,000 men', they 'declined to discuss data and did not table figures of their own'. The worry now, as far as Western analysts were concerned, was that the Soviets would agree to even-handed reductions, which, while seeming radical, 'would merely serve to give permanent status to the existing imbalances'.

Overall, the authors of the Statement said, the Soviets were augmenting their military

---

CONFIDENTIAL

Diagrams

Figures 1 and 2 will show the following information:

1. Increases in the capability of the Soviet Northern Fleet

	1963	1976	% increase
Submarines (including ballistic missile sub-marines	184 (44 nuclear-powered)	203 (101 nuclear-powered)	10 (130)
Cruisers and Destroyers	27 (6 missile-armed)	34 (22 missile-armed)	26 (270)
Frigates and Escorts	45	66	47
Fixed-Wing Maritime Aircraft	170	210	24

2. Increases in the capability of Soviet Forces in Central Europe

	1963	1976	% increase
Tanks	7,250	9,500	31
Artillery	3,200	4,000	25
Armoured Personnel Carriers (including reconnaissance and command variants)	5,300	9,450	78
Tactical Aircraft	1,655	1,975	20

- 9 -

CONFIDENTIAL

spending while claiming to be lowering it. 'It has grown by some five per cent a year in real terms.' Soviet military expenditure was believed to account for '11–12 per cent of . . . gross national product (GNP)'. A table set out plainly the problem faced by the NATO allies: large-scale re-equipment across the board. In the Northern Fleet ('the main threat to NATO in the Atlantic'), capability in submarines had risen by 10 per cent since 1963: the Soviets now had 203 in the region, of which 101 were nuclear powered. The same period had also seen a rise of 26 per cent in cruiser and destroyer numbers (from 27 to 34) and a rise of 47 per cent

in the number of frigates and escort ships.

So much for Britannia ruling the Atlantic waves; even with the support of the United States and their NATO partners, they felt they were in troubled waters. On dry land in Europe, the Soviets' advantage seemed starker still. What in 1968 had seemed a formidable force was looking well-nigh irresistible by 1976, bolstered by reinforcements in all areas. In artillery, the Soviet Army was 25 per cent stronger; they had 20 per cent more tactical aircraft on the European front ready to give aerial support to any advance. Any doubt that the Soviets were contemplating an old-fashioned fight for territorial advantage was

removed by the evidence of their investment in tanks and infantry. Over 2000 tanks had been added to what had already been a force of 7250 – an increase of 31 per cent. Soviet strength in armoured personnel carriers had been built up from 5300 to 9450 – a staggering increase of 78 per cent. The report also pointed out that the Soviets had 'a substantial helicopter assault capability' they hadn't had before, while 'the acquisition of new large jet transport aircraft is increasing the Soviet capability for airborne operations and logistic support'.

Tanks pass Lenin's Mausoleum in Moscow's Red Square in a show of Soviet strength.

Soviet Plans

Far from being daunted by the nuclear 'deterrent', the Soviet Union seemed all too ready to contemplate a conventional attack on Western Europe.

Meaning Business

Did the Soviets have plans actually to use any of this kit? It hardly mattered, the authors of the UK's 1977 Draft Statement on Defence Estimates acknowledged; these things signified an expression of resolve:

Military power is regarded by the Soviet Union as a legitimate and important diplomatic weapon and there can be little doubt that the Soviet Union could exploit to the full the opportunities which would be offered by any weakening of Western political or economic stability or by any further shift in their favour of the military relationship between East and West in Europe.

By the same token, then, the authors argued,

. . . NATO's forces must serve both a military and a political purpose. They must promise a collective defence against any military aggression, and they must underpin the confidence of each member state that the Alliance would collectively resist any attempt by the Soviet Union to derive political advantage from its

military pre-eminence over a single member, or groups of members.

Weren't the West's nuclear weapons supposed to be their guarantee of security? Yes, of course, but at the same time – and emphatically – no. Strength in conventional forces was essential if the *nuclear* deterrent was to have credibility:

If NATO were patently unable to sustain a stalwart conventional defence against conventional attack, its enemies might well conclude that an Alliance which was so neglectful of its own security would be unlikely to have

the collective determination to escalate a conflict to the nuclear level; they might thus be persuaded to take the risk of launching a conventional attack.

Show of Strength

There were other reasons for the Soviets to favour a conventional war, of course: the launch of Sputnik 1 in 1957 – the world's first satellite – had been a big, but atypical, triumph for Soviet technology. The shooting down of Gary Powers' U2 spy plane over the Urals in 1960 is rightly seen as an embarrassment and a humiliation for the Americans

The arrest and arraignment of Gary Powers, pilot of a shot-down spy plane, was a huge embarrassment to the United States.

A Colonel in Soviet Military Intelligence, Oleg Penkovsky fed vital information to the West.

(especially given the ignominious collapse of a succession of cover stories). At the same time, though, the incident revealed that for five years spy planes had been flying over Soviet airspace pretty much at will. America's technological lead was evident, though naturally denied by the Soviets, and by a US political establishment anxious to discourage complacency – as well as a Military–Industrial Complex with (it could be argued) a vested interest in the fostering of fear.

The Cold War worked itself out over the years in complex games of threat and intimidation, bluff and double-bluff, imposture and denial. Neither side dealt squarely with its own public, let alone with its enemy. Strange correspondences resulted: even as the Soviets talked up their

Defence Minister Malinovsky urged his Soviet comrades to attack the West.

A Colonel in Soviet Military Intelligence, Oleg Penkovsky fed vital information to the West.

military capabilities for all they were worth, officials in the Kennedy Administration were warning the world of a 'missile gap' in the USSR's favour.

In fact, we now know, that Oleg Penkovsky, the Americans' highly placed mole in Moscow's Military Intelligence department, had all but dismissed the Soviet menace in conversation with the US President himself in 1961. Kennedy could stand firm, he had insisted: 'Khrushchev was not ready for any war.' Penkovksy was able to be so adamant because a leading member of his country's scientific and political establishments, Djerman Gvishiani, had confided in him:

You know . . . with respect to ICBMs [intercontinental ballistic missiles], up to now we don't have a damn thing. Everything is only on paper, and there is nothing in actual existence.

Despite great strides in rocketry since World War II, the challenges of producing an effective electronic guidance system for long-range missiles had so far frustrated Soviet technicians. As Mao might have put it, the Soviet nuclear threat was something of a 'paper tiger'.

Aggressive Intent

It is strange, then, in such circumstances, to find Soviet Defence Minister Rodion Malinovsky, in May 1961, urging aggression, on the grounds that:

As a result of the existence of long-range missiles with nuclear warheads, the options have increased for launching strikes deep behind enemy lines.

zur Erfüllung der nächsten strategischen Aufgaben zu beginnen. Deshalb schaffen wir strategische Raketentruppen und halten sie in ständiger Bereitschaft, besitzen wir Truppen der Luftverteidigung und eine mindestens erforderliche Menge an Land-, Luft- und Seestreitkräften. Zur Vergrößerung ihrer Anstrengungen wird eine bestimmte Menge von Kräften und Mitteln vorgesehen, die in sehr kurzer Zeit mobilisiert werden können, was in der Regel geheim durchgeführt wird, wenn es die Lage erfordert. Bei unserer Übung wurde die geheime Mobilisierung in der sogenannten Spannungsperiode durchgeführt, die im Ergebnis der Verschärfung der internationalen Lage entstand.

Die Truppen der ständigen Gefechtsbereitschaft und diejenigen, die kurzfristig mobilisiert werden, kann man die erste strategische Staffel der Streitkräfte nennen, die für die Erfüllung der wichtigsten Aufgaben in der Anfangsperiode eines Krieges vorgesehen sind.

Zur Erfüllung anderer Aufgaben ist das Verstärken der Kräfte aus der Tiefe erforderlich, wozu die Mobilisierung der Truppen mit etwas längeren Fristen vorgesehen ist.

Der Hauptteil der Streitkräfte, die für die Erfüllung der nächsten strategischen Aufgaben vorgesehen sind, sind also sowohl bei uns als auch in den NATO-Ländern faktisch schon entfaltet und können sehr schnell ihre Handlungen beginnen. Darin besteht die wichtigste Besonderheit der Entfaltung der Streitkräfte unter modernen Bedingungen.

Wichtigste Forderung an die Streitkräfte ist jetzt das schnelle Herstellen ihrer erhöhten Gefechtsbereitschaft. Das betrifft besonders den Teil der Streitkräfte, der sich in unmittelbarer Berührung mit den NATO-Ländern befindet sowie die Raketentruppen und die Truppen der Luftverteidigung des Landes. Das Signal oder der Befehl zur Herstellung der vollen Gefechtsbereitschaft, das ist, bildlich gesprochen, das Signal "zum Start", d.h. das letzte Signal vor dem Beginn der Kampfhandlungen, die letzte allseitige Mobilisierung aller zum Handeln bereiten Kräfte. Davon, wie dieses Signal ausgeführt wird, hängt die Rechtzeitigkeit, die Kraft und die Wirksamkeit des ersten Schlages auf den Gegner ab. Das hat jetzt besonders große Bedeutung.

Doch wenn man sich beim Start nur ein wenig zu lange verweilt, wie schwer wird es dann, das Enteilte einzuholen, die verlorene Initiative auf dem kurzen Wege zu erlangen, auf dem wir den Sieg erringen müssen.

1.

Dabei gewährleistete die Artillerie- und Luftwaffenvorbereitung nur die feuermäßige Niederhaltung des Gegners. Die völlige Zerstörung seiner Kräfte wurde durch den Schlag der Truppen erreicht, die nach der Artillerievorbereitung zum Angriff mit den Panzern zu Fuß übergingen.

Als Folge des Auftauchens weitreichender Raketen mit Kernsprengköpfen vergrößerten sich die Möglichkeiten, einen Feuerschlag auf die Tiefe zu führen. Die Vernichtung des Gegners wird unter modernen Bedingungen in erster Linie durch Schläge der Kernwaffen erreicht. Die Landstreitkräfte müssen die Ergebnisse dieser Kernwaffenschläge rechtzeitig ausnutzen, es versteht sich entschlossen in die Tiefe zur Zerschlagung der Stäbe, Nachrichtenzentralen, Flugplätze, Stellungen der Raketen und der herankommenden Reserven vorzubewegen. Die zweiten Staffeln der angreifenden Truppen und die Reserven sollen den Widerstand leistenden Gruppierungen des Gegners schnell Schläge in die Flanken und den Rücken zufügen und sie vernichten.

Die Hauptaufgabe zur Zerschlagung des Gegners wird also unter modernen Bedingungen durch Schläge der Kernwaffen erfüllt. Und die Aufgabe der Landstreitkräfte ist es, seine völlige Zerschlagung auf die Perspektive zu vollenden.

In den ersten Operationen der Anfangsperiode des Krieges sollen die Landstreitkräfte vor allem die Ergebnisse der Kernwaffenschläge der strategischen Mittel, die in ihrem Angriffsstreifen eingesetzt wurden, ausnutzen, die eigenen Kernwaffen sollen sie äußerst sparsam einsetzen und maximal für die Kampfhandlungen in der Tiefe aufheben. Der Übergang zum Angriff muß unter Berücksichtigung der Strahlungslage durchgeführt werden, die sich im Ergebnis des Führens von Raketen-Kernwaffenschlägen mit strategischen Mitteln ergibt. Berechnungen zeigen, daß die Zeit, die für das Absinken des Strahlungsspiegels erforderlich ist, nach Stunden und Tagen rechnet und daß wenig Wahrscheinlichkeit dafür besteht, daß die eigenen Truppen die verseuchte Zone früher als nach 5 - 6 Stunden betreten können.

Der einzige Ausweg, das ist das möglichst schnelle Durchfahren der verseuchten Räume durch Panzertruppen und auf stark gepanzerten Schützenpanzerwagen, die die Menschen vor der Strahlung schützen, mit Hubschraubern, und wenn es möglich ist, so muß man die Abschnitte mit dem höchsten Strahlungsgrad auf üblichen

2.

TRANSCRIPT OF KEY PARAGRAPHS

Speech by Soviet Defence Minister Rodian Malinovsky on the need for Warsaw Pact Offensive Operations, May 1961

As a result of the existence of long-range missiles with nuclear warheads, the options have increased for launching strikes deep behind enemy lines.

Under modern conditions the main task of destroying the enemy is realized through nuclear strikes. And the army's ground forces will be in charge of aiming for the complete destruction of enemy forces.

During the first operations in the initial phase of war, the army ground forces mainly have to exploit in their area of attack the results of strategic nuclear strikes. Only very sparingly should they use their own nuclear weapons, instead keeping the bulk of them for battle behind the enemy lines. The transition to attack must be contingent on the level of radiation resulting from nuclear missile strikes with strategic weapons.

Calculations have shown that the time needed to lower the level of radiation can be measured in hours and days. Thus there is little likelihood that our own troops will enter the contaminated zone before

Transportmitteln und Kraftfahrzeugen.

Der Angriff soll ohne Halt geführt werden unter Ausnutzung in erster Linie der herkömmlichen Vernichtungsmittel, der Panzer und der Luftstreitkräfte. Die Truppen müssen sich zielstrebig vorwärtsbewegen.

Wenn im Verlaufe des Angriffs Kernwaffen oder große Truppengruppierungen beim Gegner festgestellt werden, so muß man sie durch Kernwaffenschläge vernichten. In einigen Fällen kann es sich als zweckmäßiger erweisen, die unversehrt gebliebenen und Widerstand leistenden Stützpunkte des Gegners zu ügehen, ohne sich mit ihm in aufhaltende Kämpfe einzulassen.

Diese Bestimmungen und Forderungen sind allen längst bekannt. Aber aus irgendwelchem Grund werden sie bei den durchgeführten Übungen nicht immer erfüllt.

Über das hohe Tempo beim Angriff.

Der hohe Grad der Motorisierung der Armeen und die Anwendung der Kernwaffen schaffen günstige Bedingungen für eine entschlossene Vorwärtsbewegung der Truppen, auf eine große Tiefe. Das hohe Angriffstempo und das breite Manöver mit Kräften und Mitteln gewinnt unter modernen Bedingungen erstrangige Bedeutung. Wir haben mehrmals darüber gesprochen und man muß sagen, daß die Generale und Offiziere in der Mehrheit diese Fragen richtig verstehen. Jedoch einige Kommandierenden begannen die Angriffstempi außerordentlich zu erhöhen. So war das durchschnittliche Angriffstempo der Truppen der ersten Zentralen Front für die allgemeine Armee 100 bis 120 km und für die Panzerarmee 140 bis 150 km am Tag geplant. Bei der zweiten Zentralen Front wurde das durchschnittliche Angriffstempo bis zu 130 km am Tage geplant. Man muß offen sagen, daß solche Angriffstempis unreal sind. In derletzten Zeit ist bei uns eine wahllose Vergrößerung des Angriffstempos zu beobachten. Von Übung zu Übung wird das Angriffstempo höher und höher und wie wir sehen, hat es bereits 150 km am Tage erreicht. Eine solche Vergrößerung des Tempos bringt außer Schaden nichts ein.

Einige Kommandeure und Stäbe entfernen sich offensichtlich im Bemühen um erhöhte Angriffstempi manchmal von der Wirklichkeit und berücksichtigen nicht immer realen Möglichkeiten der Truppen und die Lage. Natürlich ist der Wunsch, solche hohen Angriffstempi zu erreichen, eine gute Sache. Aber die Möglichkeiten

Eine moderne allgemeine Armee benötigt keine Verstärkung durch Panzer, wie es im vergangenen Krieg war. Das Vorhandensein einer großen Anzahl von Panzern und Artillerie ermöglicht es ihr, dem Gegner selbständig mächtige Schläge auf große Tiefe zuzufügen, alles von ihrem Weg fortzufegen, was ihrer Vorwärtsbewegung Widerstand leistet und sie behindert. Sie ist in der Lage, bei Notwendigkeit, mit ihren eigenen Raketen-Kernwaffen große Truppengruppierungen des Gegners zu vernichten unddamit das Kräfteverhältnis in kürzester Zeit zu ihren Gunsten bedeutend zu verändern.

Unsere modernen Panzer-Armeen - das sind die wichtigste Stoßkraft der Fronten. Sie verfügen über eine große Schlagkraft, hohe Beweglichkeit und geringste Anfälligkeit von den Massenvernichtungsmitteln des Gegners. Ihre Handlungen sollen ganz zu Beginn des Krieges das schnelle Verlegen der Hauptanstrengungen auf große Tiefe, die Zerschlagung der operativen und strategischen Reserven des Gegners, die Vernichtung seiner Kernwaffen sowie die Verhinderung der Mobilmachungsmaßnahmen, die Desorganisierung der Truppenführung und der Arbeit des Hinterlandes gewährleisten.

Die Panzerkeile sollen - wie scharfe Pfeile - tief in die operative Gliederung des Gegners eindringen, seine strategische Front aufreißen, die Anstrengungen (des Gegners) zersplittern und ihm die Möglichkeit eines weiteren organisierten Widerstandes nehmen.

Die Panzer- und allgemeine Armee sind also gleichermaßen in der Lage, den Widerstand einer großen Gruppierung des Gegners zu brechen, einen entschlossenen Angriff zu entwickeln, schnell die Hauptanstrengungen von einer Richtung in eine andere zu verlegen und selbständig Aufgaben in großen operativen Maßstab zu lösen.

Vor kurzer Zeit stellten wir der allgemeinen Armee Aufgaben auf eine Tiefe von 150 - 200 km und das Angriffstempo wurde mit 40 - 50 km am Tag bestimmt. Jetzt haben wir die Möglichkeit, die Angriffsoperation der allgemeinen Armee bis zu einer Tiefe von 400 km und für die Panzerarmee auf die Tiefe der gesamten Frontoperation bei einem durchschnittlichen Angriffstempo von 100 km am Tag zu planen.

Die Schläge der allgemeinen und Panzerarmeen sollen sich durch den Einsatz von Luftlandetruppen ergänzt werden, die geeignet sind, schneller als die Erdtruppen, die Ergebnisse der Kernwaffenschläge auszunutzen, besonders derjenigen mit strategischer Bestimmung, wichtige Objekte in der Tiefe des

3. 4.

---

five or six hours. There is only one way of avoiding this, namely to cross the contaminated area speedily with tank units and heavy armoured personnel carriers protecting the crews from radiation, with helicopters, and, if possible, to bypass the areas with the highest levels of radiation by using ordinary motor vehicles and other means of transport.

Our modern tank divisions are the most important assault force of the Fronts. They have enormous striking power, high mobility and are least vulnerable to the enemies' weapons of mass destruction. Their actions right at the beginning of the war should guarantee a rapid shift of focus deep behind enemy lines, the destruction of the enemy's operational and strategic reserves, the destruction of its nuclear weapons and the prevention of mobilization efforts, and the disruption of the command structure and efforts in the hinterland. Recently we commissioned the army to solve tasks within a range of 150 to 200km (93 to 124 miles) behind enemy lines and with a speed of attack between 40 and 50km (25 to 31 miles) per day. Now we have the capability to plan an attack by general army units up to a range of 400km (249 miles), and to [plan an attack] by tanks deep behind enemy lines with an average speed of 100km (62 miles) per day.

Nikita Khruschev delivers a tirade against the United States during a summit in Paris in 1960.

The time has come, he urges them, accordingly, to consider combined nuclear/conventional attacks, striking deep into the territory of the Federal Republic of Germany:

During the first operations in the initial phase of war, the army ground forces mainly have to exploit in their area of attack the results of strategic nuclear strikes.

In other words, nuclear weapons would create the destruction and chaos that would be the cover for an advance by conventional forces who would take territory and consolidate their hold.

Obviously, due account would have to be taken of the conditions on the ground:

Calculations have shown that the time needed to lower the level of radiation can be measured in hours and days. Thus there is little likelihood that our own troops will enter the contaminated zone before five or six hours.

Both sides showed some naiveté about the dangers of radiation in the early Cold War years, though Malinovsky's optimism suggests the Soviets may still have been some way behind the curve.

It may also, on the other hand, indicate a cynicism on the Russian's part, a belief that soldiers were expendable. Besides, Malinovsky did recommend that, 'if possible', the invaders should 'bypass the areas with the highest levels of radiation by using ordinary motor vehicles and other means of transport'. The crucial point was that there was to be no dithering while the 'five or six hours' elapsed:

Attack must be pursued without interruption by using primarily conventional weapons, tanks and the air force. The troops have to proceed purposefully.

The Defence Minister was gung-ho:

Our modern tank divisions are the most important assault force of the Fronts. They have enormous striking power, high mobility and are least vulnerable to the enemies' weapons of mass destruction.

His confidence was no doubt justified – up to a point. The Soviet Union's tank armies had demonstrated their prowess in World War II (most notably at the battle of Kursk), and this had continued to be an area of impressive strength. Yet there was surely an element of wishful thinking in his argument. Note that Malinovsky strikes an exhortatory note; they 'must', he says, rather than they 'will'):

Like pointed arrows, tank detachments must deeply penetrate the enemy's operational lineup, tear up its strategic front line, split its efforts, and deprive it of further options for organized resistance.

'Like pointed arrows'? He's imagining it all on a map, from his fantasy operations room. He talks a good war, but could his armies really fight one?

Is there a hint of denial in this desire on Malinovsky's part to go 'back to the future', to fight the war with the West on the heroically hallowed ground of Kursk? The Defence Minister goes on to discuss the details as though the radioactive fallout isn't there, as though the only issues in question were the quality of the conventional hardware and the commanders' and soldiers' skill:

Recently we commissioned the army to solve tasks within a range of 150 to 200km (93 to 124 miles) behind enemy lines and with a speed of attack between 40 and 50km (25 and 31 miles) per day. Now we have the capability to plan an attack by general army units up to a range of 400km (249 miles) and by tanks deep behind enemy lines with an average speed of 100km (62 miles) per day.

Cuban Climbdown

Malinovsky's nostalgia would perhaps make more sense the following year when Cuba became the focus of global attention and the Soviet Union suffered considerable humiliation. When US spy planes spotted Soviet missile bases under construction on Cuba, 14 days of the tensest Cold War stand-off ensued. The Cuban Missile Crisis – or 'Caribbean Crisis', as it was known in the USSR – saw the United States demanding the USSR withdraw their missiles, and Khruschev calling the US quarantining of Cuba by air and sea as 'an act of aggression propelling humankind into the abyss of a world nuclear-missile war.'

However, the 'poker game' of popular mythology was in truth to be more one-sided than most

'We do not believe the imperialists ... they are only waiting for a suitable opportunity to attack ...'

Rodion Malinovsky, 1960

A bold stroke, the siting of missiles in Cuba rebounded badly on the Soviets.

MISSILE TRANSPORTERS

12 PROB GUIDELINE MISSILES

HEAVY EQUIPMENT

5 MISSILE DOLLIES

20' LONG CYLINDRICAL TANKS

MISSILE TRANSPORTERS

OPEN STORAGE

in the West realized – or most in the Soviet Union could have conceived. Even in the highest echelons of the military and the party, it would come as a shock to find that, faced with the prospect of a nuclear shootout with the United States, the Soviet political and military established felt that it was left with no alternative but to fold. Eschewing the usual secrecy, the United States made a performance of mobilizing for war, affording a glimpse of the scale and sophistication of their nuclear forces. This was designed to be intimidating – and intimidate it did. As the USAF's Major-General Jack Catton recalled,

We had absolute superiority. Khruschev was looking down the largest barrel he had ever stared at . . .

What could he do? He cancelled leave, but that was it. Malinovsky was all for going in guns blazing then as well, but his General Secretary was forced to bow down to the reality – that the Soviet Union wasn't ready for a nuclear war. Granted, its military could put on an impressive show rolling through Red Square in the annual May Day parade, and it had a well-stocked arsenal of bombs and missiles. But this kind of hardware wasn't enough in the absence of any working early-warning or missile-tracking systems. The Soviet bear, Catton explained, was a rabbit caught in the headlights:

They did not increase their alert, they did not increase their flights, or their air defence posture. They didn't do a thing, they froze in place.

East German Options

Suffice it to say, the US invasion of Cuba didn't go ahead – however straightforward it should have been. And the Soviets soon had their hands full in East Germany. Whatever the strategic strength of the Soviet Union and its satellites, in the economic competition between the two Cold War blocs, the West was racing ahead in leaps and bounds. And nowhere more obviously than in the Federal Republic of Germany, where the *Wirtschaftswunder* ('Economic Miracle') was in full flight. And the workers of the German Democratic Republic (GDR) were pretty much leaping and bounding in their eagerness to reach the West and share in this prosperity.

These were demoralizing times for leaders in the GDR. In the weeks and months that followed Malinovsky's fighting talk, the only invasion of the Federal Republic was one of discontented Easterners moving to the West. Faced by what threatened to be an exhausting brain-drain of all its younger, most vigorous and talented citizens, the Communist authorities were reduced to constructing a physical barrier to keep them in. The Berlin Wall

The building of the Wall in 1963 left East Berliners imprisoned in their own city.

Chancellor Erhard (right) meets President Johnson, who ignored his plan to 'buy' the GDR.

went up almost overnight, from 13 August 1961.

Ironically, East Germany had been one of the better-performing Iron Curtain economies. The Soviet Union was in an utter mess. The sixth Five-Year Plan (1956–60) had been set aside just a year in, a new programme being agreed in 1957 to start in 1959. This was supposed to introduce efficiencies into what the most loyal commentators more or less discreetly acknowledged was a hopelessly unwieldy, inflexible and wasteful economy. But this Seventh Five-Year Plan had been proving no more successful than the last.

What, then, if West Germany were to offer to take the East off the Soviet Union's hands – with a handsome, hard-currency payment in return? The communists would lose a liability, and the Germans regain the national unity they'd been pining for since partition: it would be a win–win, reasoned West German Chancellor Ludwig Erhard. A booming Federal Republic could manage the $20bn cost envisaged (on an instalment plan: $2bn per annum for 10 years). It might not be *easily* affordable, perhaps, but the unification project would be worth it, if only for the incentive it gave West German workers, managers and industrialists to succeed. The Soviets, meanwhile, would be delighted both to be rid

of an irksome East German burden and to have 10 years of windfall subsidies.

In October 1963, Erhard proposed his plan to the US Ambassador, George McGhee, who seems to have been as tactful as he could in his response. Erhard's plan showed great 'originality', the Ambassador reported in his communications with Washington. It was also worked out with great thoroughness – economically, indeed, it made perfect sense. Erhard was no flake: first as Finance Minister and now as Chancellor, he had done more than anyone else to bring about the *Wirtschaftswunder*.

He did, however, McGhee believed, show a 'serious political naiveté' in putting this plan forward – and it's hard to dispute the Ambassador's conclusions. The 'Great Patriotic War' (the Soviet term for World War II) ran the 1917 October Revolution close as the defining event in Soviet history — distrust of Germany was fundamental to the Russian psyche. The idea that Germany should be allowed to grow and thrive again (and potentially re-emerge as an aggressor) was not to be borne, whatever the short term benefits.

Visiting America in 1964, Erhard put his plan to Lyndon Johnson, US President since Kennedy's assassination the previous November. Johnson was enthusiastic, but relations with the Soviets took a turn for the worse with the ousting of Khruschev a few months later.

Czech Invasion Plans

The 1960s saw the Eastern Bloc recover some of its buoyancy – and its assertiveness. Big plans were being made to take the conflict to the West.

A Plan of Attack

Khruschev's successor as Soviet premier, Leonid Brezhnev, wasn't (as Margaret Thatcher was later to say of Mikhail Gorbachev) a man the West could 'do business with'. But it wasn't just his temperament that prevented it, or the fact that – in reaction to the 'Khruschev Thaw' of the post-Stalin years – the former chill descended on East–West relations. It was also because, for a few years, at least, the Soviet economy revived. Thanks to this upturn, the Warsaw Pact was able to prepare for the NATO 'first strike' it believed was coming – the only question being exactly when.

Quite how far it went in these preparations became apparent only in 2007, when historian Petr Lunak was rummaging in the Military Archives in Prague. He uncovered a 'Plan of Action' for defence against a NATO attack.

Dated 1964, it was signed as having been 'approved' by Antonín Novotny, the President of the Czechoslovak Socialist Republic (CSSR) and Supreme Commander of its 'People's Army'. That said, the document had been handwritten in Russian (a clear indication of where true real power lay in the Soviet sphere) and appears to have represented just the Czechoslovak

Leonid Brezhnev (centre) takes the salute at the May Day march-past in Red Square, Moscow, 1964.

component in a wider retaliation plan involving all the armed forces of the Warsaw Pact.

The plan anticipated an advance on the Czechoslovak Front by a formidable array of NATO units (up to 12 in all), including:

— *The 2nd Army Corps of the FRG [Federal Republic of Germany] including: 4th and 10th mechanized divisions, 12th tank division, 1st airborne division and 1st mountain division.*

— *the 7th Army Corps of the USA including: the 24th mechanized division and 4th armored tank division;*

— *the 1st Army of France including: 3rd mechanized division, the 1st and 7th tank divisions, and up to two newly deployed units, including 6 launchers of tactical missiles, up to 130 theater launchers and artillery, and up to 2800 tanks.*

Operations of the ground troops could be supported by part of the 40th Air Force, with up to 900 aircraft, including 250 bombers and up to 40 airborne missile launchers.

The task of this invasion force would be:

To disorganize the leadership of the state and to undermine mobilization of armed forces by surprise nuclear strikes against the main political and economic centers of the country.

To critically change the correlation of forces in its own favor by strikes against the troops, airfields and communication centers.

To destroy the border troops of the Czechoslovak People's Army

Soviet Premier Leonid Brezhnev (right) takes Czechoslovak President Antonín Novotny in a comradely embrace.

in border battles, and to destroy the main group of our troops in the Western and Central Czech Lands by building upon the initial attack . . .

Red Ruthlessness

War is never won by 'over-thinking' things; nor is the battlefield any place for the conspicuously compassionate. The Western establishment was hardly jam-packed with bleeding hearts. Even so, it's hard to decide whether Warsaw Pact strategic thinking here stands out more for its naive enthusiasm or its sheer cold-bloodedness. Did leading politicians and the military brass on the Soviet side just not 'get it'? Had they failed to appreciate what it was going to be like trying to fight a conventional

'Altogether the operation will require the use of 131 nuclear missiles and nuclear bombs . . .'

Warsaw Pact Plan of Action, 1964

Утверждаю
... Главнокомандующий
вооруженными силами ЧССР

Антонин Новотный
1964 г.

План
использования Чехословацкой Народной
армии на военное время
карта 1:500.000, изд. 1963 г.

1. Выводы из оценки противника.

На Центрально-Европейском театре
военных действий в полосе наступления Чехословацкого
фронта с Д1 до Д7-8 противником может
быть использовано до 12 общевойсковых соединений
- 2АК ФРГ в составе: 4,10 мпд, 12 тд, 1 вдд и 1 гпд;
- 7АК США в составе: 24 мд и 4 бртд;
- 1ПА французов в составе: 3 нд, 1 и 7 бртд и до
двух вновь развертываемых соединений, - 6 пусковых
установок оперативно-тактических ракет, до 130
тактических пусковых установок и орудий и до
2800 танков.

Действия наземных войск может поддерживать
часть сил 4 ОТАК - до 900 самолетов, в том числе 250 самолетов-
-носителей и до 40 установок самолетов-снарядов

Исходя из группировки войск НАТО и оценки
результатов учений, проведенного командованием НАТО
можно предполагать следующий замысел действий

... В составе первого эшелона иметь 1 и 4 армии и

иметь 131 ядер-
... 96 ракет и
... ом ударе при-
... а включение
... 9 ракет и ток-
... задачи израс-
В резерве фронта

... черного удара
с объединениями
войск 7 ПА США
с оперативно-
... реки Неккар
... нить выдвигаю-
противника и
... нсон, Эпиналь,
... готовили и
... лионском

... ении Нюрнберг,
... ч; частью
... ен.

... фронта - в
... танковой
... их развертыва-

TRANSCRIPT OF KEY PARAGRAPHS

<u>Plan of Actions of the Czechoslovak People's Army for War Period, 1963</u>

Judging by the composition of the group of NATO troops and our assessment of the exercises undertaken by the NATO command, one could anticipate the design of the enemy's actions with the following goals:

To disorganize the leadership of the state and to undermine mobilization of armed forces by surprise nuclear strikes . . .

To critically change the correlation of forces in its own favour by strikes against the troops, airfields and communication centres.

To destroy the border troops of the Czechoslovak People's Army in border battles, and to destroy the main group of our troops in the Western and Central Czech Lands by building upon the initial attack.

To disrupt the arrival of strategic reserves in the regions by nuclear strikes against targets deep in our territory and by sending airborne assault troops . . .

land war in an atmosphere and environment that had been utterly saturated in radiation? Or had they decided that this simply didn't matter – that soldiers and aircrew were expendable and could be expected to go in and fight until they keeled over? Indeed, were Czechoslovak soldiers and aircrew more expendable than Russian ones?

A great deal was expected of them either way. Far from falling back in a defensive posture, they were to take the fight to the West in no uncertain terms. They would advance under the cover of a massive nuclear strike:

Altogether the operation will require the use of 131 nuclear missiles and nuclear bombs; specifically 96 nuclear missiles and 35 nuclear bombs. The first nuclear strike will use 41 missiles and nuclear bombs. The immediate task will require using 29 missiles and nuclear bombs. The subsequent task could use 41 missiles and nuclear bombs. 12 missiles and nuclear bombs should remain in the reserve of the Front.

It would then be a matter of taking the fullest possible advantage of their enemies' state of shock, to surge westward with their Iron Curtain allies across the neighbouring countries of Central Europe. They were, the orders stated:

To be ready to start advancing toward Nuremberg, Stuttgart and Munich with part of forces immediately after the nuclear strike. Nuclear strike against the troops of the enemy should be

targeted to the depth up to the line Würzburg, Erlangen, Regensburg, Landshut.

Soon they'd be in possession of the Federal Republic of Germany. Not that they would be stopping there; within a week they'd be occupying France:

Building on the results of the first nuclear strike, the troops of the Front, in coordination with units of the 1st Western Front, must destroy the main group of troops of the 7th US Army and the 1st French Army in cooperation with airborne assault troops, force the rivers Neckar and Rhine in crossing, and defeat the advancing deep strategic reserves of the enemy in advancing battle, and by D7–8 take control of the areas of Langres, Besançon, and Epinal.

Upon completion of the tasks of the operation, the troops must be ready to develop further advances in the direction of Lyon.

In pursuing these goals, Czechoslovak ground forces were to have the backing of the 57th Air Force. Together with the 10th Air Force, it would begin by finding and destroying the enemy's nuclear bunkers, its 'aviation and command and control centers with concentration of main efforts on the direction of Nuremberg, Strasbourg'. For these purposes – and for the initial strike against the headquarters of – it was to have 10 nuclear bombs at its disposal. Seven more were to be deployed against armies in the field once battle had been joined, and a further two were to be kept in reserve.

Soviet Nuclear Strategy

Signs that some on the Soviet side were waking up to the realities of nuclear conflict appeared in an intriguing report from 1964.

Revolutionary War

In some respects more measured than the 1964 Warsaw Pact planned land invasion of the West – though terrifying in other respects – is a document produced in the same year by Petr Ivanovich Ivashutin, Head of Soviet General Staff at the Main Intelligence Directorate or GRU. This was sent to Marshal Matvei Zakharov, Commandant of Moscow's General Staff Academy, who had apparently asked for thoughts on 'the development of the military art in the conditions of nuclear war'. Wide-ranging in its reference, the document is at times almost meditative as it muses on innovations Ivashutin says have brought 'revolutionary changes' to modern warfare.

Insisting on the defensive posture of the USSR's strategic forces, it suggests that a nuclear attack by the West is 'unexpected', while conceding that the country has to plan 'for the contingency where, in violation of common sense, the imperialists decide to start a thermonuclear war'.

Ivashutin shows a clearer understanding than his Soviet predecessors of the likely scale of the conflict. There's no suggestion here that it is realistic even to think in terms of fighting a limited nuclear war:

Strategic operations of nuclear forces will be characterized by unprecedented spatial expanse. They will instantaneously cover all continents of the earth, all main islands, straits, canals, i.e. the entire territory of the countries-participants of the aggressive coalition. However, the main events in all probability will take place in the Northern hemisphere – in Europe, North America and Asia.

It's not just that the Soviets will have to target the Americans' European and Asian allies – to make sure they pay the price for their support of the 'aggressor'. Nuclear war, by its very nature, can't be contained:

In this hemisphere, essentially all the countries, including the neutral countries, will suffer destructive consequences of massive nuclear strikes (spread of radiation) to some extent.

Ivashutin appears to understand that a nuclear war was not simply going to be a bigger-than-usual conventional war: there's a point at which a difference in degree becomes a difference in kind:

The strategic operation of nuclear forces is a new phenomenon in the military art. The history of wars does not know anything like it . . .

He is vague about what will be required, but clear in his insistence that the successful prosecution of such a war is going to stretch Soviet research science and technical ingenuity to the fullest:

Such operation will rely on the decisive use of the highest achievements of scientific and technological thought to ensure security of the socialist countries, and a complete defeat and physical annihilation of the aggressor, if he rushes into the abyss of thermonuclear war having lost his head.

A cool collective head will have to be kept if the 'aggressor' loses his. Ivashutin lists the 'complex and powerful technological means' that will have to be deployed – 'ballistic missiles with nuclear warheads, strategic aircraft with nuclear ammunition, and nuclear submarines with nuclear warheads . . .'

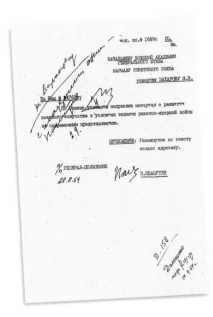

TRANSCRIPT OF KEY PARAGRAPHS

28 August 1964

To: Head of the Military Academy of the General Staff, Comrade M. V. Zakharov
From: General P. Ivashutin

Following your request, I am sending you the material on the development of the military art in the conditions of nuclear war .
. .

There are very few people left – even among the most rabid imperialist military –who would believe in the feasibility of [an unexpected first strike]. In the age of an unprecedented development of electronics, it is impossible to achieve a genuine surprise strike. The very first signs of the beginning of a nuclear attack by the imperialist aggressor will be discovered, which would give sufficient grounds for launching a retaliatory strike.

Lately the US has been increasingly concerned by the rapid weakening of its nuclear and missile power relative to that of the Soviet Union.

- 326 -

COB. CEKPETHO
экз. № 1

Таковы важнейшие особенности вооруженной борьбы в локальных войнах. Ими нельзя пренебрегать, поскольку такая война не исключена хотя бы на короткое время. Необходимо однако еще раз подчеркнуть, что локальная война, если в нее будут втянуты ядерные державы, неизбежно перерастет в мировую термоядерную войну, если не удастся быстро ее потушить. Поэтому главное наше внимание, не забывая о выучке войск для боевых действий в локальных войнах, должно быть сосредоточено на разработке и на основании способов ведения и других социалистических стран.

Стратегические операции ядерных сил

Стратегическая операция ядерных сил - основная форма использования стратегических ядерных сил и средств в термоядерной войне. Она подготавливается в ответ на угрозу внезапного ядерного нападения империалистов, на тот случай, если вопреки здравому рассудку империалисты пойдут на развязывание термоядерной войны. Это вынужденное мероприятие социалистических стран, обусловленное агрессивной политикой мировой империалистической реакции.

Империалистические государства, прежде всего США и отчасти Англия, первыми в мире стали на путь практической подготовки и теоретической разработки подобной операции. Основной силой такой операции в этих странах длительное время считалась стратегическая авиация и термоядерное оружие. Однако за последние годы правящие круги США прилагают большие усилия к развитию и накоплению межконтинентальных ракет - "Атлас", "Титан" и "Минитмэн", а также атомных подводных лодок, вооруженных ракетами "Полярис". Особое внимание уделяется созданию межконтинентальных ракет "Минитмэн" и скоростному строительству атомных подводных лодок с ракетами

It's not surprising, perhaps, that he should blame the other side, but he offers an interesting counter to the security-in-mutually-assured-destruction theory, suggesting that America is bringing the risk of conflict closer by its very vigilance, its incessant exercises and alerts:

The fact that the strategic nuclear forces of the United States are kept in the constant state of readiness for use presents a great danger for the cause of peace.

But the Soviets will be ready for them should they decide to launch a strike:

In responding to the launch of the strategic missiles of the aggressor, the Soviet Union is capable of retaliating with an even more powerful launch of its own strategic missiles, and not merely one . . .

NATO armoured vehicles exercise in Germany: each side used such manoeuvres to test the other's defences.

'Colossal destructive force allows for the instantaneous annihilation of any objects in the enemy's territory.'

Petr Ivanovich Ivashutin, 1964

Ivashutin goes on to consider more specifically what the role of Russia's nuclear strike force might be in the event of war:

The following tasks could be set for a strategic operation of nuclear forces: the destruction of the military-economic potential of the aggressor coalition; the disruption of state administration and all activity of the aggressor countries; the destruction of the armed forces, missile aviation and naval bases, warehouses and arsenals of nuclear weapons; the defeat of the formations of armed forces in the theaters of military action, i.e. a complete breaking down of the combat readiness of the enemy coalition.

Even now, though, Ivashutin is conscious that we are all in untrodden territory:

The question arises by itself: would setting such tasks for one

or several strategic operations of nuclear forces in the beginning of a thermonuclear war be realistic?

It's all about questions: this is what makes Ivashutin's musings so fascinating for us now – the glimpse they give us of the uncertainty behind Soviet nuclear militarism's iron front. Not that Ivashutin was shrinking from the challenge to the Soviet Union, or the responsibility it might have for its part in the destruction of much of the populated world. For the first time in a Soviet source, however, we encounter a real comprehension that the atomic bomb and the nuclear missile had brought a whole new meaning to the idea of 'total war':

If in past wars fighting was limited by the mutual destruction of the armed forces in the theaters of military action; in the modern conditions, the presence of nuclear weapons of vast range and colossal destructive force allows for the instantaneous annihilation of any objects in the enemy's territory, up to the annihilation of entire countries. A nuclear strike against the vital centers of a country, against its economy, its system of state administration, its strategic nuclear forces, and other armed forces is the fastest and most reliable way of achieving victory over the aggressor. The object of the military struggle has thus changed; the strike will encompass the entire territories of the belligerent countries – all that amounts to the basis of the political, economic and military power of a state will be exposed to such a strike . . .

Marx himself had famously said of capitalism that it destroyed the old illusions of social order leaving only confusion: 'All that is solid melts into air . . .' We get something of the same sense of utter disorientation here; the same sense that the old conventions, the old ways of thinking have been bankrupted but that the new 'rules' for replacing them are going to be anybody's guess.

Moscow Central?

An uneasy peace – or at least an absence of outright war – prevailed through the 1960s and 1970s. Perhaps the threat of thermonuclear armageddon had concentrated minds. The invasion of the West was very much on the agenda, despite intelligence reports bringing copious and continuing evidence of NATO superiority. How far they can really be seen as 'plans' is questionable – it's hard to dismiss the suspicion that they were more attempts to save diplomatic face and boost military morale – but strategies for an invasion of the West were constantly reviewed, and exercises staged.

Some response was considered necessary after the awe-inspiring success of 'Wintex', the biggest NATO manoeuvres yet: partly as a show of defiance; partly because it was thought that similar manoeuvres might in future be used as the springboard for an actual attack on communist Eastern Europe. Hence the organization of *Zapad* ('West') in 1977. These combined exercises seem to have highlighted considerable weaknesses in the Warsaw Pact. Authored by

TRANSCRIPT OF KEY PARAGRAPHS

By May 31, the Eastern Forces had completed mobilizing their land and naval forces and, with the goal of stopping the aggression, went ahead with their operational deployment by advancing the main groups of the 4th and 5th Fronts into the western regions of Poland and Czechoslovakia .

. .

On the eighth day of operations, conditions became more complicated when the Eastern Forces repulsed enemy invaders and went on to attack in the direction of Hamburg, Hannover, Frankfurt, and Munich.

. . . On June 10 the Western Forces made the decision to use nuclear weapons. They began immediate preparation for a massive nuclear attack.

ДОКЛАД

начальника Штаба руководства — начальника Генерального штаба Вооруженных Сил СССР Маршала Советского Союза Огаркова Н. В.

Товарищи министры обороны!

Товарищи генералы, адмиралы и офицеры!

Оперативно-стратегическое командно-штабное учение на местности со средствами связи «Запад-77», проведенное под руководством Министра обороны СССР Маршала Советского Союза товарища Устинова Дмитрия -Федоровича, является наиболее важным из всех совместных мероприятий оперативной подготовки союзных армий за последние 15 лет.

Это учение как по составу участников, так и по характеру решаемых задач имело оперативно-стратегический характер. Оно не только способствовало повышению навыков командующих, штабов и политорганов в решении учебных задач, но и позволило проверить ряд положений действующих уставов и наставлений, исследовать некоторые новые вопросы оперативного искусства.

Проведенное учение имело три характерные особенности.

Во-первых. Учение отличалось большим пространственным размахом. Командующие и штабы союзных армий работали на местности с реальным перемещением полевых пунктов управления и узлов связи на большие расстояния и с отработкой учебных вопросов в течение всего учения в реальном масштабе времени методом «час за час».

Во-вторых. Оно проводилось на учебном оперативно-стратегическом фоне, в основу которого был положен один из возможных вариантов совместных действий вооруженных сил государств — участников Варшавского Договора по отражению агрессии на Западном ТВД, и в то же время при

7

Marshal Nikolai Ogarkov, Chief of the Soviet General Staff, the official report is a masterpiece of understatement, evasion and euphemistic language ('We must note that the 5th Front . . . was in a very difficult situation'). Yet even so, it notes many technical and tactical shortcomings.

One of the problems for the Russians was the need to balance the need for centralization of authority and clarity of command structures with the need to maintain good relations with its allies. The claim that Eastern Europe was 'under the Soviet yoke' is true enough – and Hungarians and Czechoslovaks would certainly have been surprised to be told that they had national autonomy. But the reality was that, within strict limits, the Soviets did have to have some regard for their allies' feelings of national pride. Theirs was more a consent-bound 'coalition' than

Nikolai Ogarkov became Chief of the Soviet General Staff in 1977.

might be assumed. In a paper prepared for the Chiefs of General Staff Meeting held in Sofia in June 1978, Soviet General S.F. Romanov makes a point of thanking the political and military leaders of the Russians' Warsaw Pact partners before then setting out the argument for a single (Soviet) general to assume the overall command:

A future war will demand the utmost exertion of all military, economic, and spiritual forces of the socialist coalition. The conduct of such a war will only be feasible through a single body, equipped with all political, administrative, and military power, that is, through the highest politico-military leadership of the coalition.

Accordingly, the leadership of the Unified Armed Forces in strategic operations in a theater of war has to be centralized and has to be exercised by one person, who is directly responsible to the highest politico-military leadership.

'In this context', he continues, 'we must not overlook the high degree of readiness of the leadership bodies and systems of our likely enemy, the NATO forces, which have been developed and functioning for years.' By all accounts, however, this very text came to embody the very difficulties it described: the opinions of the allies having been sought, Poland alone suggested some 60 amendments.

TRANSCRIPT OF KEY PARAGRAPHS

<u>Soviet Statement at the Chiefs of General Staff Meeting in Sofia, June 12–14, 1978</u>

I merely allow myself to point out that at the regular NATO Council meeting of May 30 and 31 of this year in Washington, NATO's heads of state and government . . . paid close attention to the enhancement of what they call the command level, coordinated leadership of the allied forces . . .

The principle of centralized leadership of the armed forces in a strategic operation implies the right of the supreme commander of the United Armed Forces, . . . starting from the moment of his appointment to the official position, to give commands, directives, orders, and instructions, the fulfilment of which is mandatory for all the troops and fleets belonging to the United Armed Forces . . .

[The Supreme Command of the United Armed Forces] must exercise the immediate and direct leadership of the fronts, the fleets, the separate armies . . .

T h e s e n

des Vortrages von Generaloberst S. F. ROMANOW über
"Die Grundlagen des Entwurfs der Grundsätze über
die Vereinten Streitkräfte der Teilnehmerstaaten
des Warschauer Vertrages und ihre Führungsorgane
(für die Kriegszeit)"

Werte Genossen!

Entsprechend einem Beschluß des Politischen Beratenden Ausschusses traf das Komitee der Verteidigungsminister der Teilnehmerstaaten des Warschauer Vertrages im Dezember 1977 die Entscheidung, den Stab der Vereinten Streitkräfte gemeinsam mit den General(Haupt)-stäben der verbündeten Armeen zu beauftragen, im laufe des Jahres 1978 einen Entwurf für die Grundsätze über die Vereinten Streitkräfte der Teilnehmerstaaten des Warschauer Vertrages und ihre Führungsorgane (für die Kriegszeit) auszuarbeiten, auf der Sitzung des Komitees der Verteidigungsminister abzustimmen und anzunehmen und zur Bestätigung auf der Beratung des Politischen Beratenden Ausschusses vorzubereiten.

In Erfüllung dieser Entscheidung hat der Stab der Vereinten Streitkräfte, gestützt auf die langjährigen Erfahrungen aus der Tätigkeit des Vereinten Kommandos, auf die modernen Ansichten zum Charakter eines künftigen Krieges und auf die Erfahrungen der durchgeführten gemeinsamen und nationalen operativen und operativ-strategischen Übungen, vorläufige Vorstellungen ausgearbeitet, die man unserer Meinung nach bei der gemeinsamen Arbeit zur Vorbereitung des Entwurfs der Grundsätze über die

The Polish Invasion That Never Was

As a wave of strikes and protests swept across Poland, communist authority was shaken. Was the Soviet Union just going to stand by?

Poland may have always been a wayward member of the Eastern Bloc, but this was to take on a new and, from the Soviet perspective, more sinister form in the birth of the free trade union, *Solidarnosc* (Solidarity). In the space of a year, from 31 August 1980, a group of hands from the Lenin Shipyard in Gdansk, on Poland's Baltic coast, had built a movement comprising more than eight million people, a third of Poland's workers. Its leader, Lech Walesa, became recognizable worldwide. That the world's first Polish Pope, John Paul II – a man of enormous charisma – had recently spoken out in Poland advocating human rights, also energized the movement.

Declassified documents suggest that, despite the dangers, the Soviets were wary of getting too deeply involved. Bogged down in a war in Afghanistan, they needed no new entanglements. It was from hardline leaders in the other satellite countries, such as East Germany's Erich Honecker and Czechoslovak Gustáv Husák, that the pressure for armed intervention mostly came. Plans

Lech Walesa addresses an open-air meeting of the free trade union *Solidarnosc* ('Solidarity').

were made to invade Poland – under the cover of the latest round of military manoeuvres in Eastern Europe – Soyuz 81. Soviet soldiers would participate but would not take the lead. When these plans were passed on by Colonel Ryszard Kuklinski, the CIA's 'mole' in the Polish military, the US government revealed them to the world. It also made clear how seriously it would view a repeat of Budapest '56 and Prague '68. The times, it was becoming clear, had changed.

Mindful of this, the Socialist heads of state assembled at a conference in Moscow in December 1980, sending Poland's political leader, Stanislaw Kania, First Secretary of the Polish United Workers' Party, home,

promising he'd take firm measures to destroy the movement for democracy. His subsequent failure in the face of a rising tide of popular support for Solidarity saw his removal the following October and his replacement by General Wojciech Jaruzelski. A committed communist, Jaruzelski took charge with a career-soldier's toughness, imposing Martial Law on 13 December. Did he do so with the patriotic intent of heading off an invasion by Poland's fraternal allies, as he implied in interviews years later? Few at the time believed him.

The End of an Era?
They did, however, believe that if they didn't submit to Martial Law and to the forcible dissolution of

TRANSCRIPT OF KEY PARAGRAPHS

CIA, 27 February 1981

<u>Polish Government Plans for Possible Soviet Military Intervention and Declaration of Martial Law</u>

Prior to the VIII Plenum of the Central Committee of the Polish United Workers' Party, a group of 18 generals, all deputies and assistants to Marshal Kulikov, Commander-in-Chief of the Combined Armed Forces, made an unscheduled trip to Poland.

The visit . . . took place under the pretext of checking preparations for the "SOYUZ-81" Warsaw Pact CPX exercise.

General Gribkov proposed that . . .a large squadron of Soviet naval ships be dispatched for a visit to Polish ports beginning on 16 February.

Within the framework of the exercises of the fleets, an amphibious landing of the Combined Amphibious Forces of the Polish Armed Forces, Soviet forces and National Peoples Army of the GDR would be executed in the vicinity of Swinoujscie [north-west Poland].

Solidarity, intervention by the Soviets was bound to result. In fact, the Soviet Politburo had been mulling its alternatives just a few days earlier, and the consensus had been that this simply could not be done. The future General Secretary Yuri Andropov spoke for all present when he insisted that, whatever happened in Poland, the country's communists – and Russia's – would have to accept it. Invasion was out. 'We can't risk such a step,' he argued:

We do not intend to introduce troops into Poland. That is the proper position, and we must adhere to it to the end. I don't know how things will turn out in Poland, but even if Poland falls under the control of Solidarity, that's the way it will be . . . We must be concerned above all with our own country and about the strengthening of the Soviet Union.

By default, it can be argued, this position effectively represented a tactical retreat.

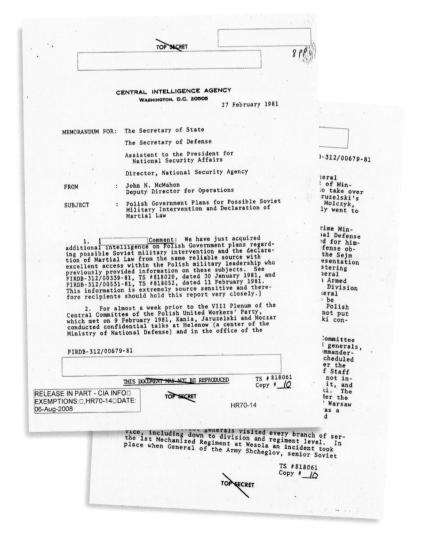

Chapter Five

America's Backyard

The United States had long worried about 'fire down below'. For Washington, there was no place for a communist revolution in any part of the Americas – north, central or south.

By the 1950s, anti-communism was well embedded in US political culture – in the US psyche, even, it might be said. So much so that it had merged with other fears of respectable America – most notably those of foreignness and brown skin. The immediate postwar period saw an influx of immigrants from Mexico, many of them undocumented. These were known as 'wetbacks' – from the assumption that they had swum the Rio Grande. In the popular mythology, they were attended by a host of ills, from knife crime to marijuana and communism.

Attorney General Herbert Brownell is even said to have called for 'wetbacks' to be shot (though where and when he said such a thing remains unclear). One thing's for sure: America's longstanding claims to be 'protector' to the western hemisphere under the 'Monroe Doctrine' had been brought into sharper focus by the sense that communist subversion was simmering in 'America's Backyard'.

President Eisenhower is warmly welcomed in the streets of Santiago, in 1960. Far-flung Chile played an improbably important part in the unfolding drama of the Cold War.

Guatemala

In a Guatemala ripe for revolution, US interests were clearly under threat. Secret plans were hatched to keep the country in safe hands.

The rhetoric of red revolution was certainly not without its appeal in Latin America. Here, the masses toiled in wretched poverty to keep a minuscule elite – an elite that owed its allegiance to the United States and which, moreover, maintained market freedom by depriving the people of key liberties. The most ardent American capitalist could appreciate that, under such conditions, workers might easily conclude with Karl Marx that revolution was worth the risk; that, in his formulation, they had 'nothing to lose but their chains'.

In several states of Central America, the United Fruit Company bankrolled a succession of tinpot dictators in return for the guaranteed right to overwork and underpay their hands. By breaking up strikes and suppressing trade unions, they ensured that the business conditions remained favourable. These countries became known as 'Banana Republics' in the outside world. Guatemala was a case in point.

Through the 1930s, the company had financed the fantasies of the 'Little Napoleon of the Tropics', Jorge Ubico y Castañeda. The dictator liked to dress up as his hero, the great

Jorge Ubico proved a friend to United Fruit.

soldier-emperor of France. United Fruit and the fruitcake made a winning team: Ubico got to strut his stuff; the company looked after the country. Under its supervision, the state legislature introduced United Fruit-friendly landholding terms and tax and customs deals; the secret police cracked down on labour organizations and protest groups.

Spring . . . For Some

In 1944, Ubico's government had been brought down by the 'October Revolutionaries' – the name obviously echoes that given to Russia's Bolshevik Revolution of 1917. The reality had been less extreme than its predecessor: while a general strike of workers brought Guatemala to a standstill, the group of army officers who

ousted the dictator were liberal in their views. Even so, they introduced real reforms: the 'Ten Years of Spring' they ushered in sent a chilly wind blowing around the business of United Fruit. When elections in 1951 swept Colonel Jacobo Árbenz to office at the expense of the company's favoured conservative candidate, United Fruit and the United States were united in dismay.

Árbenz's inaugural address wasn't that of a Lenin or a Trotsky: his pledge to his countrymen was to transform backward, feudal Guatemala into what he called 'a modern capitalist state'. In the small print, however, were commitments to make the country more self-sufficient economically and to reduce the influence of foreign corporations. And his actions spoke louder than his soothing words, a series of land reforms culminating in 'Decree 900', which provided for unused areas of big estates to be confiscated from their owners and given to local communities for their own use.

A welcome efficiency, bringing vast areas of idle land into production for the benefit of the entire economy, or communist plunder of the most rapacious kind? Full compensation was offered by the government, but Ubico had allowed United Fruit to set an impossibly low value on its landholdings to reduce its

tax liabilities; now the company insisted that they were worth vastly more.

American Ascendancy

Officially, the United States didn't interfere in the doings of its New World neighbours, but its leading role in the hemisphere was very clear. Its self-appointed policeman's role had been spelled out as early as 1823, when President James Monroe had asserted his country's rights in the region:

We could not view any interposition for the purpose of oppressing them, or controlling in any other manner their destiny, by any European power in any other light than as the manifestation of an unfriendly disposition toward the United States.

It wasn't always easy to distinguish between this kind of protectiveness and imperial proprietorship, as several countries had since discovered to their cost. The appearance of equal partnership was scrupulously maintained, and reaffirmed in the Inter-American Treaty of Reciprocal Assistance (or Rio Pact) of 1947, but no one could be in any doubt where the real power lay in the Americas.

MisFortune

No one in Harry S. Truman's White House was – that's certain. Árbenz was anathema to the Americans: his election had prompted a flurry of back-room planning before he even announced his reform programme. Talks began with Nicaraguan dictator Anastasio Somoza (who made a state visit to Washington in April, 1952), and with the exiled

Above: Military pomp and circumstance masked the ramshackle state of Guatemala. This parade was photographed in 1932.

Below: Jacobo Árbenz was no revolutionary, but he was held in deep suspicion by the United States.

'There is no place here for political institutions which serve alien masters.'

John Foster Dulles, addressing the Inter-American Conference, March 1954

Allen Welsh Dulles (left) runs into elder brother John Foster Dulles, Eisenhower's Secretary of State.

Guatemalan Colonel Carlos Castillo over ways of overthrowing this new 'communist' regime. By the middle of 1952, Operation P.B. (Presidential Board) Fortune had been planned: the CIA was going to give $225,000 and large amounts of weapons and munitions to Castillo's cause. He was going to use this to mount a coup attempt: air support would be provided by the rightist governments of neighbouring Nicaragua and Honduras, and Guatemala would be made safe for United Fruit.

In the event, this plot was discovered and had to be abandoned that October. But 'Fortune' continued, constantly evolving. That much is clear from a memorandum drafted in March the following year by Allen Welsh Dulles, Eisenhower's Director of Central Intelligence (and, as it happens, a trustee of United Fruit). Referring to Guatemala coyly as 'the country in question', it stresses

the need for political efforts to be made to create a climate in which more direct measures can be profitably pursued. America has all sorts of options in a country that, as Dulles says, 'is thoroughly dependent on its trade relations with us'. However the United States chooses to act, though, doing nothing is not considered an option. Guatemala has shown nothing but defiance:

In effect they have flaunted us and consistently got away with it. It is time they were brought to realize that this could not continue.

But America must begin by getting its own diplomatic house in order, by

. . . recalling our ambassador for consultation and sending some two-fisted guy to the general area on a trip of inspection and to report to the President.

The Dulles Doctrine

The United States' man in Guatemala City, Rudolf E. Schoenfeld, is 'timid', Dulles explains, 'and never recovered from his treatment at the hands of Anna Pauker'. (In 1950, Pauker, Romania's Foreign Affairs Minister, had ordered drastic cuts to US Embassy staff in Bucharest, leaving America no alternative but to shut down diplomatic operations in the country altogether.)

The whole Embassy should be given a look over. I just received the visit of two American citizens highly recommended who have large interests in the country. They indicated that they did not feel they could get anything whatever

TRANSCRIPT OF KEY PARAGRAPHS

<u>Memorandum from Allen Welsh Dulles, Director of Central Intelligence, 8 March 1953</u>

The country in question [Guatemala] is thoroughly dependent on its trade relations with us and has discounted the fact that we would do nothing. In effect they have flaunted us and consistently got away with it. It is time they were brought to realize that this could not continue.

Here are some of the measures which might be considered.

1. Recalling our ambassador for consultation and sending a two-fisted guy to the general area on a trip of inspection and to report to the President.
[. . .]

I just received the visit of two American citizens highly recommended who have large interests in the country. They indicated that they did not feel they could get anything whatever out of the Embassy in the way of protection of American interests and hinted at darker things.

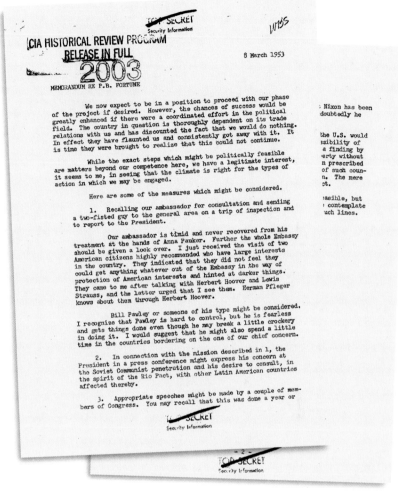

out of the Embassy in the way of protection of American interests and hinted at darker things.

Guatemala's affairs should be organized for the benefit not of the Guatemalans but of those Americans 'who have large interests in the country'. That same reasoning was to be followed over and over again in America's dealings with Latin America – and the rest of the 'Third World' – in the years to come.

Dulles realized, he confided to colleagues (in a conversation he subsequently reported to Richard Helms), that 'whatever happened in the country in question, people up here would be blamed'. As far as he was concerned,

. . . the important thing was that the operation should be successful, if there was to be one.

That same memo makes it clear – with its account of dealings with 'S' (Nicaragua's murderous dictator Somoza) and his cronies – of the extent to which the Kennedy Administration was coming to see Central America

MEMORANDUM OF CONFERENCE, MONDAY, JULY 21st WITH MESSRS. M, M, AND J

I showed the draft of the cable we proposed to send and, with the deletion of the reference to DYMAROON, the cable was approved, after explanations on my part as to the identity of the pseudonyms and as to what we had been doing with KMEGGCUP in the field of psychological warfare. The second M spoke very highly of the effectiveness of this P.W. work which he said had been handled quite largely from the country to the North. He felt that these activities might well be stepped up.

I then referred to the three questions which had been put to the second M and which BS later had put to B. There was general agreement as to the desired result. The only question was whether we could play any part in achieving it without allerting anyone as to the source of possible aid. I said that the purpose of the cable was to remove any local people from any direct or indirect contact with the activities. I also said we were calling back an undercover contact man we had in the country to the South. He might return but we would decide that after a conference.

In reply to any inquiry I said that no cash had been made available and that I had some doubt as to whether this was needed in view of the intervention of certain rich parties, whom I identified. However, it was possible that we might lead Calligeris' men or cutouts to certain hardware which was available. All activities, with respect to the hardware, would be restricted as far as we were concerned to this country and handled through cutouts.

I pointed out that whatever happened in the country in question, people up here would be blamed and that the important thing was that the operation should be successful, if there was to be one. On this point I said that most of the experts seemed to feel that this was most likely. I recognize that for every hundred rumors of this nature, only one materialized; in this case, however, it looked as though something were likely to happen.

I emphazied that we realized the very sensitive nature of this activity and that it would be handled with the utmost care.

The first M then referred to the activities of a certain Col. Mara, his relations with S, and how he had flown to N with S and had apparently come back with a report on the situation in the country of our interest, which was in the hands of the Boss. Whether this was prepared by the good Colonel or by S was not known. All this had come about after S had boasted at a luncheon with the Boss that with 600 pieces of hardware he would "knock off" A. Among others who were present and who knew all about this was S's man here in Washington. I suggested that this again was evidence that if anything happened, there would be plenty of other persons to blame for it.

SECRET

TRANSCRIPT OF KEY PARAGRAPHS

<u>Memorandum of Conference from Allen Welsh Dulles, 21 July 1953</u>

. . . M spoke very highly of the effectiveness of this P.W. [psychological warfare] work which he said had been handled quite largely from the country to the North. He felt that these activities might well be stepped up.

There was general agreement as to the desired result. The only question was whether we could play any part in achieving it without allerting [sic] anyone as to the source of possible aid.

[. . .] I said that no cash had been made available and that I had some doubt as to whether this was needed in view of the intervention of certain rich parties . . .

[. . .] I pointed out that whatever happened in the country in question, people here would be blamed . . .

All this had come about after S [Nicaragua's dictator Somoza] had boasted at a luncheon with the Boss that with 600 pieces of hardware he would "knock off" A.

President Eisenhower could be eloquent in his defence of the American Way.

as its chessboard, its politicians as pieces to be deployed. As for the region's people, America had arguably long since ceased to see them at all, except as a potential source of instability and unrest.

The Games People Play

The game of chess goes back well over a thousand years; that of its use as a metaphor for diplomacy must be almost as long. The image of choice in the Cold War era, however, had been provided by the game of dominoes. The 'Domino Theory' was well established by this time, having been introduced to the public by President Eisenhower at a press conference as early as 1954.

Strictly speaking, his image didn't draw on the game as such, but on the dominoes themselves, set up on their edges side by side in rows: when you pushed the first one, it toppled the next – and so on continuously. So it was with communism, Eisenhower had

argued: each successful revolution encouraged others in neighbouring countries; in time the momentum couldn't be contained.

It's become fashionable to deride this theory – and it's true that it has its limitations. But what Eisenhower had recognized (consciously or unconsciously) was that, where in the affluent West most people – even the comparatively poor – would feel they had too much potentially to lose from a revolutionary transformation of society, such logic did not apply through much of the world. To those who toiled away their days for scanty returns for exploitative employers under oppressive rulers, the idea of wholesale change didn't seem so scary. Indeed, it had an appeal.

Rocking the Boat, Sinking the Ship

Dulles's 'America first, last and always' philosophy helps to explain why – as Guatemala's

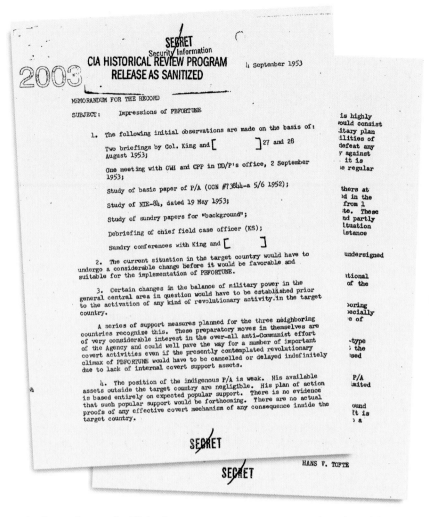

2003

4 September 1953

MEMORANDUM FOR THE RECORD

SUBJECT: Impressions of PBFORTUNE

1. The following initial observations are made on the basis of:

Two briefings by Col. King and [   ] 27 and 28 August 1953;

One meeting with CWI and CPP in DD/P's office, 2 September 1953;

Study of basic paper of P/A (CCN #73844-a 5/6 1952);

Study of NIE-84, dated 19 May 1953;

Study of sundry papers for "background";

Debriefing of chief field case officer (KS);

Sundry conferences with King and [   ]

2. The current situation in the target country would have to undergo a considerable change before it would be favorable and suitable for the implementation of PBFORTUNE.

3. Certain changes in the balance of military power in the general central area in question would have to be established prior to the activation of any kind of revolutionary activity in the target country.

A series of support measures planned for the three neighboring countries recognize this. These preparatory moves in themselves are of very considerable interest in the over-all anti-Communist effort of the Agency and could well pave the way for a number of important covert activities even if the presently contemplated revolutionary climax of PBFORTUNE would have to be cancelled or delayed indefinitely due to lack of internal covert support assets.

4. The position of the indigenous P/A is weak. His available assets outside the target country are negligible. His plan of action is based entirely on expected popular support. There is no evidence that such popular support would be forthcoming. There are no actual proofs of any effective covert mechanism of any consequence inside the target country.

SECRET

SECRET

HANS V. TOFTE

Ambassador to the United States, Guillermo Toriello, was to complain – the United States branded as 'Communist':

. . . every manifestation of nationalism or economic dependence, any desire for social progress, any intellectual curiosity, and any interest in progressive liberal reforms.

As a memo of 10 September 1953 reports, those 'critical remarks', and 'action to be taken regarding them', were discussed by intelligence officials but the consensus was that the CIA shouldn't 'rock the boat'.

Or, rather, that it should keep its powder dry, for, despite these reservations, there was general agreement that 'positive' action was 'in order'. (It was indeed taking place, and at a frenetic pace, as a glance at the CIA's log of 'P.B. Fortune Meetings' makes clear.)

Despite all this activity, though, there was growing scepticism in Washington over whether a coup at this point could succeed. The shift in attitudes is summarized in

---

TRANSCRIPT OF KEY PARAGRAPHS

<u>CIA Memorandum, 4 September 1953</u>

The military plan of action visualized by the Principal Agent (P/A) is highly questionable in view of the fact that the main forces would consist of untrained irregulars. It appears that the P/A's military plan grossly underestimates the attitude and defensive capabilities of the regular army.

According to NIE-84, this army "can defeat any force which the three neighboring countries could deploy against it -- so long as it remains united." In this connection, it is noteworthy that there is no evidence to indicate that the regular army is susceptible to defection or revolt.

According to the chief field case officer and others at WH headquarters, there is a definite time element involved in the PBFORTUNE operation. Time limits of 60, 90 and 120 days from 1 September 1953 have been indicated as desirable or ultimate.

Castillo's rebel army was well funded, but ill disciplined and untrained.

Success!

Operation P.B. Success gathered momentum in the months that followed. Castillo was given arms and funding for a private army of 400 fighters: CIA 'advisers' took charge of their training. When, dragooned by the Americans, the Organization of American States issued a condemnation of Marxist thinking in all its forms, it became clear that more direct action was on the cards. That June, Árbenz was duly overthrown. Castillo then threw his whole reform process into reverse. Hundreds of thousands subsequently died in more than a decade of civil war.

P.B. Success ultimately lived up to its name – at least from the American point of view. In the decades that followed, the United States would resort to similar strategies to topple a succession of left-leaning governments around the world. Guatemala has the dubious distinction of having been the test-bed for this way of wielding power. P.B. Fortune may never have happened, but it had already become a paradigm.

a memo drafted by Major Hans van Tofte of the Psychological and Paramilitary Operations Staff of the CIA's Deputy Directorate of Plans. Entitled 'Impressions of PBFORTUNE', it is dated 4 September 1953. For now, at least, the tide seemed to be turning against the plot as previously imagined. Not only did there seem to be no evidence that there would be sufficient support in 'the target country', but the 'position of the indigenous P/A [Principal Agent] is weak.' Castillo (or 'Pancho', or 'Rufus', as he was also known) was overoptimistic both in his military planning and in his assessment of the sort of support he could expect on the ground in Guatemala.

But if direct intervention was off the agenda, there was still a great deal that *could* be done, as the 10

September memorandum made quite clear. There was, it insisted, 'an excellent opportunity to get publicity and begin our PW campaign'. PW ('psychological warfare') having been declared, the CIA set up a radio station in Honduras within weeks. What purported to be the 'Voice of Liberation', featuring protesting voices from exiled Guatemalan patriots, was in fact the voice of the CIA, broadcast from Miami.

Increasingly, as Guatemala slipped deeper into civil strife, democracy was struggling to survive.

Cuba

In the early hours of New Year's Day 1959, Fulgencio Batista took flight from Havana. After years of struggle, Cuba was in rebel hands. The island became a beacon of revolution for the world – and an enduring thorn in America's side.

The dramatic events of the Cuban Revolution reverberated far beyond the Caribbean. The guerrillas from the Sierra Maestra were, quite simply, stars. Suddenly everyone was talking about Fidel Castro (or simply 'Fidel', for it seemed the world was on first-name terms with this most colourful of leaders). Meanwhile,

with his beard, his beret and his soulful eyes, his Argentinean friend and *compañero* Ernesto 'Che' Guevara was already well on the way to iconic status. While other statesmen blended into the background in suits, these two men strutted their stuff in combat fatigues; while others churned out an identikit rhetoric of sensitive stewardship and statistics, they promised liberation for the wretched of the earth.

That America was rattled was clear both from public pronouncements made by the Eisenhower administration and from a series of economic sanctions against Cuba. And –

to those very few who knew, at least – from the plotting that began behind the scenes almost immediately to topple the new rulers of what had been an economic satellite (and a tourist playground) for the United States. It was arguably evidenced further in the way that the incoming Kennedy administration fumbled Eisenhower's plan for an invasion of Cuba at the Bay of Pigs in April 1961. The invasion, made by Cuban exiles trained and supplied by the United States,

The Cuban Revolution brought scenes of jubilation to Havana – and dismay to Washington.

America's irregulars were routed by the Cubans at the Bay of Pigs.

was defeated on its third day by Cuban armed forces, in turn equipped by Eastern bloc countries. For all his future success as a geopolitical poker player, JFK's nerve had failed him this time: his handling of the invasion was at once irresolute and inept. And, of course, it all made Fidel that much more unbearably bodacious than he'd been before.

Under Pressure

America's immediate reaction to the Bay of Pigs debacle was to be completely stunned – and to rationalize that feeling in a view that, in the words of CIA Operations Chief Richard Helms, it was 'better to lay low'. There was an uneasy awareness that the USSR had seized the initiative. Quite bad enough on its own, the Bay of Pigs fiasco had rounded off the week from hell as far as the Americans were concerned: just

five days before, on 12 April, Russia's Yuri Gagarin had become the first man in space. That July, he made a triumphal visit to Havana, underlining both the bond between the two Communist nations and the suggestion that the future was socialist.

While the cosmonaut enjoyed the applause, more discreet diplomatic ways were also being found of increasing the pressure on the 'main adversary'. Berlin was the obvious focus for these efforts: Khruschev colourfully called it 'the testicles of the West'. To get the result they wanted in Central Europe, the Soviets were prepared to look a great deal further. In a now-notorious memo of 24 July, KGB Chief Aleksandr Shelepin set out for Khruschev a strategy of supporting national liberation movements around the world, from British East Africa to southeast Asia and Taiwan – and in Central America. In Nicaragua,

Aleksandr Shelepin saw Cuba's Revolution as a step towards Soviet dominance in the Third World.

meanwhile, Ernesto Sandino and his supporters were hatching plans to overthrow the dictator Anastasio Somoza – 'our sonofabitch', in Franklin D. Roosevelt's famous phrase. By supporting these efforts – and further, Shelepin suggested, by encouraging uprisings in Guatemala and El Salvador – the Soviets could confuse the Americans, and 'tie them down during the settlement of a German peace treaty and West Berlin'.

Operation Mongoose

A flurry of activity ensued in Washington and at the CIA's newly opened headquarters at Langley, Virginia, as spies and politicians – both now well and truly mad – plotted to get even. Down but by no means out, the United States still had formidable weapons in its armoury – not just its nuclear weapons but the mighty dollar. The Soviets are believed to have sent a bank-breaking $25,000 to the Sandinistas: President Kennedy was able to authorize a $5m budget for covert operations against Cuba – just for a start.

How to spend the money, though? The stories about depilatory-sprinkled microphones and exploding cigars are, most likely, just myths, but, judging by the record, they were by no means too improbably

extravagant to be true. If necessity is the mother of invention, the converse may also be the case: the ingenuity of US planning at this time certainly suggests a security establishment at a loss. Altogether, no fewer than 32 plans were considered under the auspices of Operation Mongoose or the 'Cuba Project'. The problem was that, crucial as it might be to bring down Castro's government, obvious American 'bullying' would be counter-productive politically – in Cuba itself, in the Caribbean and also in the wider world. The aim, therefore, was to weaken the communist regime by any underhand means available, and 'to bring about the revolt of the Cuban people'.

Red Realities

From Cuba itself, meanwhile, the signs were simultaneously encouraging and alarming: there were both positive and negative incentives to action on America's part. As Richard Helms was to report in January 1962, on the one hand, the Revolution did not enjoy unqualified support – as evidenced by 'the complexion of the refugee flow', which now included not just the expropriated landowners and industrialists but also middle-class professionals and even lower-middle-class workers. On the other, it was becoming clear that 'progress . . . toward a police and Communist state' had been more rapid than

Fidel Castro clearly revelled in the hapless hostility of the United States.

TRANSCRIPT OF KEY PARAGRAPHS

Memorandum for the
Director of the CIA,
19 January 1962

[The Attorney General
concluded that]

1) Overthrow of Castro
regime was possible

2) Sugar crop should be
attacked at once

3) Action to be taken
to keep Castro so busy
with internal problems
(economic, political, social)
that Castro would have no
time for meddling abroad
especially in Latin
America.

DETAIL: United States
Government was precluded
from destroying the
current sugar crop (1)
we were late and overly
optimistic and (b) "the
assets of the United States
Government were not
as great as we were led
to believe".

. . . a solution to the Cuban
problem today carries "The
Top priority in the United
States Government – all
else is secondary – no
time, money, effort, or
manpower is to be spared."

- 2 -

(d) With these factors in mind, the Attorney General had a discussion at the White House during the autumn of 1961 with the President, the Secretary of Defense, and General Lansdale. The Secretary of Defense assigned General Lansdale to survey the Cuban problem, and he (Lansdale) reported to the President, the Secretary of Defense, and the Attorney General (in late November) concluding:

   (1) Overthrow of Castro regime was possible

   (2) Sugar crop should be attacked at once

   (3) Action to be taken to keep Castro so busy with internal problems (economic, political, and social) that Castro would have no time for meddling abroad especially in Latin America.

DETAIL: United States Government was precluded from destroying the current sugar crop (1) we were late and overly optimistic and (b) "the assets of the United States Government were not as great as we were led to believe".

(e) Accordingly, a solution to the Cuban problem today carries "The top priority in the United States Government — all else is secondary — no time, money, effort, or manpower is to be spared. There can be no misunderstanding on the involvement of the agencies concerned nor on their responsibility to carry out this job. The agency heads understand that you are to have full backing on what you need."

(f) Yesterday (18 January 1962), the President indicated to the Attorney General that "the final chapter on Cuba has not been written" — it's got to be done and will be done.

(g) Therefore, the Attorney General directed those in attendance at the meeting to address

it had been in any country in Eastern Europe over the equivalent period of time.

Did continuing US hostility drive Cuba ever deeper into the Soviet camp? Were America's paranoid prophecies self-fulfilling? Historians are still divided. What is clear is that, for whatever reason, what amounted to an Iron Curtain country was taking shape before America's eyes in the Caribbean.

In America, the discussion intensified. Thinking was evolving along increasingly exotic lines, as – under the general heading Operation Northwoods – a range of more or less dirty tricks was planned. Its aim was summed up baldly by a memorandum dated 13 March: to provide the 'pretexts which could provide justification for US military intervention'. Or, as another official was to

'We could develop a Communist Cuban terror campaign in the Miami area, in other Florida cities and even in Washington'

Caribbean Survey Group, March 1962

put it, in a more bureaucratic style:

The desired resultant from the execution of this plan would be to place the United States in the apparent position of suffering defensible grievances from a rash and irresponsible government of Cuba and to develop an international image of a Cuban threat to peace in the Western Hemisphere.

Guantánamo Games

If the summary is stark, the detail is jaw-dropping. It is spelled out in a report by the Caribbean Survey Group to the Joint Chiefs of Staff. At the forefront of their thinking was their consciousness that the United States had its own firm foothold on Cuban soil, at Guantánamo.

This base on the island republic's southern coast had been secured by the United States in 1933 – in return, ironically, for an undertaking never again to interfere in Cuba's affairs.

The planners' aim was to unsettle the Castro regime by covert means and in so doing precipitate some rash action on

TRANSCRIPT OF KEY PARAGRAPHS

Justification for US Military Intervention in Cuba, 13 March 1962

Incidents to establish a credible attack (not in chronological order):
- Start rumors (many). Use clandestine radio.
- Land friendly Cubans in uniform "over-the-fence" to stage attack on base.
- Capture Cuban (friendly) Saboteurs inside the base.
- Start riots near the base main gate (friendly Cubans)
- Blow up ammunition inside the base
- Capture militia group which storms the base.
- Sabotage ship in harbor; large fires, napthalene
- Sink ship near harbor entrance. Conduct funeral for mock-victims.

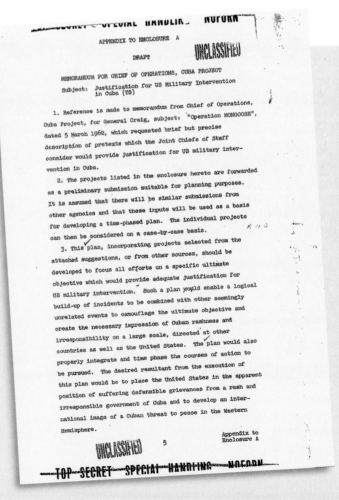

Cuba's part, which would in its turn seem to justify more direct action by the United States:

Harassment plus deceptive actions to convince the Cubans of imminent invasion would be emphasized. Our military posture throughout execution of the plan will allow a rapid change from exercise to intervention if Cuban response justifies. [. . .] A series of well coordinated incidents will be planned to take place in and around Guantánamo to give genuine appearance of being done by hostile Cuban forces.

A succession of 'false-flag' operations was envisaged, the idea being to sow doubt and confusion in the Cuban government and population and to persuade the world that US interests were in immediate danger.

The 1898 sinking of the USS *Maine* inspired a 'false-flag' operation.

The Maine Chance

Items 9 and 10 in the list of ways to justify intervening in Cuba (see panel left) recall the synthesized 'attack' and outrage that had been taken to justify the Spanish–American War of 1898, the blowing-up of the USS *Maine* in Havana Harbor. This had almost certainly been an accident, but the Americans had seized on the chance to blame the Spanish as the excuse to start a war. That modern officials were mindful of the historic parallels became clear when, a few lines later, they suggest that 'A "Remember the Maine" incident could be arranged in several forms':

a. We could blow up a US ship in Guantánamo Bay and blame Cuba.

b. We could blow up a drone (unmanned) vessel anywhere in the Cuban waters . . . The presence of Cuban planes or ships merely investigating the intent of the vessel could be fairly compelling evidence that it was taken under attack. [. . .] The US could follow up with an air/sea rescue operation covered by US fighters to 'evacuate' remaining members of the non-existent crew. Casualty lists in US newspapers would cause a helpful wave of national indignation.

Bringing it On Home

That was nothing to the 'national indignation' that would have been caused if the Caribbean Survey Group's next bright idea had come to public knowledge:

We could develop a Communist Cuban terror campaign in the Miami area, in other Florida cities and even in Washington.

Would it have made things better if steps had been taken to avoid the loss of innocent American lives?

The terror campaign could be pointed at Cuban refugees seeking haven in the United States. We could sink a boatload of Cubans enroute to Florida (real or simulated).

Such cynicism makes the plan to attack the Dominican sugar crop with '"Cuban" B-26 or C-46 type aircraft' sound high-minded. ('Soviet Bloc incendiaries could be found.') There were suggestions too that 'MIG type aircraft' flown by US pilots could provide

Kennedy brothers Robert (left) and John made Cuba a priority.

of the Cuban Revolution with youthful idealism had already been established – and that clearly rankled in administration minds.

This Time It's Personal

No one in Washington was wild about the idea of a communist Cuba – a Soviet outpost less than 160km (100 miles) from the Florida Keys. For the Kennedys, family honour was at stake. Painstakingly built up during his presidential campaign, with the help of his father's friends in Hollywood, John F. Kennedy's reputation as a war hero – he'd commanded a patrol torpedo boat in the Pacific – had started to unravel with the Bay of Pigs. Hence the otherwise eccentric decision to appoint the Attorney

'additional provocation' if used to harass civil flights and surface shipping. Trying to get hold of an actual MIG would carry its own security risks, of course, but it was believed that 'reasonable copies . . . could be produced from US resources in about three months'.

'It is possible', the report's author argued,

. . . to create an incident which will demonstrate convincingly that a Cuban aircraft has attacked and shot down a chartered civil airliner enroute from the United States to Jamaica, Guatemala, Panama or Venezuela.

Warming to his theme, the author pointed out that the passengers (all Company plants, of course) 'could be a group of college students off on a holiday'. Fidel and Che, the slaughterers of innocent kids? At this point, the Hippie subculture lay some years in the future, but the association

7. Hijacking attempts against civil air and surface craft should appear to continue as harassing measures condoned by the government of Cuba. Concurrently, genuine defections of Cuban civil and military air and surface craft should be encouraged.

8. It is possible to create an incident which will demonstrate convincingly that a Cuban aircraft has attacked and shot down a chartered civil airliner enroute from the United States to Jamaica, Guatemala, Panama or Venezuela. The destination would be chosen only to cause the flight plan route to cross Cuba. The passengers could be a group of college students off on a holiday or any grouping of persons with a common interest to support chartering a non-scheduled flight.

   a. An aircraft at Eglin AFB would be painted and numbered as an exact duplicate for a civil registered aircraft belonging to a CIA proprietary organization in the Miami area. At a designated time the duplicate would be substituted for the actual civil aircraft and would be loaded with the selected passengers, all boarded under carefully prepared aliases. The actual registered aircraft would be converted to a drone.

   b. Take off times of the drone aircraft and the actual aircraft will be scheduled to allow a rendezvous south of Florida. From the rendezvous point the passenger-carrying aircraft will descend to minimum altitude and go directly into an auxiliary field at Eglin AFB where arrangements will have been made to evacuate the passengers and return the aircraft to its original status. The drone aircraft meanwhile will continue to fly the filed flight plan. When over Cuba the drone will being transmitting on the international distress frequency a "MAY DAY" message stating he is under attack by Cuban MIG aircraft. The transmission will be interrupted by destruction of the aircraft which will be triggered by radio signal. This will allow ICAO radio

Annex to Appendix
to Enclosure A

10

UNCLASSIFIED

TOP SECRET SPECIAL HANDLING NOFORN

TRANSCRIPT OF KEY PARAGRAPHS

Top Right: Minutes of meeting of the Special Group on Operation Mongoose, Oct 1962.

It was agreed that four major points emerged from today's discussion:
a. We ought to go all out for increased intelligence.
b. There should be considerably more sabotage.
c. Restrictions on attributability can be relaxed so that training and other preparations can be subject to some short cuts.
d. All efforts should be made to develop new and imaginative approaches to the possibility of getting rid of the Castro regime.

Bottom Left: [How the staged shooting down of a US civilian aircraft by Cuba would work.]

When over Cuba the drone will be transmitting on the international distress frequency a "MAY DAY" message stating he is under attack by Cuban MIG aircraft. The transmission will be interrupted by destruction of the aircraft which will be triggered by radio signal.

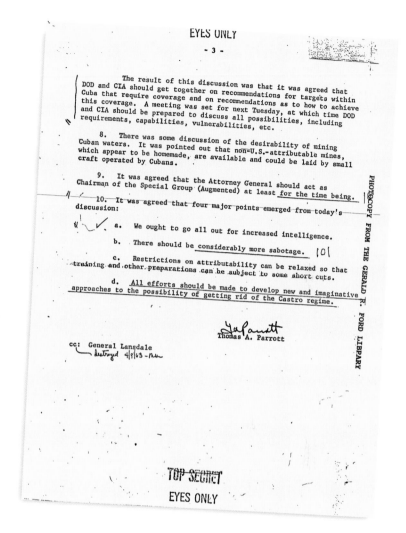

EYES ONLY
- 3 -

The result of this discussion was that it was agreed that DOD and CIA should get together on recommendations for targets within Cuba that require coverage and on recommendations as to how to achieve this coverage. A meeting was set for next Tuesday, at which time DOD and CIA should be prepared to discuss all possibilities, including requirements, capabilities, vulnerabilities, etc.

8. There was some discussion of the desirability of mining Cuban waters. It was pointed out that non-U.S.-attributable mines, which appear to be homemade, are available and could be laid by small craft operated by Cubans.

9. It was agreed that the Attorney General should act as Chairman of the Special Group (Augmented) at least _for the time being._

10. It was agreed that four major points emerged from today's discussion:

a. We ought to go all out for increased intelligence.

b. There should be considerably more sabotage.

c. Restrictions on attributability can be relaxed so that training and other preparations can be subject to some short cuts.

d. All efforts should be made to develop new and imaginative approaches to the possibility of getting rid of the Castro regime.

Thomas A. Parrott

cc: General Lansdale
destroyed 4/9/63 - mm

PHOTOCOPY FROM THE GERALD R. FORD LIBRARY

TOP SECRET
EYES ONLY

General to oversee Operation Mongoose. Brother Bobby would see that Castro got what was coming to him.

By comparison with John, Robert FitzGerald Kennedy was a pallid figure, quiet and reserved. But still waters ran deep, and he'd been profoundly stirred by his family's humiliation. 'Bobby was always extremely emotional,' Ray Cline, sometime CIA Chief Analyst, afterwards recalled. 'He was perpetually on the CIA's case about the Cubans.' He was still on it in October 1962, as the minutes of a meeting make clear:

The Attorney General opened the meeting by saying that higher authority is concerned about progress on the MONGOOSE program and feels that more priority should be given to trying to mount sabotage operations.

Ten days later, such stunts started to seem trivial by comparison with the diplomatic drama then unfolding after the discovery that secret sites on Cuba were being built to hold Soviet missiles.

Chile

Far as it was from the centres of Cold War power, Chile had a way of forcing itself into the thick of things. Visionaries of both left and right ideologies sought to realize their dreams there – and violence was the invariable result.

Chile has always been prone to seismic shocks, but November 1970 brought a different kind of earthquake. The accession of Salvador Allende as Latin America's first democratically elected Marxist President sent a tremor through the Washington establishment. That a people could freely have chosen to be governed by a group of communists was not just outrageous but upsetting; the more so because of a regretful sense of what might have been. Less than a decade before, plans had been drawn up for what was to be arguably the most ambitious attempt ever to engineer ethnic harmony, civil obedience and social conformism in the country: Chile as the capitalist Camelot.

Free-Market Myths
The name originally given to the court of King Arthur in the English legend 'Camelot' was familiar to Americans from its application to the Kennedy White House. In this use, it was more immediately derived from T.H. White's novel *The Once and Future King* (1958). That fantasy, made more famous

Salvador Allende's improbable victory caused consternation in the United States.

by the Lerner-Loewe musical of 1960, saw Arthurian England as a land of contentment, peace and chivalry. If the brutish realities of medieval Britain could be so idealized, why not a Chile that, as the CIA itself reported in its National Intelligence Estimate for 1963, had 'a longstanding tradition of respect for constitutional order and civil liberties'? Why shouldn't a country with 'human and material resources . . . adequate to provide a decent living for its rapidly growing population' be made a utopia of market freedom and social peace?

It says much for the temper of the times that a serious project should have been named after an unabashedly confected fairy tale,

without apparent appreciation of the ironies involved.

Reality Check
The authors of the National Intelligence Estimate were themselves aware that Chile currently fell short of utopian ideals. Despite the resources and skills available to the economy, they pointed out:

for half the population real wages have been declining since 1950, and a large proportion of the population is ill-housed, ill-clothed and ill-fed.

Allende already exercised a wide appeal – the CIA's analysts could see this clearly. Fortunately, a rival candidate had fatally divided the left in 1958.

Liberation Struggles

Whether it was the result of toppling dominoes or just a reluctance any longer to accept colonial rule, national liberation movements had been emerging around the world. The Soviets had regarded their 'struggles' as an opportunity to make life difficult for America and its friends. The significance of this Soviet support might be debated – the sums involved were often negligible by CIA standards – but the fact of this interference wasn't to be denied.

In a speech of November 1960, Nikita Khruschev had proclaimed 'New Victories of the World Communist Movement'. The Americans were already at work trying to stop them from being won. They had fought a 'proxy war' with the Soviets in the Congo

The CIA took an intense interest in the destiny of Chile.

(1960); the Soviets had supported Egypt's intervention in Yemen (1962–63). Nicaragua's Sandinistas had also been backed by the Soviets; now, with whatever reluctance (this itself was hotly debated), Castro's Cuba was a client of the USSR as well.

Strategic Psychology

US spooks were also, of course, quite capable of interfering in the affairs of other countries, but they did feel haunted by the attentions of a free and inquisitive media and a judgmental public. Less obviously (and less consciously, perhaps), they were under the spell of science. This was a country currently racing to catch up with the Soviets in the Space

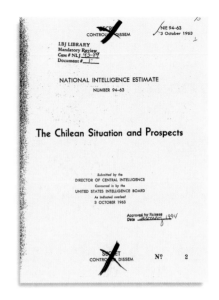

Below: Allende's popularity was rooted in the plight of Chile's poor.

The United States backed the Belgian colonial authorities in the Congo.

'Organized espionage, under the appearance of sociological investigation ... is being carried out'

Chilean Communist Deputy, Jorge Montes, 1965

Race. But science was also encroaching on what had been 'softer' areas of study. And, conversely, the 'social sciences' were carving out a niche for themselves in strategic thinking.

Psychological Warfare had been a part of US strategic thinking since World War II (it had, of course, had an important role in both P.B. Fortune and P.B. Success), but an increasing emphasis was being placed on it. By now these tactics were being renamed Psychological Operations – if only because it seemed embarrassing to use the word 'warfare' for practices as

often as not employed on populations supposed to be friendly, like Guatemala.

But what in those days had been little more than a box of clever tricks – leaflet-drops, phony broadcasts, loudspeaker announcements – was now developed with something like scientific rigour. The Special Operations Research Organization (SORO) led the way. Its brief was to carry out 'non-material research' in support of the military. And while it was affiliated to the American University in Washington DC, it was much more closely linked to the Department of Defense and the Army Office of Research and Development. Its Director, Professor Theodore Vallance, had himself been a practitioner of Psychological Warfare during World War II.

Academic Attack

First proposed in 1963, Project CAMELOT set out to harness the insights of modern social science to the fight against communism. Or, as Vallance himself put it in a statement of 1964:

Project CAMELOT is a study whose objective is to determine the feasibility of developing a general social systems model which would make it possible to predict and influence politically the politically significant aspects of social change in the developing nations of the world.

Sociology, psychology, cultural anthropology . . . they would all play a part. An army of academics was to be mobilized, not just from SORO itself but from other research institutions in the United States and overseas. Libraries were to be combed; learned articles anatomized; research papers filleted; experiments repeated and taken further. A budget of $6m was set aside for what was going to be a large-scale enterprise. Could a country be revolution-proofed? Researchers were going to try and see. Was it possible to identify the earliest signs of what the left were calling 'national liberation struggles'? The whole body of available scholarship was going to be trawled in search of an answer, and further researches would be conducted to investigate potential leads.

A comprehensive survey of the existing literature would be followed by 21 historical case studies, tracing the origins and courses of insurgencies since World War II. A further five analyses of current insurrections would take Latin America as their focus; finally, an in-depth study would be conducted into a single country: Chile.

TRANSCRIPT OF KEY PARAGRAPHS

Memorandum from Secretary of State Rusk to President Johnson, 30 June 1965

Camelot is an Army sponsored project being carried out by the Special Operations Research Office. It is a large-scale unclassified project calling for an estimated 140 professional man hours of work and a budget of more than $4,000,000. The proposed study would attempt to make a scientific analysis of international tension and war and insurgency and counterinsurgency. Considerable case work abroad is envisaged, including studies of Bolivia, Colombia, Paraguay, Peru and Venezuela. [. . .]
Such studies made by private social scientists would probably elicit little attention . . .

(d) With these factors in mind, the Attor[ney] General had a discussion at the White [House] during the autumn of 1961 with the Pre[si]dent, the Secretary of Defense, and G[eneral] Lansdale. The Secretary of Defense a[sked] General Lansdale to survey the Cuban [problem] and he (Lansdale) reported to the Pres[ident,] the Secretary of Defense, and the Atto[rney] General (in late November) concluding:

(1) Overthrow of Castro regime wa[s] possible

(2) Sugar crop should be attacked at once

(3) Action to be taken to keep Cas[tro] so busy with internal problems (economic, political, and soci[al]) that Castro would have no tim[e] meddling abroad especially in Latin America.

DETAIL: United States Government was precluded fro[m] the current sugar crop (1) we were late an[d] optimistic and (b) "the assets of the Unit[ed] Government were not as great as we were le[d to be]lieve".

(e) Accordingly, a solution to the Cuban [problem] today carries "The top priority in th[e United] States Government — all else is seco[nd,] no time, money, effort, or manpower i[s] spared. There can be no misunderstan[ding of] the involvement of the agencies conce[rned] on their responsibility to carry out [...] The agency heads understand that you have full backing on what you need."

(f) Yesterday (18 January 1962), the Pres[ident]

Medici plans

Anxious that social injustice would foster revolutionary ferment in Latin America, the Americans found a strongman in the new dictator of Brazil.

If forming an alliance with a dictator was an unfamiliar way for the United States to wage war, it certainly produced some unexpected language. Here is Lieutenant-General W. Dick discussing the phenomenon of the Third World revolution before a congressional committee in 1965:

There is a general consensus that the problem is intimately related to the social structure, culture, and behavioral patterns in the countries involved.

He stops short of identifying economic injustice or political oppression as factors, instead implying that the 'problem' – the insurrectionary urge – is little more than a cultural quirk; however, there's still something unmistakably liberal-sounding about his speech. With its emphasis on the need to understand, rather than simply to attack, this isn't the stereotypical discourse of the soldier.

Forget the cultural differences between America and Chile, then: what of the culture clash between the military and intelligence community and their recently recruited comrades-in-arms in academe? Just how long could this collaboration last?

Cancelot

Unsuprisingly, the union didn't last long, although it wasn't the military that ran out of patience first. In fact, academics rebelled at the sense that they were being used. Ill-advised attempts to conceal the nature of the project and convince Chilean scholars that their work was sought for a project funded by the National Science Foundation (NSF) blew up in the organizers' faces, making Project CAMELOT seem still more sinister than it actually was. There was a furore in Chile, whose politicians queued up to denounce the project and whose government (never consulted) protested in outraged terms. 'Yankees Study Invasion of Chile', ran the headline in the leftist press – and to many in Chile it seemed all too believable. Almost as upset was Ralph Dungan, the US Ambassador to Chile, who had been left out of the loop but had to deal with the fallout when it all collapsed.

THE SOVIET ROLE IN LATIN AMERICA

THE ESTIMATE

1. Over the past few years, the political environment in Latin America has altered dramatically, and the pace of change is clearly accelerating. Radical approaches to problems are gaining ever wider support. In several countries, leaders of a new stripe have taken over and have begun to make far-reaching changes. Nationalism is a powerful motive force in this process. The Soviets are well aware of these developments, and their interest and their activities have grown. This paper examines recent trends in the area (excluding Cuba) and their implications for the position of the US and the future role of the USSR, in the main for the next five years or so, but sometimes for longer periods. Its main conclusions are contained in paragraphs 34-41.

I. THE CHANGING ENVIRONMENT IN LATIN AMERICA

2. The process of change in Latin America is mainly in response to forces operating there, rather than to US or Soviet actions. Yet the process has important implications for the roles played by both Washington and Moscow in the area. The preponderant position of the US is eroding, and at an accelerating pace, for complex reasons rooted in economic developments, social pressures, and history. Conversely, the Soviet Union and other countries as well are more and more looked to by nationalistic elements as a balance to American preponderance, often for purely opportunistic reasons.

3. Nationalism is a strong and growing force in Latin America, and it is increasingly taking on an anti-American coloration. This is so because the US is the dominant external force, and the Latins have bitter memories of political and economic pressures going back many decades. Local leaders, eager to stress their independence, frequently complain about US hegemony and paternalistic interference. US firms are the ones most affected by schemes of nationalization. The Latins occasionally take actions which they recognize as affronts to the US, such as the capture by Ecuador of US tuna-boats operating within the 200 mile territorial limit that it claims. Several governments are actively seeking to diversify their purchases of arms, sources of aid, and trading partners.

SECRET

1

TRANSCRIPT OF KEY PARAGRAPHS

<u>CIA REPORT 1971 – 'The Soviet Role in Latin America'</u>

(Left) The process of change in Latin America is mainly in response to forces operating there, rather than to US or Soviet actions. Yet the process has important implications for the roles played by both Washington and Moscow in the area. The preponderant position of the US is eroding, and at an accelerating pace, for complex reasons rooted in economic developments, social pressures, and history. Conversely, the Soviet Union and other countries as well are more and more looked to by nationalistic elements as a balance to American preponderance . . .

(Right) In many ways, Latin American governments are casting off US influences because they feel capable of directing more of their own affairs. In a sense they are right. More than most countries in the Third World, the advanced nations in Latin America have the skills needed to modernize their societies . . .

SECRET

4. The spread of nationalism creates both opportunities and problems for the Soviets. It provides the USSR with an opening for policies and actions designed to speed the erosion of US influence and to increase its own. The Soviets have something to offer to those who seek a counterweight to the US and a diversification of purchasing and trading patterns. At the same time, the concern of Latin Americans to run their own affairs places a constraint on the expansion of Soviet influence. The military-populist government in Peru, for instance, is certainly out to assert its independence of the US, and it has sometimes done so abruptly and abrasively, but it remains wary of the Soviets and is of no mind to become the client of any power. The Mexican Government's belief that the USSR was involved with the Revolutionary Action Movement (MAR) was sufficient to get five Soviet diplomats expelled from the country.

5. To a greater or lesser degree, all Latin American countries suffer from deep-seated economic and social problems which resist solution. Increasing social unrest and unfulfilled popular expectations have contributed to political instability and the growing radicalization of Latin American institutions. Income is unevenly distributed, and in most of the countries small ruling classes still possess most of the money, land, and material goods. Unemployment and underemployment, high birth rates, overcrowded and rapidly growing cities—all contribute to social and political tensions and to impatience with present institutions. None of these conditions is entirely new, but modern means of communication and a growing political awareness have combined to raise the level of expectations of the increasing numbers of underprivileged, and to reveal the gap between what is and what could be.

6. Latin American intellectuals, socially-minded military officers, and clerics are increasingly persuaded that drastic changes in the established order are necessary. The US is seen as the center of capitalism and as the advocate of free enterprise, and thus as an opponent of such change. Consequently, the US and what it stands for are on the defensive. The local oligarchs, moreover, have been traditionally associated in the public mind with US businessmen and diplomats. US aid is increasingly regarded as politically motivated and self-serving; the Alliance for Progress is widely considered a failure.

7. The Soviets, claiming to be the exemplars of socialism and supporters of the working man, stand to gain from this growing anti-capitalist, anti-US sentiment. Marxism has long had a considerable following among Latin American intellectuals, especially at the universities. Unfamiliarity with the Soviet Union makes it easier for Moscow to appear as a counterbalance to US influence in the region. To many Latin Americans, US concepts appear familiar and shopworn, in contrast to those of the Soviets. Latins share little history with Russia but, as they see it, rather too much with the Colossus of the North.

8. In many ways, Latin American governments are casting off US influences because they feel capable of directing more of their own affairs. In a sense they are right. More than most countries in the Third World, the advanced nations in Latin America have the skills and resources needed to modernize their societies and some prospects for developing new markets and sources of capital. Among the important constraints have been the lack of institutions to suit societies growing more mature, a reluctance to invest at home for the long term, and their own lethargy and willingness to rely on the US and others to do things for them. The political, social, and economic reforms now being ap-

2   SECRET

Waiting for Revolution

Guatemala, Cuba, Camelot . . . the list was already long – and, for many, damning. A CIA report of 1971 into 'The Soviet Role in Latin America' is admirably clear:

Nationalism is a strong and growing force in Latin America, and it is increasingly taking on an anti-American coloration. This is so because the US is the dominant external force, and the Latins have bitter memories of political and economic pressures going back many decades.

No Marxist would have found much to quibble with in the report's description of 'deep-seated economic and social problems which resist solution' or their attribution to the uneven distribution of the region's wealth:

in most . . . countries small ruling classes still possess most of the money, land, and material goods. Unemployment and

Brazilian leader Emílio Garratazu Médici.

underemployment, high birth rates, overcrowded and rapidly growing cities – all contribute to social and political tensions and to impatience with present institutions.

Communism had the value of novelty – and it came ready-airbrushed: few people this far from the Soviet Union had much awareness of its evils:

To many Latin Americans, US concepts appear familiar and shopworn, in contrast to those of the Soviets. Latins share little history with Russia but, as they see it, rather too much with the Colossus of the North.

A 'New Course'

But Brazil, as a National Intelligence Estimate of 1972 enthused, was following a 'new course' courtesy of Emílio Garrastazu Médici's military junta – the most ruthlessly repressive

the country had yet seen. So admirable an institution deserved all the support the United States could give it, so it was gratifying for the Estimate's author to be able to report that 'Médici's state visit to Washington in December 1971 [had done] much to increase his stature at home'.

It had certainly enhanced his stature in Washington, where President Richard Nixon had given him the warmest possible welcome. 'I wish he were running the whole continent,' the President had confided in a call to Secretary of State William Rogers a few days before. Médici met Nixon and adviser General Vernon Walters at the White House. Cuba, Paraguay, Peru, Bolivia, Uruguay and Argentina all came up in the conversation, but the most important common ground was to be found on Chile, where a Marxist president had just been voted in:

The President then asked whether President Médici thought that the Chilean Armed forces were capable of overthrowing Allende. President Médici replied that he felt that they were, adding that Brazil was exchanging many officers with the Chileans, and made clear that Brazil was working towards this end.

But Nixon was eager that America should do its bit towards the destruction of democracy in the name of freedom: 'it was very important', he said, 'that Brazil and the United States work closely in this field'. 'We could not take direction,' he insisted – conscious, perhaps, that some loss of US dignity might be involved in this new friendship with the South American strongman –

. . . but if the Brazilians felt that there was something we could do to be helpful in this area, he would like President Médici to let us know. If money were required or other discreet aid, we might be able to make it available. This should be held in the greatest confidence.

The meeting came to a cordial close, Nixon expressing his hope for continuing cooperation, as 'there were many things that Brazil as a South American country could do that the U.S. could not.'

Binning the Ballot

Was one of those things the undermining of the democratic process in Uruguay? There the right-wing president (and future dictator) Juan Maria Bordaberry had been swept to power in November 1971. Harassment of opposing candidates had been quite open, while widespread rumours of electoral fraud were subsequently to be confirmed. National Security Adviser Henry Kissinger's account of Nixon's meeting with British Prime Minister Edward Heath a few weeks later shows the President in anything but apologetic mood. 'The Brazilians rigged the Uruguayan election,' he crows. 'There are forces at work which we are not discouraging,' he goes on. 'Castro is still bent on Hemispheric subversion.'

Uruguayans should perhaps be grateful that Bordaberry's ballot-

rigging had worked: it's widely believed that, had his left-wing *Frente Amplio* opponents had their victory, Médici intended to invade, with America's support. As for Chile, it was firmly set on its own new course; one that would bring a violent crescendo of CIA-sponsored subversion – and, ultimately, Augusto Pinochet's bloody coup.

'The Brazilians rigged the Uruguayan election ... There are forces at work which we are not discouraging.'

President Nixon, 20 December, 1971

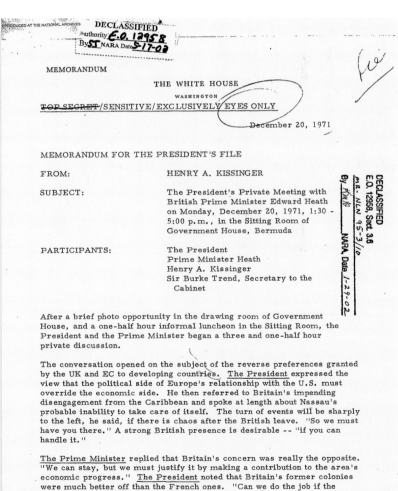

Chapter Six

The East is Red? Asia

The Soviet Union was not the only major communist power: behind its 'Bamboo Curtain' loomed China. It was vast and populous, but what were its ambitions in Asia?

With a population approaching 700 million, China had enough people to be a world unto itself; it certainly seemed to be a world apart. And it was a country with its own epic history: Mao's Long March to victory over the Nationalist forces of Chiang Kai-Shek had given way to a still more gruelling slog towards totalitarianism, as the Great Leader bent a broken country to his will. Well over a million people were killed in the making of this People's Republic. Many millions more were to die in the 'Great Leap Forward' from 1958 to 1961 – in a China ravaged by famine and terrorized by state repression.

With all its troubles, Mao's China had from the first been very obviously the major power in the Far East – even if it seemed as inscrutable as it was clearly influential. Yet, if it could not be comprehended, it had still to be contended with: that was the challenge facing the West in Asia.

Colonial occupiers in Asia were feeling increasingly beleaguered. The plight of the French in Vietnam was a case in point.

Taiwan

Chiang Kai-Shek's Republic of China was a running, rankling sore for the People's Republic – and a potential flashpoint for a nuclear conflict.

China was happy enough to maintain a role as the 'junior partner' in the communist alliance. Mao felt bound by ideological loyalty to the Soviet Union. Indeed, in 1949, a CIA analyst suggested that it was

. . . the intention of the Soviet Union to advance toward its goal of eventual world domination by adding to the Soviet orbit the enormous territory and population of China, and by employing China to facilitate Soviet expansion into other Far Eastern areas.

And yet, he stressed, 'the process of consolidation of Soviet control over China will unquestionably encounter considerable difficulty' – on everything from the acceptance of US aid to the control of 'peripheral areas' and – a key stumbling-block – the question of assistance to communist movements in other countries of the region.

For the People's Republic of China (PRC) was showing little interest in territorial expansion. With well over five million men under arms, it wasn't that it lacked raw strength. But plans were already afoot for the numbers of the People's Liberation Army (PLA) to be cut by half.

The General and the Generalissimo: Douglas MacArthur and Chiang Kai-Shek in 1950.

China had enough difficulties of its own without taking on other territories – and other problems.

True, when conflict flared in Korea, China's communists stepped in to support their North Korean comrades – but North Korea's Kim Il Sung was Stalin's protégé, not Mao's. (Even when Kim went ahead and sent his armies southwards to attack UN-supported South Korea, the Chinese preferred to hover on the sidelines – until, flushed with his early success against the invaders, US General MacArthur mounted an unsanctioned counter-invasion of North Korea.)

Taiwan Trouble

The PRC's aggression towards Taiwan (the Republic of China, or ROC) was not inconsistent with this policy, given that the communists never acknowledged the government of Chiang Kai-Shek or his Kuomintang. Taiwan and its associated islands were just offshore fragments of the Chinese homeland, they believed.

Evacuated from the mainland by the Americans with a million supporters, Chiang had established himself on Taiwan after the civil war. He in his turn claimed dominion over the mainland. The two republics faced one another across the Taiwan Strait in mutual denial. America and Britain saw that the ROC was the 'China' represented at the United Nations – leaving the PRC out in the international cold until 1971, at which point the positions were reversed. And, long after the PRC's capital had been renamed 'Beijing', the Americans still referred to it as 'Peiping' – the old Qing-era title still in use among the Nationalists.

Dire Strait

The confrontation across the Taiwan Strait was a war-in-waiting. It came in 1954, when the PRC landed troops on some of Taiwan's offshore island groups. Critics claimed that mixed signals from the Truman administration (1945–53) had encouraged Chinese aggression. The Joint Chiefs of Staff urged President Eisenhower to make nuclear strikes against mainland China; the hawks were upset all over again when he refused. They considered the PRC's annexation of the Yijiangshan Islands and the forced evacuation of the Tachen group to be a shameful defeat for the United States. Another way of looking at it, though, was that the communists' determination to take Taiwan had actually been frustrated.

Raising the Stakes

The crisis had certainly sounded an alarm call, though; and as everyone clearly understood, it had very possibly been a warning of worse to come. Washington would have been remiss if it hadn't looked to the likelihood of a fresh attack further down the line. And it would have been surprising, considering the lead the United States still had in the arms race, if it hadn't given some thought to the playing of the nuclear card. The more so in

After their evacuation from the mainland, the Kuomintang had set up their own 'China' in Taiwan.

~~TOP SECRET~~

SINO-SOVIET AND FREE WORLD REACTIONS TO US USE OF NUCLEAR WEAPONS IN LIMITED WARS IN THE FAR EAST

THE PROBLEM

This estimate was requested by the NSC as a result of a study prepared by the Departments of State and Defense and the Joint Chiefs of Staff, with appropriate participation of the Central Intelligence Agency, on *US and Allied Capabilities for Limited Military Operations to 1 July 1961*, 29 May 1958. Among the limitations under which this study was prepared were that it did not examine US and Allied capabilities against overtly employed Soviet armed forces; nor against an enemy employing nuclear weapons, since the latter case was construed as overt employment of Soviet forces. On the other hand, it was assumed that the US used nuclear weapons selectively from the outset in four hypothetical cases involving Communist aggression in the Far East.

This estimate examines whether or not the enemy would employ nuclear weapons if the US employed them, and assesses the impact on world attitudes if either the US or both sides employed them. It confines itself to assessing the above reactions in the four hypothetical cases given in the State-Defense study where the US employed nuclear weapons at the outset in response to Communist aggression through mid-1961: (1) North Korean invasion of South Korea, (2) Chinese Communist attack on Quemoy and Matsu, (3) Chinese Communist attack on Taiwan, and (4) North Vietnam attack on South Vietnam and Laos. It is based on the hypothetical situations which are developed in Appendices A–D of the State-Defense study and which are summarized at the outset of Sections III–VI of this estimate.

CONCLUSIONS

1. We believe that if the US used nuclear weapons in meeting Bloc local aggression in the Far East, there would be a grave risk that the Communists would retaliate in kind. Indeed any Far East Communist state, taking into account the possibility of such US action, would be unlikely to launch a local aggression without having received assurances of Soviet support.

2. We estimate that, though the USSR will be determined to avoid courses of action gravely risking general war throughout the period concerned, it probably calculates that its growing military capabilities likewise increasingly deter the US from taking such risks. Therefore, the Soviets would probably estimate that local Communist use of nuclear

~~TOP SECRET~~

1

... attempt to win without using nuclear weapons or seek to break off the action. However, even if the US nuclear response were limited to the immediate area of Korea, Taiwan, Quemoy and

~~TOP SECRET~~

2

... and Laos, we cannot ... lity that the Communi ... in kind, possibly in ... acks against US bases ... to minimize the addi ... l war.

... governments and ... pressed and encour ... t US resistance to ... n, but the US use ... would arouse wide ... al war and would ... unist responsibility ... s. The US would ... y popular opinion, ... the use of nuclear ... that the adverse ... dow the favorable ... s.

... would be miti ... e quickly halted ... sing large civil ... t for US power ... n so, the stigma ... nitiation of the ... ould not be re ... d, if the Com ... nuclear weapons ... nged and ex ... ar would rise ... sure would be ... a settlement.[1]

... gence, the Joint ... onclusions that: ... nmunist aggres ... n Bloc response ... the first two cases ex ... ed and less likely in the second two cases.

b. Considerable adverse political and psychological reaction, particularly in Asia, would initially result from US nuclear attacks.

The DDI, Joint Staff, disagrees, however, with certain lesser estimative judgments and estimative yardsticks applied in these conclusions and in the supporting discussion. He believes:

(Footnote continued on page 3)

TRANSCRIPT OF KEY PARAGRAPHS

A US prediction of Sino-Soviet and Free World Reactions to US Use of nuclear weapons in Limited Wars in the Far East, 1958

This estimate . . . confines itself to assessing the . . . reactions in the four hypothetical cases . . .
1) North Korean invasion of South Korea, 2) Chinese Communist attack on Quemoy and Matsu,
3) Chinese Communist attack on Taiwan and
4) North Vietnam attack on South Vietnam and Laos.

The adverse reaction would be mitigated if the US response quickly halted the fighting without causing large civilian casualties, and respect for US power would be enhanced. Even so, the stigma resulting from the US initiation of the use of nuclear weapons would not be removed.

On the other hand, if the Communists responded with nuclear weapons and hostilities were prolonged and expanded, fears of general war would rise even higher, and great pressure would be exerted on the US to reach a settlement.

that strategists had been feeling paradoxically hamstrung by the sheer destructive power of the atomic bomb and intercontinental ballistic missiles: a credible tactical use was something of a holy grail. A 1958 report on 'Sino-Soviet and Free World Reactions to US Use of Nuclear Weapons in Limited Wars in the Far East' weighs the risks of raising the nuclear stakes in the Far East:

The likelihood of Communist retaliation with nuclear weapons would be greatest if the US mounted nuclear attacks deep into Communist China, creating a situation to which Moscow and Peiping would almost certainly feel compelled to respond by attacks on US bases and nuclear capable forces in the Far East.

A Calibrated Conflict?

A more measured reaction by America might be expected to prompt a more measured reaction – the possibility of fine-tuning the conflict was there, it seemed:

If, in the case of Communist aggression against South Korea or Taiwan the US nuclear response were limited to Korea or the Straits area, the Communists would probably respond in kind in the same area.

What of the Western allies, and more particularly America's friends in the Far Eastern region?

Many Free World governments and countries would be impressed and encouraged by the prompt US resistance to Communist aggression, but the US use of nuclear weapons would arouse widespread fear of general war . . .

Changing the nature of the game so radically, moreover, would 'tend to obscure Communist responsibility for initiating hostilities'.

The US would be widely condemned by popular opinion, especially in Asia, for the use of nuclear weapons. We believe that the adverse reactions would overshadow the favorable effects in most countries.

A rapid success, however, would go a long way towards allaying these anxieties, the writer concluded: American thinking was a little less cautious than it might at first appear.

Running Out of Options

Was this just a government doing its 'due diligence' strategically, considering every option, weighing the alternatives? Was there ever really any possibility of such a strike? In fact, it came a great deal closer than might be thought.

In early August 1958, it seemed likely that the conflict would be renewed as PRC forces stepped up their pressure on the islands around Taiwan. America had been building up the ROC's armed strength – most recently with forces of the new F-86 and F-100 fighters – but the communists appeared to be unfazed. No amount of conventional strength was going to see off the attackers, it seemed. What option was there but the nuclear one?

Desperate Remedies?

Fearing that sporadic harassment would escalate into a determined bid to cut off or even occupy the

There's no mistaking the map location of China's first atomic test in 1964. It was harder to be sure who the target would be now.

islands, America's defence chiefs felt forced into a tough response. The plan, as sketched out by General Nathan F. Twining, Chairman of the Joint Chiefs of Staff, was that:

American planes would drop 10- to 15-kiloton bombs on selected fields in the vicinity of Amoy. This blow, he hoped, would cause the Communists to lift their blockade. If not, the United States would have to attack airfields as far distant as Shanghai. These more extensive strikes, General Twining admitted, might bring down nuclear vengeance on Okinawa as well as Taiwan, but he considered this a risk that would have to be taken if the offshore islands were to be defended.

Down to Detail

Drastic counsel. Nevertheless, by the middle of the month the strategy had hardened to such an extent that 'five Strategic Air Command (SAC) B-47's on Guam

went on alert to conduct nuclear raids against the mainland airfields.' The SAC further ordered its units to stand ready

. . . to prepare to destroy the Chinese cities and industries in the event the initial strikes touched off a major conflict.

A USAF report of 1962 confirms this account, whilst filling in some details. The decision to use Guam-based bombers had been taken to allay the fears of the Japanese: the plan had originally been for planes of the Thirteenth Air Force to take off from Clark Air Base in the Philippines and from Kadena in Okinawa. Though Okinawa remained a US military possession, the Japanese government had to be consulted, since these flights would have needed 'tanker, tactical and reconnaissance support' from the Fifth Air Force, stationed in Japan.

As so often was the case, President Eisenhower was a voice of calm and caution: even when communist artillery began bombarding the islands of Matsu and Quemoy. Much to Chiang's disgust, the President called for defensive actions only, and for these to be restricted to conventional weapons. In the event, the massing of an impressive show of US naval and air power concentrated minds in the People's Republic: within weeks, the communists had backed down.

Stopping China's Bomb

China came late to the nuclear arms race. It didn't conduct its first test until 1964, by which time the West's fears were eased to some extent by knowledge of the Sino–Soviet Split. Mao and Khruschev had fallen out over the latter's handling of the Cuban Missile Crisis, the Soviets' weakness encouraging the PRC to strike out alone.

But the idea of a nuclear-armed China still caused concern: a November 1963 memo reveals how much. Tantalizingly, General Maxwell D. Taylor's note to the Joint Chiefs of Staff is just the cover to a longer report, now lost. Even so, it suggests that a 'coordinated program of covert activities' was then being contemplated. A range of 'technological, scientific, economic and industrial' aspects of the Chinese nuclear development project were to be targeted so that the date of its conclusion might be 'materially deferred'.

DECLASSIFIED
Authority NND941071
By CMV NARA Date 4/26/96

REPRODUCED AT THE NATIONAL ARCHIVES

CM file

TOP SECRET - SENSITIVE

THE JOINT CHIEFS OF STAFF
Washington 25, D. C.

CM-1024-63
18 November 1963

MEMORANDUM FOR: GENERAL LEMAY
GENERAL WHEELER
ADMIRAL McDONALD
GENERAL SHOUP

Subject: Chinese Nuclear Development

1. Much has been written on the emergence of Communist China as a nuclear power and its potential effects upon the world. Thought has been given as to how we might combat Chinese employment of their nuclear capability in Asia and how we might deter them from using their capability once it has been acquired. Nothing has been written, so far as I know, on how we can prevent or delay the Chinese from succeeding in their nuclear development program.

2. That is the purpose of the attached paper. It has its basis in the fact that nuclear development, at best, is fraught with troubles - technological, scientific, economic and industrial. If these inherent problems are intensified by a coordinated program of covert activities there is reason to believe that the date on which the Chinese nuclear program matures may be materially deferred.

3. Due to the very sensitive nature of the subject and of the proposals set forth in the paper, only one copy of the paper is being delivered personally to each Chief. Following discussion by the Joint Chiefs of Staff all papers shall be collected. This subject will appear on the agenda as "Unconventional Warfare Program BRAVO."

Maxwell D Taylor
MAXWELL D. TAYLOR
Chairman
Joint Chiefs of Staff

Attachment

TOP SECRET - SENSITIVE

TRANSCRIPT OF KEY PARAGRAPHS

Joint Chiefs of Staff MEMO, 18 November 1963

Much has been written on the emergence of Communist China as a nuclear power and its potential effects upon the world. Thought has been given as to how we might combat Chinese employment of their nuclear capability in Asia and how we might deter them from using their capability once it has been acquired . . .

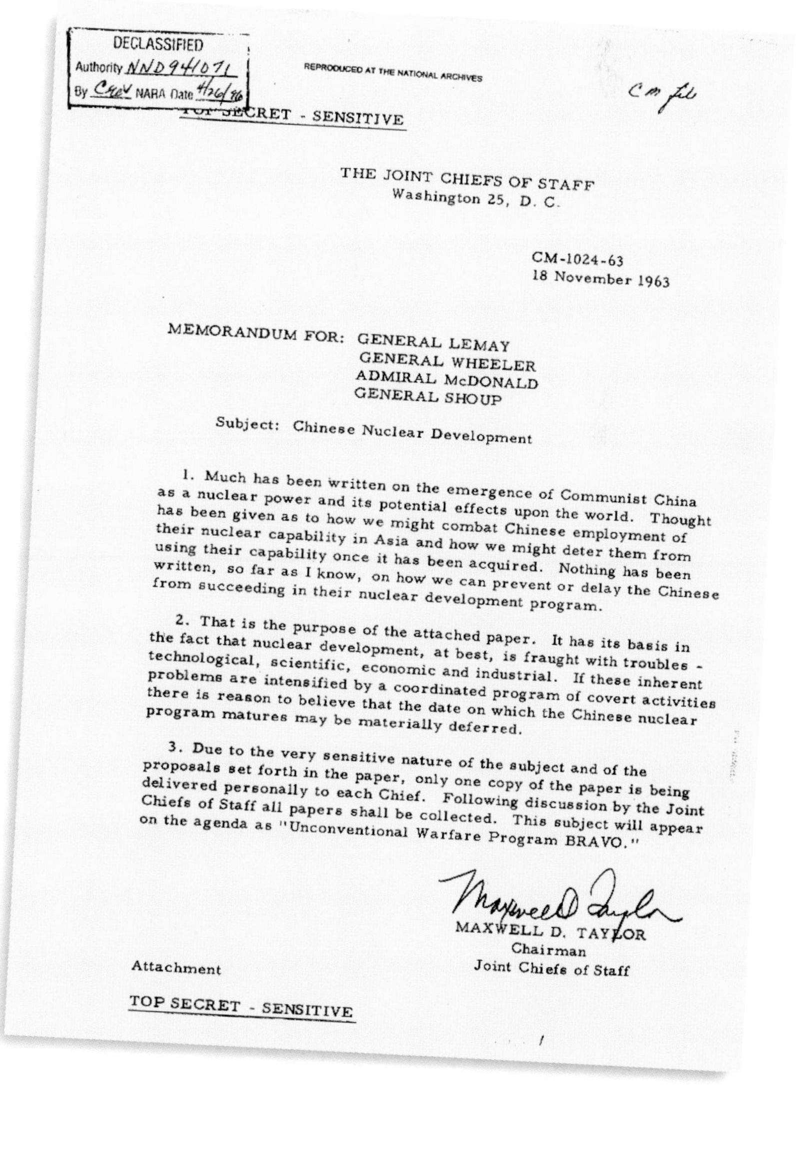

[This paper] has its basis in the fact that nuclear development, at best, is fraught with troubles – technological, scientific, economic and industrial. If these inherent problems are intensified by a coordinated program of covert activities there is reason to believe that the date on which the Chinese nuclear program matures may be materially deferred.

Due to the very sensitive nature of the subject and of the proposals set forth in the paper, only one copy of the paper is being delivered personally to each Chief.

Vietnam

The legitimate desire of a freedom-loving people to rule themselves? That's not how the Western powers were prepared to view the struggle of the Vietnamese.

The confrontation between capitalism and communism may have provided postwar history with its 'grand narrative', but it wasn't the only story, by any means. Most obviously, there was the unravelling of the colonial empires built up before World War I by the great European powers – in Africa, Asia and elsewhere.

Independence and Ideology

Nothing in principle connected the one with the other: there was nothing inherently Marxist about the nationalist impulse. (On the contrary, Karl Marx had seen nationalism as just another instrument of oppression for the working people; he'd also dismissed the idea that an undeveloped peasant society could attain a 'real' revolution.) That said, it seemed only natural for the nationalists to look to their enslavers' enemies – especially when these held out the promise of people-power.

Rightly or wrongly, the word 'communism' didn't have the taboo quality it had for most in the developed countries of western Europe and North America; neither, conversely, did people feel any reverence for the 'democratic' values of a West that had taken them – often brutally – in thrall.

China's suspicion was in part a result of bullying and exploitation by the colonial powers – though more recently, of course, it had suffered at the hands of Japan, an imperialist power of the East. Mao's view (and few economic historians would disagree with him) was that, in the longer term, modern China's economic development had been distorted by its relationship with the West. By rewriting Marx to give the rural peasantry a role analogous to that of the German master's militant industrial proletariat, the Chairman had also given Asian radicals a working philosophy of revolution.

From India to Indochine

But the first important sign that the sun was setting on the British Empire came in 1947, when India was granted its independence – a painful blow to Britain's imperial pride. Further to the east, France was fighting frantically to stay in charge of its Asian possessions. *Indochine française* included not only Vietnam but what became Cambodia and Laos. Once World War II had started, the region had been captured by the Japanese: the decision to return it to the French in 1946 sparked a war of independence by the guerrilla forces of the Viet Minh, who were led by the brave and resourceful Ho Chi Minh.

The 'reds-under-the-bed' paranoia of the Americans in particular could prompt them to see any nationalist movement as

India gained its independence in August 1947.

communist-inspired, but Ho Chi Minh made no secret of his communist allegiances. Converted to the cause as a student in Paris, he'd completed his ideological education during extended stays in the Soviet Union and in China.

For France, though, Ho's political agenda was less immediately important than the fact that he was making their Indochinese colonies ungovernable. Though centred in Tonkin – the north of Vietnam – his insurrection extended across the whole of *Indochine*. Despite a determined counter-insurgency campaign, his rebel army was prevailing. By 1954, the main French force was more or less marooned – under relentless artillery and infantry attack – near the north Vietnamese village of Dien Bien Phu.

Imperial Rescue

The Americans felt affronted, not so much that French imperial power was being attacked as that the forces of a NATO ally should be under siege by a communist enemy. It was in response to this unfolding crisis that, on 7 April, President Eisenhower first enunciated what became known as the 'Domino Theory'.

As Foreign Secretary Anthony Eden briefed the British Cabinet – at a couple of meetings held on 27 April 1954, the US Secretary of State Allen Dulles was seriously alarmed. 'It now seemed inevitable', Eden reported, 'that the French garrison at Dien Bien Phu would be overwhelmed or compelled to surrender.'

Mr. Dulles feared that this would be promptly followed by the collapse of all French resistance throughout Indo-China . . .

To avert this, Eden said, his US counterpart favoured 'some dramatic gesture of Anglo-American intervention'. The word 'gesture' is revealing here, as, perhaps, is that of 'resistance', with its echoes of the French underdog's determined refusal finally to bow down to Nazi terror.

But real action was envisaged: not just the deployment of ground forces but squadrons of heavy bombers (perhaps even nuclear-armed) with fighter support, backed by a beefed-up US naval presence in the Gulf of Tonkin. Dulles *had* been thinking of some arm's-length action by the US Air Force, 'but he had now been persuaded that this could not in fact save the garrison there'. While he still wanted air strikes of some sort, he saw this as no more

Above: The French fought ferociously to hold on to their possessions in Southeast Asia.

Below: Ho Chi Minh was the venerable father of Vietnamese independence.

than 'a means of rallying French and Viet Namese morale elsewhere in Indo-China with a view to preventing a general collapse'.

Domino Dread

That collapse would not necessarily be confined to Southeast Asia, it was pointed out. France's power in Africa would also be weakened. And nor was that the only problem:

French morale was undoubtedly at a low ebb. If the garrison at Dien Bien Phu were overwhelmed or compelled to surrender, it was very likely that the French government would fall. It might be succeeded by a neutralist Government.

In other words, the solidity of NATO's stand in Europe was now at stake.

Despite impeccable credentials as a Cold War warrior, Winston Churchill was a son of the British Empire first and foremost. He had his own white-man's-burden take on what a French defeat would mean. 'It would', he maintained,

. . . be greeted throughout Asia as a notable triumph of Communism over capitalism, and of Asians over Europeans.

Likewise, he had his imperialist's version of the 'Domino Theory'. He foresaw the consequences spilling over into 'Siam and Burma and ultimately . . . Malaya'.

CONFLICT IN CONTEXT

Despite the name, it was never just the 'Vietnam War'. The ousting of the French from *Indochine* had allowed the emergence of three separate countries – four, if you count North and South Vietnam (the 'Democratic Republic' and 'Republic' respectively). Yet Communist parties across the region made common cause, fighting together to keep the Americans at bay.

Vive la liberté! Vietnamese soldiers celebrate their freedom from the French.

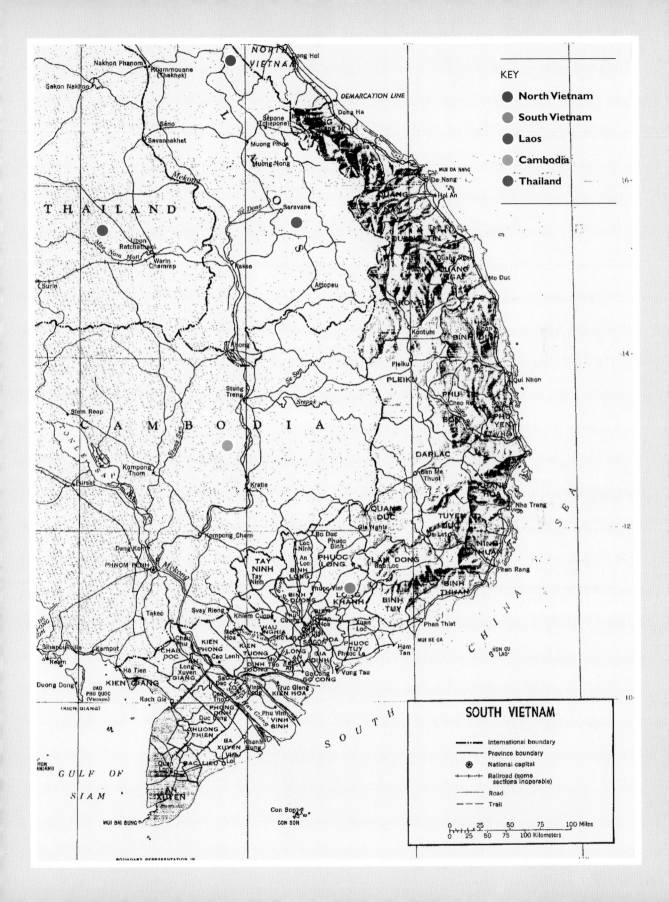

KEY

● North Vietnam
● South Vietnam
● Laos
● Cambodia
● Thailand

SOUTH VIETNAM

International boundary
Province boundary
⊗ National capital
Railroad (some sections inoperable)
Road
Trail

0   25   50   75   100 Miles
0 25 50 75 100 Kilometers

The Vulture Fails to Fly

Yet Britain shrank from what it feared might easily be an open-ended commitment: 'it seemed likely that very substantial forces might be required over a long period.' In conclusion, with some reluctance, the meeting:

Agreed that the United Kingdom Government should not associate themselves with any immediate declaration of intention to afford military assistance to the French in Indo-China . . .

Eisenhower being loath to go it alone, Britain's reluctance proved to be decisive: Operation Vulture was quietly dropped.

Into the Maelstrom

Britain's caution seemed justified. It was to appear so again when, a decade later, Harold Wilson's Labour Government steered clear of any direct involvement with the United States in Vietnam. The US involvement steadily escalated throughout the 1960s, resulting in a quagmire from which it was difficult for America to withdraw. Vietnam has often been referred to as an 'American Tragedy'.

If the Vietnam War was a drama, it was half-'Theatre of Cruelty', half-'Theatre of the Absurd' – and wholly bewildering for the Americans who served. It hardly helped that there were no clear territorial objectives. Signing up to fight for right and freedom, soldiers found themselves drawn into frantic (and largely futile) 'search-and-destroy' operations by a Vietcong enemy who,

blending in with the general populace, seemed simultaneously pervasive and maddeningly elusive. The result was that all-but-existential disorientation summed up so well by the Vietnam veteran and novelist Tim O'Brien in works like *Going After Cacciato* (1978):

They did not know even the simple things: a sense of victory, or satisfaction, or necessary sacrifice. They did not know the feeling of taking a place and keeping it, securing a village and then raising the flag and calling it a victory. No sense of order or momentum. No front, no rear, no trenches laid out in neat parallels. No Patton rushing for the Rhine, no beachheads to storm and win and hold for the duration.

At a Loss

For commanders too, the war seemed obdurately to defy comprehension – to fly in the face of all strategic logic even. If US

TRANSCRIPT OF KEY PARAGRAPHS

CIA MEMORANDUM

The Vietnamese Communist Will To Persist

To direct the execution of their insurgent campaign, the Communists have developed a party apparatus in the South estimated to number around 100,000 members, supported by a somewhat smaller youth auxiliary. The Communists have also probably enrolled around 700,000 people in some component of their front organization, the "National Front for the Liberation of South Vietnam."

[. . .] We estimate that total Communist losses in South Vietnam alone – killed in action, captured, seriously wounded and deserted – ranged from 80,000 to 90,000 during 1965, counting both North and South Vietnamese. We estimate that during 1966 these losses may range from 105,000 to 120,000. We further estimate that the Communists may incur an additional 65,000 to 75,000 losses during the first sixth months of 1967, if current rates of combat are maintained . . .

suggests that our holdings on the numerical strength of these irregulars (now carried at around 110,000) may require drastic upward revision.* To direct the execution of their insurgent campaign, the Communists have developed a party apparatus in the South estimated to number around 100,000 members, supported by a somewhat smaller youth auxiliary.** The Communists have also probably enrolled around 700,000 people in some component of their front organization, the "National Front for the Liberation of South Vietnam." This total apparatus must be controlled, funded and supplied, although most of its requirements may be met from resources within South Vietnam.

6. Casualties the Communists have incurred and are incurring in ever increasing numbers represent another major element of human cost. We estimate that total Communist losses in South Vietnam alone--killed in action, captured, seriously wounded and deserted--ranged from 80,000 to 90,000 during 1965, counting both North and South Vietnamese.*** We estimate that during 1966 these losses may range from 105,000 to 120,000. We further estimate that the Communists may incur an additional 65,000 to 75,000 losses during the first six months of 1967, if current rates of combat are maintained and presently projected troop strengths are achieved.

---

*Details on Communist military forces in South Vietnam are given in Annex IV.

**Around 25,000 party members and somewhere between 15,000 to 20,000 members of the youth auxiliary are thought to be serving in the Communist armed forces. They would be included in the military strength totals already cited. If our estimate of the number of Communist irregulars proves to require upward revision, our estimate of the size of the party apparatus in the South and of its youth auxiliary will also require compensating adjustments. Details on the Communist organization in South Vietnam are given in Annex III.

***See Annex IV.

290 Foreign Relations, 1964–1968, Volume V

of this project is Practice Nine. As you will recall, the initial phase calls for construction of a series of strong points just south of the DMZ extending inland a distance of approximately 30 KM. Secretary McNamara has given the go-ahead for the preliminary work on this portion of the system. Plans for a westward extension using air-dropped mines and sensors are still in a preliminary stage.

2. On March 9 CINCPAC/MACV was given authority to proceed with improvements to the port of Hue which will be receiving most of the Project Nine material and to Route One north of Hue. The next step will be to acquire the necessary right of way for the strong point system and to make arrangements for relocating civilians who will be displaced by the construction work or who will find themselves in the no-man's land between the line of strong points and the Demarcation Line between North and South Viet-Nam. MACV estimates that between 13,000 and 18,000 civilians will have to be relocated.

3. We have queried Saigon about GVN receptivity to this project and about the political, sociological and economic problems which it might create (Tab D).³ Saigon responded to the effect that the Mission saw no major difficulties, provided Washington was convinced that the cost of the project in manpower and matériel was justified (Tab C).⁴

4. DOD has now proposed that we send a Joint State/Defense message to Saigon asking the Embassy to approach the GVN to secure its support in the acquisition of land and the relocation of civilians (Tab A).⁵

5. While we believe the initial 30 KM section of the system will be of limited military value as an anti-infiltration measure (it might have somewhat more utility as an impediment to an overt invasion) we can perceive no political problems associated with it which would justify our interposing an objection. However, it is important to bear in mind that to be fully effective against infiltration the system will

(Ibid.) As a result, in a March 6 memorandum to the JCS, Secretary of Defense McNamara, upon the positive recommendation of Wheeler and despite protests from the service chiefs and Sharp that the diversion of forces and funding for the scheme could not be arranged in the time called for, directed that preparations for the execution of the strong-point obstacle system go forward and that the system be in place by November 1. (Ibid.)
³ None of the tabs is printed. Tab D is telegram 156207 to Saigon, March 16, which informed the Embassy in Saigon that the Department would send it a joint State-Defense message requesting procurement of GVN support for the project.
⁴ Tab C is telegram 20625 from Saigon, March 17, in which Lodge suggested that the GVN approved of the plan and would likely bring it up at the Guam conference.
⁵ Tab A is a draft of telegram 164440 to Saigon which was sent on March 29, a joint State-Defense message directing the Embassy to approach the GVN in regard to Practice Nine. A copy of this telegram as it was transmitted is in the National Archives and Records Administration, RG 59, Central Files 1967–69, POL 27 VIET S.

292 Foreign Relations, 1964–1968, Volume V

2. That you sign a letter to Assistant Secretary McNaughton noting that approval of Phase One of this plan does not constitute approval of the details of subsequent phases of Project Nine (Tab B).⁷

⁷ Tab B is a March 27 letter from Kohler to McNaughton, which informed him that the State Department approved the first phase of the project. As indicated in footnote 1 above, the measure was approved. In memorandum JCSM-204-67 to McNamara, April 17, the Joint Chiefs recommended that full implementation of the barrier concept be delayed until April 1, 1968, but requested that funds be allocated as soon as possible in order to initiate the line's construction and other operational requirements. (Department of Defense, Official Records of the Joint Chiefs of Staff, 911/321 (Jan 67) IR 1160, Sec. 6) In a memorandum to the JCS on April 22, McNamara approved the implementation of measures designed to support the plan. He continued to hold to the November 1 deadline for completion. (Ibid.)

122. Telephone Conversation Between President Johnson and Secretary of State Rusk¹

Washington, March 28, 1967, 4:14 p.m.

President: [Robert Kennedy] is doing it all over Europe, and so on and so forth. So he brought it up himself. He has no business doing it. I told him not to go over there and start explaining Vietnam; talk about others things until they brought it up, [then] he could answer it. But he just did it. I think maybe we ought to send him something from what you said today.² So, I guess that tickers will have it over there. So, you could say that we replied affirmatively, definitely, and positively, and they again said no.

Rusk: I'll get my transcript right over to him.

President: I think that would be good. Now, I see you're going to be on "Today,"³ in the morning. I think that if they ask that question—or they ought to ask it—on did we harden ourselves, I think we ought to say no. We've taken the position that if they want us to stop, they had to be reciprocate [sic] and say, "Now, don't you think this would

¹ Source: Johnson Library, Recordings and Transcripts, Recording of Telephone Conversation Between Johnson and Rusk, March 28, 1967, 4:14 p.m., Tape F67.10, Side A, PNO 2. No classification marking. This transcript was prepared in the Office of the Historian specifically for this volume.
² For Rusk's statement, which was critical of the North Vietnamese leadership for its apparent rejection of the recent peace formula proposed by U Thant, see Department of State Bulletin, April 17, 1967, pp. 618–624.
³ The "Today" show, a morning news program on broadcast television.

---

fortunes were mixed, it wasn't just a matter of good news and bad news. Rather, a top-secret CIA 'Analysis of the Vietnamese Communists Strengths, Capabilities and Will to Persist in Their Present Strategy in Vietnam' (August 1966) seems to suggest, the good news actually was the bad news.

Soaring losses among North Vietnamese Army (NVA) and Vietcong (VC) – estimated by the Americans as having risen from as much as 90,000 killed, wounded or deserted in 1965 to as much as 120,000 in 1966 – didn't seem to be impacting on the communists' ability to wage war. Any more than the heavy bombs dropped on North Vietnam's 'industrial plant', which, the Americans admitted, made 'only the most marginal contribution to Vietnamese Communist military strength' (the country's very backwardness made it a tougher target). Or than the millions of tons of high-explosive expended over the weeks and months of Operation Rolling Thunder, aimed at preventing supplies and matériel from being brought in on foot and by bicycle couriers on the 'Ho Chi Minh Trail' through Laos and Cambodia. Indeed:

Despite the disruptions inflicted, the North Vietnamese transport and logistic system is now functioning more effectively after almost 18 months of bombing than it did when the Rolling Thunder program started.

TRANSCRIPT OF KEY PARAGRAPHS

Telephone conversation between President Johnson and Secretary of State Rusk, 28 March 1967

President Johnson: Robert Kennedy is doing it all over Europe . . . I told him not to go over there and start explaining Vietnam; talk about other things until they brought it up, [then] he could answer it. But he just did it. I think maybe we ought to send him something from what you said today. [Rusk's statement had been critical of the North Vietnamese leadership for its apparent rejection of the peace formula proposed by U Thant.]

President Johnson: [. . .] So, you could say that we replied affirmatively, definitely, and positively, and they again said no.

President Johnson: I see that you're going to be on "Today" [TV news programme] in the morning. I think that if they ask that question . . . on did we harden ourselves, I think we ought to say no. We've taken the position that if they want us to stop, they had to be reciprocate [sic]. .

How to make sense of such a conflict? The pressure was on to find a way of imposing some sort of order on a situation in which chaos and confusion reigned.

Practice Makes Perfect?

It's hard to resist a suspicion that the desire for some such resolution prompted Project Practice 9, a plan whose first feasibility study was ordered by Defense Secretary Robert McNamara in September 1966 and which, on 12 January 1967, was given the 'highest national priority' by President Johnson. It involved the construction of an 'anti-infiltration barrier' across the northern edge of South Vietnam and southern Laos. What Hadrian's Wall had done for Roman England, this fixed frontier would do for Vietnam – help mark out a civilized South from a barbaric (in this case communistic) North.

Like Hadrian's Wall, its significance was going to be as much psychological as strategic, though it would present a formidable barrier to the other side. A series of static bases with ground obstacles in between, it was to be 'air, ground and electronically supported'. In Laos, that meant mobile teams of troops conducting regular reconnaissance in the forests and cutting off would-be infiltrators before they could make their way into South Vietnam. A 500m (1640ft) strip of ground having been cleared by bulldozers, it was going to be sown from the air with 20,000 electronic sensors and many millions of anti-personnel mines.

The human component of the Practice 9 barrier would collectively be codenamed Dye

Robert McNamara was determined to stop the traffic down the 'Ho Chi Minh Trail'.

'We Americans are a do-it-yourself people ... an impatient people ... This trait has been carried over into our foreign policy.'

President Richard Nixon, November 1969

The war provoked protests from an increasingly vociferous 'counterculture' in America itself.

Marker, and their operations on the ground as Prairie Fire. Backing them from above would be a concerted series of air operations. These were to be known as Muscle Shoals.

The McNamara Line
The scheme was outlined in a little more detail in an 'Action Memorandum' of 27 March 1967, from Leonard S. Unger, Deputy Assistant Secretary of State for East Asian and Pacific Affairs to Foy D. Kohler, Deputy Under-Secretary of State for Political Affairs. It described:

. . . a strong point-obstacle system designed to inhibit infiltration into the northern portion of South Viet-Nam. . . The initial phase calls for construction of a series of strong points just south of the DMZ extending inland a distance of approximately 30km [18 miles]. Secretary McNamara has given the go-ahead for the preliminary work on this portion of the system. Plans for a westward extension using air-dropped mines and sensors are still in a preliminary stage.

Work was already under way, wrote Unger, on improvements to the facilities at the port of Hue, and on Route 1 to the north, to ease the large-scale movement of materials and equipment.

The next step will be to acquire the necessary right of way for the strong point system and to make arrangements for relocating civilians who will be displaced by the construction work or who will find themselves in the no-man's land between North and South Viet-Nam. MACV [Military Assistance Command, Vietnam] estimates that between 13,000 and 18,000 civilians will have to be displaced.

The Joint Chiefs of Staff were sceptical: work on the barrier would tie down huge numbers of military engineers (and the troops to guard them). It would also make them sitting targets for the enemy – whose forces would, in any case, only push deeper eastwards into Laos to outflank these frontier defences, extending the scope of a war that had already spilled too far across Southeast Asia.

Frustrated Firepower
It has become a cliché that the US military had to 'fight with one arm tied behind its back' in Vietnam. The claim is at best half-true. An all-out offensive on the ground, whatever it might have done to the enemy, would have exacted more US casualties than could politically be sustained. Sure, the United States could have all but obliterated North Vietnam with its nuclear weapons – but at

Henry Kissinger meets South Vietnamese Premier Nguyen Van Thieu, 1972.

the obvious risk of starting World War III. Even hawks like Henry Kissinger recognized the need for America to walk a tightrope: if this was frustrating for US forces, that was tough.

Who's Breaking Who?
By 1969, however, patience was running out – not least because tolerance on the Home Front was wearing thin. This was the most unpopular war anybody could remember. It hardly helped that there was so little sign that it was being won. Respectable America tried hard to dismiss the youth-protest movement as just another aspect of a hippy counterculture it disdained – and to some extent, for a great deal of the time, it was successful. But the fact that the world's greatest nation was, if not actually being beaten, then persistently failing to win against a no-account crew of Asian peasants, grew ever more

demoralizing as the months went by. 'I refuse to believe that a little fourth-rate power like North Vietnam does not have a breaking point,' said Kissinger. He failed to see, of course, that North Vietnam's *strength* lay in its insignificance; its lack of development (or anything much to lose in the way of infrastructure).

'Great Consequence and Force'
That July, then, an ultimatum was given by President Richard Nixon to Ho Chi Minh: America wanted a 'just peace', but not at any price. Nor would it wait indefinitely: if no substantial progress had been made by 1 November, Nixon wrote, he would have no choice but to resort to 'measures of great consequence and force'. But what were those 'measures' to be exactly? Deliberately left vague in the message to the North Vietnamese leader, the answer was unclear to the Americans

TOP SECRET/SENSITIVE

PRELIMINARY ASSESSMENT

INTRODUCTION

The two essential elements of the military concept are

-- a mining operation sufficient to seal off the sea approaches to North Vietnam and thus NVN's supply of waterborne imports,

-- collateral bombing designed to destroy or damage supplies, industrial capacity, and critical parts of the transportation system, thereby intensifying the economic strains brought about by the mining.

A detailed assessment of this concept involves analyzing

-- their capabilities to counter the effects of the mining and bombing,

-- required actions on our part -- e.g. reseeding the minefields, destroying lighters, cutting rail lines and highways -- to prevent their countermeasures from being successful.*

A rough preliminary assessment is as follows:*

NVN Countermeasures and Our Responses

General. North Vietnam has stockpiles of food, industrial supplies, and petroleum sufficient to last several months. Upwards of 30-40% of their petroleum stocks, 50,000 tons or so of imported supplies, and perhaps 1000 trucks could be vulnerable to our initial attacks. Nevertheless, remaining stocks are largely dispersed and difficult to destroy by bombing. These stocks can sustain NVN for a few months.

Countering the Mining. North Vietnam would attempt to counter the effects of the mining in three ways:

-- sweeping or otherwise breaching the minefields,

-- rerouting imports through rail and highway approaches from China,

-- airlift from or through China.

_____
* The concept assumes that we surprise North Vietnam and that bad weather will not force major changes in the military plan. Later we will analyze what we do if these assumptions prove false.

themselves: indeed, within the administration, it was a matter of furious debate.

What *does* seem to have been agreed is spelled out in a memo, dated 2 October, to the President from Henry Kissinger, in his capacity as President's Assistant for National Security Affairs. Kissinger envisaged

. . . a series of short, sharp military blows against North Vietnam designed to bring them to serious negotiations and an honorable settlement.

Operation Duck Hook was to be a massive air offensive, aimed at the very heart of North Vietnam. A 'Preliminary Assessment' clearly sets out US thinking. Earlier attempts to confine attacks to 'targets directly related to Hanoi's capacity to support the war in the south' had proven insufficient: now it had been concluded that 'hitting targets of more general strategic importance would be more effective'. The Americans would take the war to the North

TRANSCRIPT OF KEY PARAGRAPHS

<u>US National Security Council Documents relating to Operation Duck Hook, 1969</u>

(Left) The two essential elements of the military concept are:
– a mining operation sufficient to seal off the sea approaches to North Vietnam and thus NVN's supply of waterborne imports
– collateral bombing designed to destroy or damage supplies, industrial capacity, and critical parts of the transportation system, thereby intensifying the economic strains brought about by the mining.

(Right) <u>NVN Counter-measures and Our Responses</u>
North Vietnam, even with Chinese help, probably cannot sweep the minefields in a way which allows large ships to continue to dock. She can attempt to unload ships beyond the minefields into barges and other small craft . . .

It is more likely that North Vietnam will seek to have imports rerouted through China.

TOP SECRET/SENSITIVE

North Vietnam, even with Chinese or Russian help probably cannot sweep the minefields in a way which allows large ships to continue to dock. She can attempt to unload ships beyond the minefields into barges and other small craft and sweep the fields well enough to allow cargo to move ashore this way.

If they try this, we can easily lay more mines. We can also attack and attempt to destroy the barges and lighters with naval gunfire and tactical aircraft.

It is more likely that North Vietnam will seek to have imports rerouted through China.

-- Ships with goods bound for North Vietnam could unload in Chan-chiang, 560 miles from Hanoi by direct rail line, or Canton, which is much further by rail from Hanoi; (see attached map)

-- China herself could supply petroleum, food and some other supplies to North Vietnam by rail or highway.

The general strain on Chinese supplies and transportation capability would not be great because North Vietnam's requirements [for 16 million people] are relatively small. There will be local strains, however, and it will take time (we are analyzing how long) to assemble rail cars and divert supplies from their normal routes.

Our response to a major overland operation to supply North Vietnam could be to attack repeatedly the rail lines, marshalling yards, sidings, bridges and highways from China in an attempt to stop the supply flow. We could also bomb supply concentrations.

We should be more effective in this than we were when bombing North Vietnam before; we can concentrate our efforts instead of bombing targets all over North Vietnam. We still will not have complete success, however. Weather, darkness and the difficulty of policing the long border with China will provide opportunities for some supplies to get through.

Vietnamese by mounting heavy raids on the capital, Hanoi. At the same time as disrupting their war effort, they would also send a signal of defiance to the country's communist allies by undertaking (against specific Soviet warnings) the mining of Haiphong Harbour.

Nuclear or Not?

Would these 'short, sharp military blows' against North Vietnam include atomic explosions? US nuclear capability was at once a temptation and a taboo. While it offered (or appeared to offer) freedom from an impossible situation, the political costs – both internationally and domestically – might be immense. Nor was this the only matter to be resolved: the ruminations recorded by Kissinger's staff in a list of 'Important Questions' raise several others. This, though, was the crucial one.

The Americans' dilemma was summed up by staffers Tony Lake and Roger Morris, commenting on a draft plan by Captain Rembrandt C. Robinson. (The latter, as adviser to the Chairman of the Joint Chiefs of Staff, had been in charge of plans for Operation Duck Hook.) The President, Lake and Morris had argued, would have to accept 'two operational concepts'. The first was that

. . . the action must be brutal and sustainable. Brutal, because of the proven tenacity of NVN in the face of actions which did not strike at their existence in society. Sustainable because we must assume that even in this extreme case they will be evasive and rely

TRANSCRIPT OF KEY PARAGRAPHS

<u>White House Memorandum, 29 September 1969</u>

We think the basic memorandum to the President should be extensively reworked . . . Our criticisms in summary are:
- There is no analysis, beyond an assertion of "reasonable expectation", of the predictable results of the action.
- There is no adequate treatment of [. . .] how we would respond to a favorable reaction from NVN.

In our view, the study must assume that the President has decided:
- That NVN has judged our present policy untenable and was therefore settling in for a slow but sure victory, notwithstanding a decrease in infiltration, etc . . .

ORANDUM

THE WHITE HOUSE
WASHINGTON

TOP SECRET/SENSITIVE   September 29, 1969

MEMORANDUM FOR CAPTAIN ROBINSON

FROM: Tony Lake and Roger Morris

SUBJECT: Draft Memorandum to the President on Contingency Study

We think the basic memorandum to the President should be extensively re-worked, both as a matter of general concept and specific points. It does not adequately lay out the questions to be asked and alternative answers, but rather makes a number of assumptions. The contingency group should not be arguing at this point for or against the decision. As we understand it, our job is to present clearly and fully all the implications of the action, <u>should</u> the President decide to do it.

Our criticisms in summary are:

-- The present draft offers only one package of actions. It should present alternative military programs for achieving the objective.

-- There is no analysis, beyond an assertion of "reasonable expectation", of the predictable results of the action.

-- There is an adequate treatment of possible reactions by others, but no clear presentation of the probability of those reactions or of what we might do in each case.

-- There is no adequate treatment of our specific diplomatic objective, how we would measure success, or how we would respond to a favorable reaction from NVN.

In our view, the study must assume that the President has decided:

-- That NVN had judged our present policy untenable and was therefore settling in for a slow but sure victory, notwithstanding a decrease in infiltration, etc. and,

TOP SECRET/SENSITIVE

on pressures in this country to deflect our action . . .

The second:

that the action would be self-contained. The President would have to decide beforehand . . . how far we will go. He cannot, for example, confront the issue of using tactical nuclear weapons in the midst of the exercise. He must be prepared to play out whatever string necessary in this case.

Some of their wording reappeared in the memo Kissinger sent to Nixon a few days later. The need for brutality was underlined (quite literally: 'the action must be brutal') and the assistants' distinctive figure of speech was also echoed.

To attempt this course and to fail would be a catastrophe . . . we must be prepared to play out whatever string necessary.

Offering an Out

But Kissinger's idea of brutality stopped short of nuclear attack. Hawk though he was, he had his eye on the diplomatic tightrope which he felt America had to walk. It was vital, he warned, in another memo to the President,

. . . to convey to Hanoi and others that our goal is not the total destruction of the country or the regime, which would invite major outside intervention . . .

Thus, to present the Soviets and Chinese with actions too limited to justify a military confrontation with us, yet effective and firm enough to forestall circumvention and promote their eventual influence on Hanoi to compromise.

Duck Hook Ducked

In a speech a few weeks later, on 3 November, famous for its appeal to the 'silent majority' of Americans, Nixon tried to sell his Duck Hook strategy as a final push towards a successful conclusion to the war. In the end, however, it was overtaken by events: Nixon and Kissinger had already outmanoeuvred themselves, having opened up a secret front in Cambodia earlier that same year. While the ousting of the neutral Laotian Prince Sihanouk by pro-US General Lon Nol was a coup for the Americans, it also brought the North Vietnamese into the war and boosted support for the communist Khmer Rouge. The conflict was now spiralling out of control.

As Cambodia's political climate worsened, the neutral posture adopted by Prince Sihanouk became unsustainable.

'To attempt this course and fail would be a catastrophe . . .'

Henry Kissinger, on Operation Duck Hook, 1969

Laos

If only the 'Vietnam War' could have been confined to Vietnam. But the conflict was a tangled web, and America tied itself up in knots in its efforts to shape the outcome.

In Joan Didion's 1996 novel *The Last Thing He Wanted*, the reporter-protagonist muses on a sort of story she feels she's read over and over, in one form or another, down the years. It is, we're told,

> . . . *the kind of two-inch wire story that has to do with chartered aircraft of uncertain ownership that did or did not leave one or another Southern airport loaded with one or another kind of cargo.*

It's true: the same essential narrative kept cropping up during the 1980s, the era of Iran–Contra, at the time when Didion's character was cutting her journalistic teeth, and mysterious shipments were flying back and forth between the United States and Central and South America. But the same kind of story might as easily have been told – had the US press been less ingenuous, less trusting – decades before, at the very start of the 1960s. Then, though, it was Southeast Asia that was in the secret spotlight.

Sidling into Southeast Asia

The United States had for some years been sidling gradually deeper into the Vietnam War – just a few advisers to begin with, and lots of aid for Saigon strongman General Ngo Dinh Diem. The Kennedy administration stepped up assistance markedly: though the first combat troops were still not to be sent for a few years yet, the United States was doing everything it could behind the scenes.

Already, there was unease: Diem was an unappealing figure (a murderous tyrant, it might even be said), though Vice-President Johnson felt obliged to acclaim him as the 'Winston Churchill of Southeast Asia'. There were questions too, even at this early stage, about the extent to which the developing conflict could be contained. French *Indochine* had included Laos and Cambodia as well as Vietnam, and – whatever their rulers did, it seemed – communist cross-contamination between all three. For America, the region was a row of dominoes, ready to collapse one into another: the problem was, how to prevent this without openly intervening.

A Princely Prize

Laos was easily overlooked, but as a 1959 CIA report pointed out, this 'primitive and remote country' was now 'a highly-prized piece of real estate':

Laos's Prince Souphanouvong was a disciple of Ho Chi Minh.

TRANSCRIPT OF KEY PARAGRAPHS

CIA Geographic Intelligence Memorandum. September 1959

The Kingdom of Laos, a primitive and remote country, today constitutes a highly prized piece of real estate. [. . .]

Terrain

. . . The main Annam [mountain chain] range and its outliers . . . comprise imposing obstacles to east-west traffic. Since the stream divide is near the eastern edge of the range, eastward-draining valleys are short, narrow, and steep.

The westward-draining valleys within the Mekong watershed have gentler slopes and are more open. Consequently, military movement across the mountains is easier from west to east than in the opposite direction.

Effect on Military Operations

Factors of military geography suggest that guerilla tactics will, to a large extent, characterize the pattern of military operations in Laos – particularly during the rainy season.

SECRET

Introduction

The Kingdom of Laos, a primitive and remote country, today constitutes a highly prized piece of real estate. The strategic importance of the country derives from its location -- bordering on Communist China and North Vietnam on the north and east, and having common borders with non-Communist Burma, Thailand, Cambodia, and South Vietnam. Should Laos fall to the Communist Bloc, the limits of Communist-controlled territory would be brought into direct contact with Thailand and Cambodia and would be extended to the western flank of South Vietnam. Whatever the outcome of the current situation, the same natural and cultural factors that have established the character of the current military operations will profoundly handicap the future achievement of economic and political stability in Laos.

Terrain

The terrain of Laos is predominantly rugged and mountainous with relatively level areas restricted to a few plateaus and the river plains. Northern Laos, the area north of Vientiane, consists of parts of what traditionally have been known as the West Tonkin Highland and the West Laos Highland, the boundary between them being the divide between the Mekong drainage system on the west and the drainage systems of streams flowing eastward to the Gulf of Tonkin. The province of Sam Neua (more properly called Houa Phan) lies largely within the West Tonkin Highland. Here the predominant trend of the major mountains and valleys is northwest-southeast, and egress from the eastern ends of the valleys is toward the Vietnam coast. In the West Laos Highland the major trend is north-south. In both areas, many of the mountains are steep sided, commonly reaching elevations of 3,000 to 6,000 feet and occasionally more than 8,000 feet. The intervening valleys are narrow, in many cases almost impassable gorges. Secondary ridges and valleys that branch off the main features have created an intricate network of spurs and valleys that makes movement, even on foot, very difficult. Locally, small plateaus, mainly of limestone, are bounded by precipitous scarps.

South of these northern highlands and extending in a northwest-southeast direction to the southern border of Laos is the mountainous belt known as the Annam Chain. Elevations of 8,000 feet are numerous near the northern limits; but, in the latitude of Savannakhet, only a few peaks exceed 4,000 feet. Immediately to the south, in the eastward extensions of the range, elevations again increase and some peaks exceed 8,000 feet. The main Annam range and its outliers -- such as the rugged limestone areas northeast of Thakhek -- comprise imposing obstacles to east-west traffic. Since the stream divide is near the eastern edge of the range, eastward-draining valleys are short, narrow, and steep. The westward-draining valleys within the Mekong watershed have gentler slopes and are more open. Consequently, military movement across the mountains is easier from west to east than in the opposite direction.

The chief areas of relatively level surface in Laos are found on two plateaus -- Tran Ninh and Bolovens -- and in plains areas along the Mekong River. To the southeast of Luang Prabang, roughly centered on Xieng Khouang, is the rectangular-shaped Plateau du Tran Ninh, which has been compared to a high fortification surrounded by many lines of ramparts and moats. Its military importance lies in its extensive areas of level land, which provide sites for air bases, in the midst of very rugged mountains. The plateau, at an elevation of about 3,700 feet, is made up of 3 plains separated by hills, the largest being the Plaine des Jarres. The Plateau des Bolovens is east of Pakse, has an undulating surface and an elevation of about 4,000 feet. Currently (1959), a jeep trail is being bulldozed from Dak To in South Vietnam to Attopeu in Laos which will connect with the route from Pakse that crosses the Plateau des Bolovens.

Of the river plains the most important are those centered on Savannakhet and on the capital city of Vientiane. The Savannakhet plain, an area of undulating surface between the Mekong and the Annam Chain is approximately 100 miles long by 80 miles wide. It is the site of the large military air base of Seno. The strategic route between Mukdahan, Northeast Thailand, and Quang Tri, South Vietnam, crosses the Savannakhet Plain. The plain centered on Vientiane, some 70 miles long from north to south and 20 to 40 miles wide, is almost flat, but it is largely swamp and marsh covered. The rail line from Bangkok terminates at Nong Khai, Thailand, across the river from the Vientiane area.

Climate

Laos has a monsoonal climate with pronounced wet and dry seasons and relatively uniform temperatures ranging from moderate to high. The mean annual temperature in Luang Prabang, at about 1,000 feet elevation, is 78°F. In January, freezing temperatures may occur at high elevations; and uncomfortably cold nights may be experienced at medium elevations not only in January but also during the rainy

---

The strategic importance of the country derives from its location – bordering on Communist China and North Vietnam on the north and east, and having common borders with non-Communist Burma, Thailand, Cambodia, and South Vietnam. Should Laos fall to the Communist Bloc, the limits of Communist-controlled territory would be brought into contact with Thailand and Cambodia and would be extended to the western flank of South Vietnam.

The country defied all the obvious conventions. Even under French colonial rule, it had remained a monarchy. And where else would a prince be proud to be numbered among the communist

President Kennedy defends a now-considerable political investment in the affairs of Laos.

leadership? But the 'Red Prince' Souphanouvong was only one of the players in a fast-moving game of power politics in which alliances were formed and dissolved, and loyalties shifted, with dizzying speed.

Laosed Up

By the beginning of 1960, however, it was possible to identify the broad outlines of a struggle between the Royalist Forces Armées de Laos (FAL) and the Pathet Lao. This group wasn't just communist: it was strongly linked to the Vietnamese, and backed by North Vietnam's Soviet sponsors too. The 'Neutralist' forces of Kong Le had joined it in coalition, leaving the FAL substantially outnumbered and outgunned.

The Pathet Lao Puzzle

The enemy's motives were puzzling, CIA analysts admitted in February 1961. 'Bloc support' for the Pathet Lao

. . . appears to be in excess of the present needs of the PL–Kong Le forces . . . Also, we believe that the PL forces have a somewhat greater capability than they have yet chosen to exercise.

It wasn't that the Pathet Lao were sweeping all before them: there was something of a stalemate. Yet,

. . . the PL do not have to maintain their military effort at a very high level to serve Communist aims in Laos.

'Longer range trends', they concluded, were 'toward the Communists'. In the event, they didn't have to wait for the longer

range. Within weeks, the Pathet Lao were advancing across the Plain of Jarres.

Mill Pond

President Kennedy called for a plan on 9 March; Project Mill Pond was promptly hatched. It was officially approved on 21 March.

The idea was that B-26 Invader bombers should be brought in to support a FAL fightback: if the Pathet Lao had Soviet help, why shouldn't the Royalists have American assistance, albeit secret? The decision was taken, therefore, that these elderly planes – veterans of Korea and, in some cases, World War II – should have their identifying insignia removed and be 'sanitized' from USAF inventory records. Some 16 were brought from US base Camp Chenen, Okinawa, Japan and Akena Air Base in the Philippines and then flown to Takhli in northern Thailand.

Eighteen Air Force pilots were brought in. They too had to be 'sanitized' or 'sheepdipped': they went through the whole rigmarole of (officially) leaving the Air Force and were given completely new identities (so there would be absolutely no record of them if they were captured or killed). Flown to Thailand, they were sent up-country to Takhli with papers identifying them as employees of an enterprise called Bangkok Contract Air Services. All this time, it seems, their flight logs were being meticulously updated – but for flights with the Air Force Reserve back at Andrews, in the United States.

Bay of Pigs' Ear

On 16 April, they were fully briefed, their planes all loaded and fuelled-up for their first bombing raid on the Pathet Lao positions in Laos when – without warning, and at the very last moment – the cancellation came. Another wave of B-26s had been in action on the other side of the world, mounting diversionary attacks in preparation for an invasion of Cuba that, though it had barely begun, was already obviously ending badly. Kennedy, unnerved, called a halt to Operation Mill Pond. The Pathet Lao were to remain a thorn in America's side; Laos a contested piece of 'real estate' – and a vital supply-conduit for the Viet Cong.

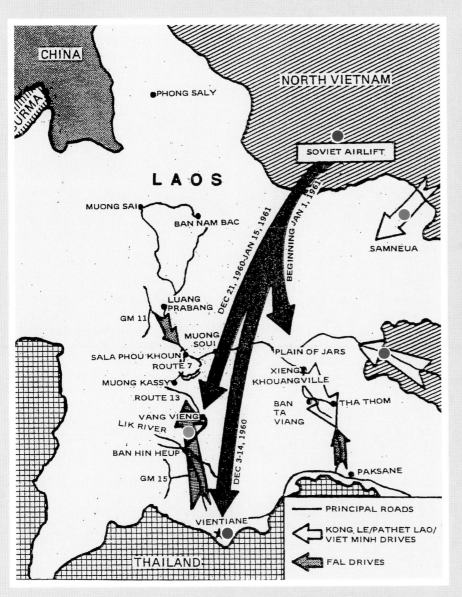

THE FAL AT BAY

Northern Laos was becoming a battlefield with a combined force of communist and 'neutral' guerrillas converging from the north and east. The communists were themselves a coalition, including native Pathet Lao, North Vietnamese regular troops and South Vietnamese Viet Cong guerrillas – all backed by a Soviet airlift from North Vietnam. Supplied by the West through Thailand, the Royalist Forces Armées de Laos (FAL) fought back, but ultimately to no avail.

KEY

- 🔴 Soviet airlift
- 🔴 Main advance of NVA
- 🔴 VietCong forces from South Vietnam
- 🟠 Main northward drive by FAL capital
- ⚫ Vientiane, Laotian capital

Bartering Bodies

Swap your spy for our revolutionary . . . ? That's the offer the communists made to the Western democracies in the case of Edgar Sanders and Lee Meng. Both the United States and Britain took it extremely seriously.

With Japan's defeat in 1945 and the old colonial powers too remote – and too war-weary – to intervene effectively, the region was now up for grabs. In Indonesia, the Dutch were ousted; in Indochina, France now fought vainly to re-establish its hold; and in Malaya, Marxist guerrillas began a war of liberation.

Against the Western Way
Communism had been quick to exploit the will to independence. And Marxism-Leninism (and Soviet assistance) were not without their appeal. Why would Asian freedom-fighters sign up to the economic approach that had inspired and underpinned the colonialist project, or embrace a democratic system that had brought oppression to the East? Britain's handling of its 'Malayan Emergency' from 1948 was a brutal case in point: half a million people were forcibly relocated; thousands of suspected guerrillas (and civilians) killed.

Trial and Trade
In 1952, a young Malay-Chinese guerrilla, Lee Meng, was captured.

A British court sentenced her to death for the possession of a hand-grenade. Before her sentence could be carried out, however, the British 'businessman' (and former intelligence officer) Edgar Sanders was arrested in Budapest and convicted of spying. The Hungarians then made an astonishing suggestion: to trade Sanders for Lee Meng.

Did the Hungarians seriously regard Sanders as a spy (though it is true that he had pleaded guilty), or was he nothing more than a counter with which to bargain? In a memo dated 23 February, Britain's Foreign Secretary, Anthony Eden, showed himself flabbergasted at the businesslike aplomb with which the request was made:

115

(THIS DOCUMENT IS THE PROPERTY OF HER BRITANNIC MAJESTY'S GOVERNMENT)

SECRET   COPY NO. 70

C.(53) 75

25TH FEBRUARY, 1953

CABINET

SANDERS/LEE MENG EXCHANGE

Memorandum by the Secretary of State for Foreign Affairs

I have given further thought to this tragic problem.

We have no further sanctions that we can impose upon Hungary. We have stopped all trade. Hungary has no Consulates to close. We have restricted the movements of their diplomats and we shall gain nothing by closing their Legation.

2. The Hungarians might be willing to release Sanders in exchange for important concessions in the way of delivery of essential raw materials, e.g. they have hinted that they might do something for 5,000 tons of copper together with supplies of other strategic materials. I do not think that we can contemplate any deal of this kind. We could not allow strategic raw materials to pass behind the iron curtain, even to save a man's life.

3. There remains only the possibility of this exchange. As it seems to me, it could be viewed as an exchange of prisoners in the cold war. There is a risk that the Hungarians might arrest other British subjects, but I do not rate it high now. The numbers of British subjects in Hungary have been greatly reduced and travel behind the iron curtain, except by Communist sympathisers, is rare. There is always of course a certain danger to junior members of our own Legation staff, but to arrest one of them would be another category of offence.

4. I am however concerned about the position of our businessmen in China, and before finally advising the Cabinet again in the matter I would like to consult Mr. Lamb, our representative in Peking. I am doing this and will submit a further paper to the Cabinet when I have his reply.

A.E.

Foreign Office, S.W.1.

25TH FEBRUARY, 1953.

TRANSCRIPT OF KEY PARAGRAPHS

<u>Memorandum by the British Secretary of State for Foreign Affairs, 25 February 1953</u>

I have given further thought to this tragic problem. We have no further sanctions that we can impose on Hungary. We have stopped all trade. Hungary has no Consulates to close. We have restricted the movements of their diplomats and we shall gain nothing by closing their Legation.

[. . .] There is a risk that the Hungarians might arrest other British subjects, but I do not rate it high now. The number of British subjects in Hungary have been greatly reduced and travel behind the iron curtain, except by Communist sympathisers, is rare. There is always of course a certain danger to junior members of our own Legation staff, but to arrest one of them would be another category of offence.

I am however concerned about the position of our businessmen in China . . .

Edgar Sanders (left) returning to Britain on his release by the Soviets for spying in 1953.

The Hungarians might be willing to release Sanders in exchange for important concessions in the way of delivery of essential raw materials, e.g. they have hinted they might do something for 5,000 tons of copper together with supplies of other strategic materials.

He wasn't persuaded:

We could not allow strategic materials to pass behind the iron curtain, even to save a man's life.

Oddly, it might be thought, he considered that the freeing of a convicted terrorist represented less of a problem:

There remains only the possibility of this exchange . . . it could be viewed as an exchange of prisoners in the cold war.

A Cynical System

As *Time* magazine observed, the episode underlined the extent to which world communism spoke – and negotiated – with a single voice:

Rarely has Russian diplomacy so blatantly acknowledged its real control over Communists everywhere. The barter proposal showed how fast, when the Reds want to make a deal, they cynically drop the pretense of a rebel band of local 'patriots' fighting 'colonialism' in Malaya, or of a 'People's Republic' having a genuine sovereignty in Hungary.

No Deal

Despite Eden's inclinations to reach agreement, his Prime Minister was having none of it: on 15 March, Churchill announced that his Government had resolved that no deal would be done. Lee Meng's sentence was commuted on representations from the Malaysian Federation (Malaya's British-backed 'official' government). A decade later, Lee Meng was released, handed over to the People's Republic of China. What inducements, if any, were offered, is unknown.

Chapter Seven

Mobilizing Science

Necessity was the mother of some extraordinarily off-the-wall Cold War inventions and technical ingenuity was taxed to the utmost on both sides.

For much of the twentieth century, a better future was an article of faith. Between the rampant confidence of capitalism and the utopian promises of socialism, all agreed that technological development was going to guarantee continuous 'progress' in every area of life.

This included the dealing of death. Technology had always played its part in warfare, from the first flint blade to the machine gun. But in the Cold War, the scientific stakes seemed so much higher. The single greatest force in modern military technology, nuclear fission, was still mysterious to the uninitiated, as were the complexities of delivery. The chemistry of rocket fuels, the aerodynamics of missile-design, the development of navigation systems: these involved knowledge and understanding drawn from the forefront of modern science. So too did nuclear submarines lurking in the ocean's depths for months on end and planes that could fly at several times the speed of sound.

President Kennedy signs the 1963 Test Ban treaty on behalf of the United States. Supporters in the White House look on warily.

Carrier Grudge

The heavy bomber became the vehicle of choice for the US nuclear deterrent in the 1950s – but not before other options had been mooted and early difficulties ironed out.

Louis A. Johnson had served with distinction as a soldier before being appointed by Franklin D. Roosevelt in 1937 as Assistant Secretary of War. It was also with Roosevelt's approval that, in 1943, Johnson was appointed to the board of one of America's biggest aviation suppliers, Consolidated Vultee Aircraft Corporation, or 'Convair'.

Although Eisenhower had yet to coin the term, hindsight sees Johnson as the 'military–industrial complex' personified. Naturally enough, the Army and the Air Force were happy when, in March 1949, President Harry S. Truman made Johnson his Defense Secretary. The Navy,

however, was more wary. Johnson's predecessor, James Forrestal, had been very much the Navy's man – a former Navy flier, he had actually opposed the creation of a separate and independent USAF in 1947.

Forrestal's Fleet

The US Navy had 'had a good war', making the difference in the Pacific in particular. And it could look forward to the peace with confidence too – especially because it was already understood that this would be no ordinary peace: the Cold War would bring an arms build-up on an unprecedented scale. And, in Forrestal's vision, the Navy was going to be in the forefront, the spearhead for America's nuclear capability. The first of a new type of vast and state-of-the-science 'super carrier' was already being built. Weighing in at 58,976 tonnes (65,000 tons), the flush-decked

James Forrestal – a former navy flier.

vessel was designed to carry, not the usual fighters and fighter-bombers, but full-sized strategic bombers – if necessary, nuclear-armed. The USS *United States* was to be followed by four further 'super carriers' from which nuclear attacks might be mounted anywhere in the world.

There were celebrations when, on 18 April 1949, the *United States'* keel was completed, but these were to some extent overshadowed by the suicide of a burned-out James Forrestal a few weeks before. And if its mood was sombre now, the Navy was to be hurled into shock and outrage five days later when abruptly, in one of his first decisions as Defense Secretary, Johnson called the whole 'super carrier' programme to a halt.

Secretary of Defense Louis A. Johnson was closely identified with the Air Force – and the aviation industry.

Why the cancellation? Cost-cutting came into the decision: the *United States* was going to come in at $190m, but this figure was massively misleading, given that she wasn't going to be able to go to sea without a supporting task force of 32 further, specially commissioned ships. The overall cost, accordingly, was therefore more likely to be in the region of $1.25 *billion*.

Sunk by the SAC?

But few believed this was the sole or even the primary reason, given the impetus that it gave the Strategic Air Command (SAC). Certainly not the naval chiefs, who soon made their disgust apparent in what became known as the 'Revolt of the Admirals'. In the event, by the end of the 1950s, the advent

Below left: The *United States'* keel had already been laid when the order came for her cancellation.

Below right: The 'super carrier' was to be a fully nuclear-capable floating air force base.

of the nuclear submarine would go much of the way towards restoring the initiative to the Navy, while the appearance of bigger, better intercontinental ballistic missiles (ICBMs) had weakened the hold of the SAC. For the moment, though, the Navy felt bitterly betrayed.

From Super Carrier to Super Bomber

No super carriers? No problem . . . Johnson's friends at Convair would see America right. Indeed, they had just the plane – a bomber awe inspiring in both scale and range. The B-36 'Peacemaker' was a formidable beast by any standards: powered by six 28-cylinder engines, with a wingspan of 70m (230ft), it could carry a payload of over 27 tonnes (30 tons). Flown by a crew of 15, it had a range of over 9656km (6000 miles), so could take the Atlantic Ocean in its stride. Its development had begun in 1941, when it seemed all too possible that the United Kingdom would be taken by the Nazis and America left without a base to continue the war in Europe.

Not So Super?

By the time it entered service in 1948, America's strategic needs had changed – the B-36 wasn't quite what was required. Impressive as its range was, it couldn't cope with the round-trip to Russia. (The good news, in this regard, was that Britain had not been 'lost to the enemy', after all, and that the US also had the use of bases in Franco's Spain. The bad news was that the first prototype of the B-36 had such heavy landing-gear that only three airfields had runways strong enough to receive it – and all of those were in the United States.)

With a cruising speed of only 346km/h (215mph), the B-36 wasn't exactly sprightly (it was a 'lumbering cow', according to its critics), but since its engines could call on supplementary jet-power for brief bursts of speed, it could achieve 560km/h (350mph) in short spurts when needed. It could also climb to 11,580m (38,000 feet), and cruise quite comfortably at 9144m (30,000ft) – above both the range of the jet

Forrestal's death spelled the end for the whole super carrier project.

fighters of the day and of ground-based anti-aircraft batteries.

War of Words
But the B-36 was under fire; even before it came into service in 1948, it had been branded 'obsolete and unsuccessful', a 'billion-dollar blunder'. There were suggestions that its commissioning had been corrupt. It was, of course, no coincidence that these criticisms came from opinion-formers close to the US Navy, who saw the B-36 as usurping the 'super carrier' fleet of which it had had such high hopes.

The Air Force returned fire – and then some. The 'super-carrier' would be nothing but a big and cumbersome white-elephant. Useless against the Soviets, its construction would have been nothing more than an ego trip for the Navy chiefs. Altogether, this was a most unseemly squabble: it

was easy to forget that these services were on the same side in what was supposed to be a Cold War against the Soviets.

The only answer seemed to be for the B-36 to silence its critics, and the obvious way for it to do that was to extend its range. And the obvious way for it to do *that*, given the limitations of all existing or as yet imaginable jet engines, was for it to be driven by nuclear power.

A Nuclear Plane
Research into the potential for nuclear-powered planes had, in fact, already been taking place for some time – ever since the inauguration, in May 1946, of the Nuclear Energy for the Propulsion of Aircraft (NEPA).

As with nuclear weapons, so too with other aspects of nuclear technology: once the initial fascination with the sheer

enormity of the untrammelled atomic chain reaction had worn off, interest quickly focused on ways in which it might be managed on a smaller scale – not just in military but civilian applications. Some of these now seem completely normal: the nuclear submarine is the obvious example. But others sound hopelessly far-fetched: suggested – in all seriousness – in 1958, the Ford Nucleon was to be a nuclear-powered family car.

Eternally Airborne
By these standards, the Convair X-6 sounds like a sober, sensible development. Based on the B-36, it was to be a nuclear-powered jet. Rather than running on (readily exhaustible) liquid fuel, its General Electric J47 turbojet engines were to be driven by a 3-megawatt nuclear reactor. Air taken in at the front would be superheated. Instantly expanding – yet at the same time compressed by the engine's spinning turbofans – it would escape behind with explosive force, propelling the plane at up to 640km/h (400mph) – and for just about any distance. In principle, there was nothing to prevent a plane like this remaining airborne for weeks on end.

Radiation Woes
Too good to be true? Well, yes. In the first place, how was the radiation from the reactor to be contained? Even for an age as insouciant as this about the dangers of atomic energy, the difficulty just couldn't be ignored. After all, one key advantage of the

A giant of the skies, the B-36 had backward-mounted engines.

'The Air Force can do anything the Navy can do nowadays, so that does away with the Navy.'

Defense Secretary Louis A. Johnson, 1949

atomic plane was supposed to be its ability to patrol for extended periods. What of those on board, soaking up radiation all that time? This worry went beyond humanitarianism: aircrews' skills and experience were precious and hard-won; a rapid turnover could not be sustained.

Some precautions were taken. In the prototype X-6, the reactor was placed as far back as possible – the aft bomb-bay was adapted to this purpose. A shield of lead and rubber kept the cockpit from the worst of the radiation, even if much escaped from underneath the reactor and on either side.

Issues of Weight

Full protection would not have been practical given the weight involved. The shield weighed 10.8 tonnes (12 tons); anything more substantial and there'd have been no way of carrying bombs.

And it wasn't just the radiation: while it 'cooked' the air coming into the engines, the reactor also raised the general temperature – potentially by thousands of degrees. Factor in the need for concrete insulation, miles of piping for coolant (or both) and you were looking at a craft that would be doing very well to take off at all.

Faced with such technical challenges, the whole X-6 project struggled to get itself off the ground. It was cancelled in 1958. Even so, the potential benefits of nuclear-powered flight were such that it remained something of a holy grail for the US defence establishment: research went on into the early 1960s.

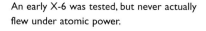

An early X-6 was tested, but never actually flew under atomic power.

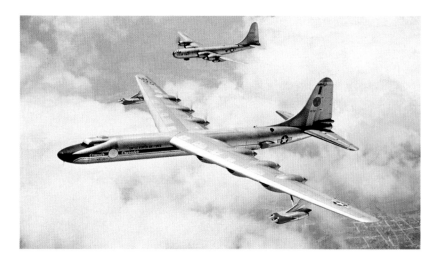

Shooting for the Moon

As if global confrontation wasn't enough, the superpowers had started to look beyond the earth, to space – and so the 'final frontier' became a new front in the Cold War.

'Mr President,' blurts the panicked White House aide, 'the Russians are up there right now, painting the moon red!' 'Then get a rocket up there with some white paint, and write "Coca-Cola on it"', comes the calm reply . . . The Cold War-era joke acknowledges what the political establishments on either side weren't quite so ready to: that the 'Space Race' was about bragging rights and branding. Neither superpower was comfortable with the idea of being behind in the eyes of the watching world – whether in science, technology, enterprise or vision. Neither wanted its ideological outlook or economic system shown up as second best.

Unfortunately for the United States, that was very much the way it was beginning to look after 4 October 1957, when the Soviets successfully launched the first-ever artificial satellite, Sputnik 1. And it got worse when, within a month, Sputnik II was launched (carrying with it Laika, the first dog in space). The humiliation was then

The Soviets could afford to be humorous about Sputnik. America, on the other hand, had to take it seriously.

emphatically underlined when, after weeks of publicity, on 6 December 1957, the Vanguard TV3 rocket blew up during its launch at Cape Canaveral.

The Character Issue
It's hard now to imagine the crippling effect this had on American morale. The United States' early lead in atomic science had long since been lost and the widespread perception was that, overall, they were lagging behind now. The fear in Washington was that, in the eyes of the wider world, communism appeared to have prevailed over capitalism; that it might even be 'burying' it, to use Nikita Khruschev's phrase.

Hence the need for some convincing show of strength, of technological accomplishment and moral resolution – for something like Project A119, in short. The Americans weren't quite going to write 'Coca-Cola' on the moon but they were going to do the next best thing. What was envisaged was, almost literally, a 'moonshot'; they were going to detonate a nuclear device on the moon, for all to see. A rocket (or a missile; they were, of course, substantially the same thing) would be targeted so as to impact just out of sight over the horizon, on the dark side of the moon; the cloud of dust it produced would be spectacularly illuminated by the sun. Given the weakness of the moon's gravity and the absence of atmosphere, it wouldn't be a 'mushroom cloud' of the now-classic sort.

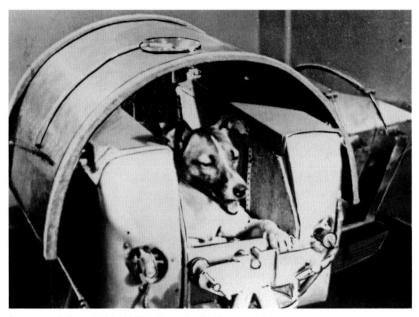

Sent up with Sputnik II in 1957, Laika sadly died from overheating.

A lofty concern with the quest for knowledge, with the pursuit of scientific understanding for its own sake? Perhaps not, but at least these are genuinely technical concerns. More shocking is the all-but-frank acknowledgement of what Reiffel himself later called the 'one-upmanship' agenda. Even if 'the political motivations' are, as here he coyly insists, 'outside the scope of the present work', he makes a point of mentioning them anyway:

Obviously . . . specific positive effects would accrue to the nation first performing such a feat as a demonstration of advanced technological capability.

That said, he also recognizes the potential for negative effects:

It is also certain that, unless the climate of world opinion were

Putting on a Show

Under the direction of the distinguished physicist Leonard Reiffel, a team of researchers set to work exploring the possibilities for such a stunt. That word is used advisedly. Reiffel himself was in no doubt as to the object of all their efforts:

The foremost intent was to impress the world with the prowess of the United States. It was a PR device, without question.

The scientists involved in 'Project A119' included the young Carl Sagan, destined to find fame as a popular science writer and broadcaster. Though backed by the Air Force Special Weapons Research Center in Kirtland, New Mexico, the bulk of the research was undertaken in Chicago at the Illinois Institute of Technology's Armour Foundation.

'Specific Positive Effects'

Much of the research material Project A119 produced was subsequently destroyed. But one 'Study of Lunar Research Flights', authored by Reiffel himself, has survived. This densely written document bristles with facts and figures, and with statistics on everything from particle dynamics to plasma. Yet the essential issues are evidently simpler:

. . . it is quite clear that certain military objectives would be served since information would be supplied concerning the environment of space, concerning detection of nuclear device testing in space and concerning the capability of nuclear weapons for space warfare.

Intended as America's answer to Sputnik, Vanguard barely made it off the ground.

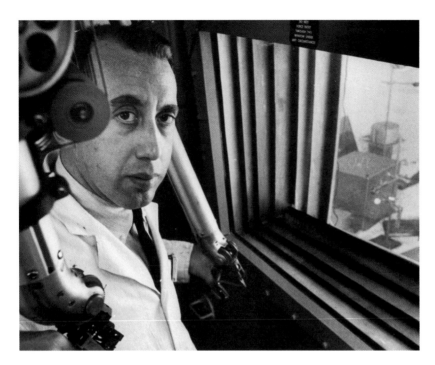

Physicist Leonard Reiffel led the team working on Project A119.

'The foremost intent was to impress the world with the prowess of the United States.'

Leonard Reiffel, recalling Project A119

well-prepared in advance, a considerable negative reaction could be stimulated.

Indeed. However cynical the Soviet Union's enemies might be, the Sputnik programme could at least be claimed to have some serious scientific basis and to have as its ultimate object the advancement of humanity. It's hard to see how the same could possibly have been said for Project A119. At very best, this nuclear blast was going to be viewed as a vainglorious firework display in space; at worst as a vaunting threat by an aggressive and bullying United States.

Interviewed in 2000, when the whole astonishing story was first revealed to the public,

Reiffel confessed himself outraged. 'I am horrified that such a gesture to sway public opinion was ever considered.' By this time, people had become more conscious of the environmental damage done by human activity on earth, and this threw the contemplated vandalism of 1958 into stark relief.

Science Takes Sides

Why did Reiffel cooperate, if he felt so strongly? In hindsight it's easy to condemn, and yet few scientists of his generation would feel comfortable casting the first stone. It's easy to forget now how completely the Cold War dominated every aspect of public, institutional and even scientific life in the 1950s and 1960s.

'Within the Revolution, everything. Outside the Revolution, nothing,' Fidel Castro was to tell Cubans in 1961. That sort of thinking prevailed on both sides in the conflict. It extended

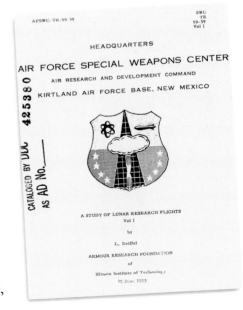

TRANSCRIPT OF KEY PARAGRAPHS

STUDY OF LUNAR
RESEARCH FLIGHTS
by Leonard Reiffel

Chapter 1 - Introduction
Rapidly accelerating progress in space technology clearly requires evaluation of the scientific experiments or other human activities which might be carried out in the vicinity of the earth's natural satellite. Among various possibilities, the detonation of a nuclear weapon on or near the moon's surface has often been suggested. The motivation for such a detonation is clearly threefold: scientific, military and political.

The scientific information which might be obtained from such detonations is one of the major subjects of inquiry of the present work. On the other hand, it is quite clear that certain military objectives would be served since information would be supplied concerning the environment of space, concerning detection of nuclear device testing in space and concerning the capability of nuclear weapons for space warfare.

into every area of intellectual life, into the most seemingly disinterested areas of artistic enterprise or scientific enquiry. It wasn't all tanks, submarines and soldiers: the Cold War set playwrights against poets, abstract impressionist artists against ballet companies. As for physicists, given the intensity of the superpowers' struggle for predominance in nuclear and space technology, they could hardly have avoided finding themselves in the frontline.

A Semblance of Science

But if science was going to come a poor second to the promotion of American prestige, it wasn't going to be dispensed with altogether. Project A119 was to involve the placing of

. . . three identical instrument packages at arbitrary locations on the visible face of the moon prior to any possible nuclear detonation. These instrument packages would be equipped to make a variety of measurements . . .

radiological contamination, only the last of which is unique to the nuclear weapon. While the present efforts have been designed to explore scientific aspects of lunar experimentation, including detonation of a nuclear weapon among other possibilities, we nevertheless have felt some obligation to consider the obstacles listed above and at least a beginning has been made in an evaluation of some aspects of the contamination problems.

A central theme, which runs through many of the projected experimental situations, envisions placing of a maximum of three identical instrument packages at arbitrary locations on the visible face of the moon prior to any possible nuclear detonation. These instrument packages would be equipped to make a variety of measurements treated in the following chapters, and, as such, only certain operations would require a nuclear detonation. The instrument packages, in general, would accumulate very valuable information on the way to the moon, while emplaced on the moon before any detonation, as well as during and after a possible nuclear detonation. The location of the instrument packages need not be pre-determined but is presumed to be known by virtue of suitable markers.

Clearly, the landing of three complex instrumentation packages on the lunar surface with "state of the art" techniques, either today or in the near future, must be considered a maximum effort. It is presumed obvious to the reader that many valuable measurements could be performed with only one instrument package, and for certain of the observations to be treated in the present work, only terrestrial observations are required. In no case have we attempted to detail the design of a suitable instrument package

3

**TRANSCRIPT OF
KEY PARAGRAPHS**

STUDY OF LUNAR
RESEARCH FLIGHTS (ctd.)
by Leonard Reiffel

Chapter 1 - Introduction
(ctd.)

A central theme, which
runs through many of
the projected experimental
situations, envisions
placing of a maximum of
three identical instrument
packages at arbitrary
locations on the visible
face of the moon prior to
any possible nuclear
detonation.

These instrument packages
would be equipped to
make a variety of
measurements . . . The
instrument packages, in
general, would accumulate
very valuable information
on the way to the moon,
while emplaced on
the moon before any
detonation, as well as
during and after a possible
nuclear detonation.

The location of the
instrument packages need
not be pre-determined but
is presumed to be known
by virtue of suitable
markers.

They would also, Reiffel emphasized – clearly keen to keep up the pretence that this was some sort of scientific venture – 'accumulate very valuable information on the way to the moon'.

And in fairness, of course, there *was* a real opportunity for genuine investigatory work to be done into the nature and the origins of the moon itself. As Reiffel was at pains to remind his reader:

Seismic observations on the moon are of great potential interest from the viewpoint of fundamental theories of the development of the solar system and of the moon itself . . .

From here, though, the justifications he used become ever more tortuous:

It is not certain how much seismic energy will be coupled into the moon by an explosion near its surface, hence one may develop an argument that a large explosion would help ensure success of a first seismic experiment.

You can almost feel the grimace as, with the carefully worded phrase 'one may develop an argument', Reiffel establishes a fastidious distance between his professional integrity and the opportunistic nonsense he's writing at this point. But the scientist gets the upper hand as he goes on:

On the other hand, if one wished to proceed at a more leisurely pace, seismographs could be emplaced upon the moon and the nature of possible interferences determined before selection of the explosive device. Such a course would appear to be the obvious one to pursue from a purely scientific viewpoint.

Reiffel does in fairness point to certain 'obstacles' to the project: these centre on 'environmental disturbance, biological contamination and radiological contamination'. Questions of this kind are explored in fascinating detail later, with attention being paid to the possibility that the lunar surface and atmosphere might support (or might at some point in the past have supported) rudimentary forms of life. There is a long and painstaking examination of the risks that bacteria or spores brought up from the earth might compromise the lunar environment or the possibility for its later development. But it's hard to imagine the military brass paying particular attention to this.

In the final analysis, was this project at all technically feasible? Reiffel was subsequently to insist that it certainly was, and with the kind of ICBM that was then already in use. Such a missile typically reached over 1125km (700 miles) in altitude at the highest point in its intercontinental flight. All that would be needed would be for it to be targeted at the moon, rather than at Russia. This being the case, it seems most likely that the project was shelved when political considerations came into play, and that the decision was taken that the 'negative reaction' to an explosion on the moon would outweigh the 'positive effects'.

Acoustic Kitty

If the idea seemed too improbable to be true, the reality bore that suspicion out. America's attempts to train electronically equipped cats to serve as listening-posts proved unavailing.

From cavalry horses to carrier pigeons, there have always been animals in the frontline in human conflict. Dogs have performed a range of roles: as combatants, guides, guards, detectors of explosives. What of our other most familiar household pet? The record of the cat has not been so illustrious. Not that this is really so surprising. Dogs are companionable, cooperative: 'man's best friend' is only too glad to be of service. Cats could hardly be more different. For Rudyard Kipling, the cat was the animal that 'walked by himself': wilful and independent minded, it shows little sign of a desire to please.

Wired for Sound

On the other hand, in its aloofness the cat can be infinitely more discreet than a dog can be. Even after millennia of domestication, this natural hunter can slink on its way unnoticed; so closely does it mind its own business that we barely register that it's there. This must be why, then, in the 1960s it seemed sensible to the CIA's Science and Technology Directorate to disregard so many centuries of precedent and to

Victor Marchetti was a CIA insider.

attempt to enlist the cat in the cause of the Cold War.

The idea, essentially, was that cats might be trained to serve as mobile eavesdropping agents. Fitted up with microphones and transmitters (these were to be implanted surgically, so as not to be discernible), the 'acoustic kitty' could get up close to conversations as they were happening, allowing officers at some distance off to listen in.

'They Made a Monstrosity'

More than $20 million was ploughed into a programme that for the most part is still secret (more, one suspects, for reasons of embarrassment than of continuing significance). Victor Marchetti, at the time a special assistant to CIA Director Richard Helms, later recalled,

. . . they slit the cat open, put batteries in him, wired him up.

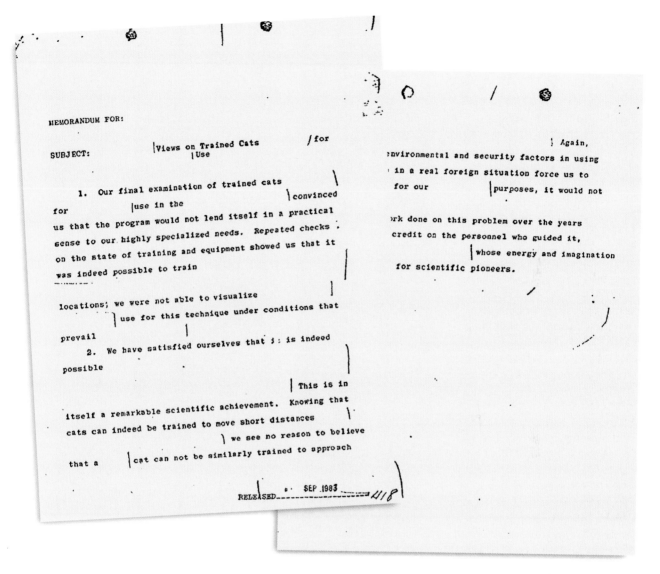

MEMORANDUM FOR:

SUBJECT: |Views on Trained Cats   /for
           |Use

1. Our final examination of trained cats \
for |use in the   \convinced
us that the program would not lend itself in a practical
sense to our highly specialized needs. Repeated checks .
on the state of training and equipment showed us that it
was indeed possible to train
----

locations; we were not able to visualize
          |use for this technique under conditions that
prevail
2. We have satisfied ourselves that i: is indeed
possible

                          | This is in

itself a remarkable scientific achievement. Knowing that
cats can indeed be trained to move short distances
                    \ we see no reason to believe
that a |cat can not be similarly trained to approach

RELEASED----------------SEP 1983-------418

| Again,
environmental and security factors in using
in a real foreign situation force us to
for our |purposes, it would not

ork done on this problem over the years
credit on the personnel who guided it,
          |whose energy and imagination
for scientific pioneers.

The tail was used as an antenna. They made a monstrosity. They tested him and tested him. They found he would walk off the job when he got hungry, so they put another wire in to override that. Finally, they're ready. They took it out to a park bench and said 'Listen to those two guys. Don't listen to anything else – not the birds, no cat or dog – just those two guys!' . . . They put him out of the van, and a taxi comes and runs him over. There they were, sitting in the van with all those dials, and the cat was dead!

A *little* more light is shed on this particular project by a memorandum of 1967, 'Views on Trained Cats'. The full title isn't available, and much of the text has been redacted too, though enough remains to give the sense of officials working hard to put a positive spin on a fiasco. 'We have satisfied ourselves that it is indeed possible . . .' to do something unspecified, they maintain; something or other unnamed 'is in itself a remarkable scientific achievement'. In short, it all sounds very (if vaguely) encouraging. Even so, they concluded that the program would not lend itself in a practical sense to 'our highly specialized needs'.

Big Ivan

'It seemed to suck the whole world into it,' one witness reported. But the big brother of all H-bombs proved unexpectedly unintimidating. How could it conceivably be deployed?

Nikita Khruschev declared in January 1960 that 'the Soviet army today possesses such combat means and fire power as no army has ever had before'. It could 'wipe the country or countries that attack us off the face the earth'. Soon after, he claimed that the Soviet Union was 'now the world's leading military power'.

Quoting Khruschev, a CIA staff study of 6 March 1964 is triumphant. Not only had the First Secretary been bluffing, but his 'strategic deception' had

... *done irreparable damage to the USSR by stimulating a major improvement of the defense posture of the United States, thereby resulting in a substantial widening of the actual U.S. military lead.*

Yet if Khruschev had overplayed his hand, his claims hadn't been entirely without foundation: elsewhere in his report the CIA analyst refers to 'high yield explosions' and 'super-bombs'.

Ivan the Terrible?
They didn't come much more super than the RDS-220. Big Ivan, or the *Tsar Bomba*, as Western officials called it. But just how

'terrible' was this Tsar? The nickname, only part-admiring, made mocking reference to the *Tsar Pushka*, a giant sixteenth-century cannon built chiefly for show. Even Soviet experts wondered what the RDS-220 was really going to offer: 'Building up yields in this simple fashion looked both trivial and useless,'

one technician of the time recalled later.

Miniaturization was the big thing then, for the Soviets as for the Americans, so a weapon on this scale seemed perverse. There *was* a certain desperate logic to it, though – the same as had prompted the Americans to develop the 25-megaton Mark 17.

strategic deception, as an integral part of Soviet policy, had as objectives not only compensation for an unavoidable, adverse imbalance in strategic power, but also the conceal-ment from the West that the Soviet ICBM force programmed for the period 1958-1962 would not close the gap and might even permit it to widen substantially. The effort to deceive, moreover, was intended not merely to deter an attack on the Soviet Union, but to secure political gains as well.

Khrushchev's public confidence in the deterrent ef-fect of Soviet deceptive missile claims reached a high point in early 1960. In his speech to the Supreme Soviet in Janu-ary of that year he boasted that the USSR was "several years" ahead of the United States in the "mass production" of ICBMs, and that the "Soviet army today possesses such combat means and fire power as no army has ever had before," sufficient "literally to wipe the country or countries that attack us off the face of the earth." Consequently, Khru-shchev said, "the Soviet people can be calm and confident; the Soviet army's modern equipment ensures the unassail-ability of our country." At the end of the following month he would announce unambiguously that the Soviet Union is "now the world's strongest military power."

Over the same period, the principal military element in the Soviet deterrent scheme was the massive force intended for war against Europe. This might have been a meaningful anti-U.S. strategy in a purely military sense had the with-drawal of SAC forces from Europe not coincided with the emergence of the Soviet MRBM force. The real deterrent against the United States, hence, was largely indirect; Europe, as Khrushchev would acknowledge (in September 1961), was a "hostage."

By the end of 1961, the Soviet leaders realized that the strategic deception scheme had backfired; not only was it exposed to the whole world but in the meantime it had done irreparable damage to the USSR by stimulating a major improvement in the defense posture of the United States, thereby resulting in a substantial widening of the actual U.S. military lead. Furthermore, it was by that time clear to the Soviet leaders that the effectiveness of the counter-Europe threat had been undermined by the proven inability

– 8 –

TRANSCRIPT OF KEY PARAGRAPHS

CIA STUDY – March 1964

Khruschev's public confidence in the deterrent effect of Soviet deceptive missile claims reached a high point in early 1960. In his speech to the Supreme Soviet in January of that year he boasted that the USSR was "several years" ahead of the United States in the "mass production" of ICBMs [Intercontinental ballistic missiles], and that the "Soviet army today possesses such combat means and fire power as no army has ever had before," sufficient "literally to wipe the country or countries that attack us off the face of the earth."

Consequently, Khrushchev said, "the Soviet people can be calm and confident; the Soviet army's modern equipment ensures the unassailability of our country."

[. . .]

The real deterrent against the United States [. . .] was largely indirect; Europe, as Khrushchev would acknowledge (in September 1961), was a "hostage."

The *Tsar Bomba* throws up the first Marxist-Leninist mushroom cloud.

This was the need – in the heat of nuclear war – to make good the lack of reliable intelligence on enemy weapons, facilities and troop deployments by wiping out whole areas.

Too Big to Use?
Originally, the RDS-220 was to have a 'yield' equivalent to 100 million tons of TNT. Imagine the total power of Hiroshima's Little Boy and Nagasaki's Fat Man bombs, then multiply that by 1400, and you have some idea of its explosive force. But prohibitive amounts of fallout, which would waft back across to Russia and her allies as deadly 'blowback', were likely to be generated by this blast. (Or, rather, these blasts: initial fission triggered a second, thermonuclear explosion, which in its turn set off a third, still greater eruption – the *Tsar Bomba* was what's called a 'three-stage' device.) Hence its subsequent downsizing to 'just' 50 megatons – which had the added advantage of cutting fallout by much more than half. Even at this reduced size, however, it was going to take a specially modified Tupolev Tu-95 aircraft to deliver the RDS-220 – and at a lumbering speed that would make it a sitting duck in a wartime situation.

Even so, the *Tsar Bomba* was successfully tested: its descent retarded by a parachute, it was detonated at approximately 3960m (13,000ft) above the Mityushikha Bay test site on the western side of Arctic Russia's Novaya Zemlya Island. The results were certainly impressive. So completely was the island's surface 'levelled, swept and licked' by the blast that it looked like a 'skating rink'; the mushroom cloud lofted 64,000m (210,000ft) into the air; the town of Severny, 56km (35 miles) away, was razed.

BIBLIOGRAPHY

Anderson, David L., *The Columbia History of the Vietnam War* (New York: Columbia, 2011)

Betts, Richard K., *Nuclear Blackmail and Nuclear Balance* (Washington, DC: Brookings Institution, 1987)

Blum, William, *Killing Hope: US Military and CIA Interventions Since World War II* (London: Zed Books, 2003)

Bragg, Christine, *Vietnam, Korea and US Foreign Policy* (London: Heinemann, 2005)

Burnett, Thom, *Conspiracy Encyclopedia* (Stuttgart: Franz Steiner Verlag, 2006)

Didion, Joan, *The Last Thing He Wanted* (New York: Knopf, 1996)

Edwards, Paul M., *Combat Operations of the Korean War: Ground, Air, special and Covert* (Jefferson, NC: McFarland, 2009)

Friedman, Norman, *The Fifty-Year War: Conflict and Strategy in the Cold War* (Annapolis, MD: Naval Institute Press, 2007)

Haas, Michael E., *Apollo's Warriors: United States Air Force Special Operations During the Cold War* (Maxwell, AL: Air University (US) Press, 1997)

Hastedt, Glenn, *Encyclopedia of American Foreign Policy* (South Riding, VA: Infobase, 2004)

Herman, Ellen, The Romance of American Psychology (Berkeley, CA: University of California Press, 1995)

Karnow, Stanley, *Vietnam: A History* (London: Viking, 1983)

Loth, Wilfried, *Overcoming the Cold War: A History* (Basingstoke: Palgrave Macmillan, 2002)

Miller, David, *The Cold War: A Military History* (London: John Murray, 1998)

Millett, Allan R., *The Korean War*, volume 3 (Lincoln, NE: University of Nebraska Press, 2001)

Olson, James J., *Dictionary of the Vietnam War* (Westport, CT: Greenwood, 1988)

Painter, David S., *The Cold War: An International History* (London: Routledge, 1999)

Sandler, Stanley (ed.), *The Korean War: An Encyclopedia* (New York: Garland, 1995)

Steinberg, Blema S., *Shame and Humiliation: Presidential Decision Making on Vietnam* (Montreal: McGill-Queen's University Press, 1996)

Trahair, R.C.S., *Encyclopedia of Cold War Espionage* (Westport, CT: Greenwood, 2004)

Tunzelmann, Alex von, *Red Heat: Conspiracy, Murder and the Cold War in the Caribbean* (London: Simon & Schuster, 2011)

Woodward, Bob, *Veil: The Secret Wars of the CIA, 1981–1987* (New York: Simon & Schuster, 1987)

INDEX

PICTURE CREDITS

í Главнокомандующий
ными силами ČSSR

Антонин Новотный
1964 г.

План

использования Чехословацкой Народ
армии на военное время
карта 1:500.000, изд. 1963 г.

1. Выводы из оценки противника

На Центрально-Европейском теа

WAR OFFICE SPECIFICATION FOR AN ATOMIC LAND MINE

This specification represents an attainable ideal as foreseen by the W
ice. If the realisation of the specification indicates unreasonable co
plexity or difficulty of maintenance whether in development, production
, it is requested that the War Office be informed accordingly at the ear
sible stage.